A General Theory of Crime

A GENERAL THEORY OF CRIME

Michael R. Gottfredson and

Travis Hirschi

Stanford University Press   1990

Stanford, California

Stanford University Press
Stanford, California
© 1990 by the Board of Trustees of the
Leland Stanford Junior University
Printed in the United States of America

CIP data appear at the end of the book

TO THE TAILGATERS OF '88
Karol, Kate, Bryan, Anna, Kendal, Karen, Nathan,
Janice, Justine, and Phil

Because he was concerned about children, one day his mind was illuminated. He thought, *Something can be done for them.*

To believe in something not yet proved and to underwrite it with our lives: it is the only way we can leave the future open. Man, surrounded by facts, permitting himself no surmise, no intuitive flash, no great hypothesis, no risk is in a locked cell. Ignorance cannot seal the mind and imagination more surely.

—Lillian Smith, *The Journey* (New York, 1954, pp. 12, 256)

Acknowledgments

John Hagan and John Kaplan read the manuscript of this book and offered valuable advice and encouragement. We are grateful for their efforts and hasten to add that they may not agree with all we have to say about crime.

Students and colleagues at the University of Arizona read and reacted to various versions of our manuscript, and they also offered valuable advice. They include Gary Jensen, David Rowe, Chester Britt, Lenore Simon, Jeffrey Klotz, Mary Ann Zager, Theron Quist, David Sorenson, Carolyn Uihlein, Linda Markowitz, and Barbara Costello.

Readers of the book will soon discover that we have intellectual debts we do not always take the time to recognize in the text. Far beyond acknowledgments that may be found in footnotes or references, we have been influenced by the work of Ronald Akers, Lee Robins, David Matza, Marcus Felson, Lawrence Cohen, Ronald Clarke, Jackson Toby, John Hagan, Donald Cressey, Yohji Morita, Gerald Patterson, John Laub, Robert Sampson, Ruth Kornhauser, Robert Burgess, Timothy Hope, Chuen-jim Sheu, Pat Mayhew, Ernest van den Haag, Gwynne Nettler, Daniel Glaser, David Bordua, Rodney Stark, Carl Klockars, Martin Killias, Kenneth Land, John Lofland, Irving Piliavin, LaMar Empey, and Walter Gove. We would not suggest that those listed would agree with what we have to say; we would suggest that we have tried to take seriously what they have had to say.

We would be remiss in our duty to friendship not to mention the daily stimulation we once enjoyed from our colleagues Michael Hindelang (at the University at Albany) and Maynard Erickson (at the University of Arizona).

At Stanford University Press, Grant Barnes reacted to our manuscript with the mix of enthusiasm and criticism that only lucky authors experience. We are grateful that he was willing to devote his talent and energy to our book. Julia Johnson Zafferano responded to our request for proactive editorial assistance with a zeal that would make users of such terms as "proactive" shudder. As a consequence, the book is now much better than it was.

Portions of some chapters are rewritten from materials published elsewhere. We are grateful to the publishers for allowing us to use those materials here. Specifically, we are grateful to the University of Chicago Press for "Age and the Explanation of Crime" (*American Journal of Sociology* 89: 552–84); to the American Society of Criminology for "The True Value of Lambda Would Appear to Be Zero" (1986, 24: 213–34), "The Methodological Adequacy of Longitudinal Research on Crime" (1987, 25: 581–614), "Science, Public Policy, and the Career Paradigm" (1988, 26: 37–55), and "Causes of White Collar Crime" (1987, 25: 949–74); to ICS Press for "Crime and the Family" (pp. 53–68 in James Q. Wilson, ed., *Crime and Public Policy*, 1983); to Transaction Publishers for "The Distinction Between Crime and Criminality" (pp. 55–69 in T. F. Hartnagel and R. Silverman, eds., *Critique and Explanation: Essays in Honor of Gwynne Nettler*, 1986) and "A Propensity-Event Theory of Crime" (pp. 57–67 in F. Adler and W. Laufer, eds., *Advances in Criminological Theory*, Vol. 1, 1988); to the Cultural and Social Centre for the Asian and Pacific Region for "A General Theory of Crime for Cross-National Criminology" (pp. 44–53 in *Proceedings of the Fifth Asian-Pacific Conference on Juvenile Delinquency*, 1988); and, finally, to Sage Publications for "Career Criminals and Selective Incapacitation" (pp. 199–209 in J. E. Scott and T. Hirschi, eds., *Controversial Issues in Crime and Justice*, 1988).

M.R.G.
T.H.

Contents

Tables and Figures

Preface

We have for some time been unhappy with the ability of academic criminology to provide believable explanations of criminal behavior. One after another, the disciplines have staked a claim to crime, and each has ended up saying about crime what it says about nearly everything else. No explanation consistent with a disciplinary perspective seems to have the ring of truth. Public policies have pretty much exhausted the possibilities available to those who would use the criminal justice system to combat crime, moving from rehabilitation, through deterrence, to incapacitation. Policymakers ask in vain for ideas to justify pursuing one solution rather than another, and as a result they are at the mercy of whatever proposals come along, from more police to fewer drugs, from more career-criminal programs to fewer furloughs, from sting operations to neighborhood watch.

We have also been unhappy with the "interdisciplinary" solution to this state of affairs. Within the university, criminology has always been the prototypical *sub*discipline, a derivative field of study hoping to achieve truth and status by accepting the insights of its parent disciplines. In fact, criminology shows that interdisciplinary attention is the road to theoretical and practical obscurity.

We find this situation paradoxical. Few topics seem more important than the bases of social and political order, more interesting than the question of human nature, or more practical than the understanding of theft and violence. Students seem to agree. Few courses attract more students to the classroom. Why should those interested in crime grant ownership of the area to one or another of the basically uninterested disciplines?

We have tried to write a book that is free of the constraints of disciplinary perspectives but that is useful in tracing the outlines of reasonable public policy toward crime. We have also tried to write a book consistent with the results of competent research, whatever the discipline producing it and whatever it may say about the limits of our ability to control crime.

To write such a book, we have looked again at the view of crime that prevailed before the disciplines came into being, the view that saw crime as the natural consequence of unrestrained human tendencies to seek pleasure and avoid pain. This view, known within criminology as the classical tradition and outside of criminology as the rational-choice model, was abandoned by criminologists long ago in favor of the view of science embodied in the disciplines. This disciplinary view of science, referred to as positivism, has dominated criminology throughout the twentieth century. It emphasizes causation and determinism, and it denies the self-seeking model of human nature embodied in the classical school.

Upon inspection, we found that we could not simply resurrect the classical model as a solution to the theoretical and policy problems of criminology. With all its difficulties, modern positivism has assembled many facts that do not combine easily with an unqualified interpretation of classical theory. For example, although classical theory tends to lead to concern with the legal costs of crime, much research shows that the operations of the criminal justice system are of little consequence for the crime rate. Classical theory also tends to ignore the role of the family in crime causation, a stance unjustified by research.

At the same time, the classical image of human nature and the classical conception of the criminal act seemed to us better able than any positivistic theory to accommodate the finding that crime is only part of a much larger set of deviant acts, acts that include accidents, victimizations, truancies from home, school, and work, substance abuse, family problems, and disease. It is also known that crime is heavily concentrated among the young, and that differences between people in their propensity to crime are reasonably stable over long periods.

The disciplines routinely begin by asking "What causes crime?" Not surprisingly, each discipline answers the question by pointing to its own central concepts. Thus sociology looks to social class, culture, and organization; psychology looks to personality; biology looks to inheritance; and economics looks to employment or work. We begin in Chapters 1 and 2 with a different question: "What is crime?" Unlike

nearly all previous work, we thus begin with crime itself, exploring its
essential nature before attempting to explain it. This turns out to be a
profitable strategy. Social scientific and popular conceptions of crime
are misleading. Crime does not require deprivation, peer influence,
or the gang; it says little about one's biological past and is in no way
akin to work. It requires no planning or skill, and "careers" in crime
go nowhere but down. Nearly all crimes are mundane, simple, trivial,
easy acts aimed at satisfying desires of the moment, as are many other
acts of little concern to the criminal law. This helps us understand
why so many social problems and forms of deviant behavior are
concentrated in the same individuals. Crime in fact bears little resemblance to the explanations offered by the disciplines or to explanations popular in the media and in law enforcement propaganda.

For this reason, the task of putting classical and positive criminology together turned out to be more difficult than we had anticipated.
The harder we looked at the empirical claims of the disciplines, the
less certain we were of their validity. Chapters 3 and 4 recount our
assessment of the truth of disciplinary claims about crime, from the
currently popular idea that crime is to some extent passed on through
the genes to the older but more settled idea that crime may be explained by a psychological trait called aggression. These chapters also
examine the economic view of crime as work and the sociological
conceptions of crime as normal learned behavior or as the expression
of frustrated aspirations. In all cases, we conclude that such concepts
are contrary to the nature of crime and, interestingly enough, to the
data produced by the disciplines themselves. We conclude that these
explanations survive more from their value to the disciplines than
from their value as explanations of criminal behavior.

In Chapter 5, we derive a conception of the criminal consistent
with the nature of crime. This offender is neither the diabolical genius
often portrayed by the police and the media nor the ambitious seeker
of the American dream often portrayed by the positivists. On the
contrary, the offender appears to have little control over his or her
own desires. When such desires conflict with long-term interests,
those lacking self-control opt for the desires of the moment, whereas
those with greater self-control are governed by the restraints imposed
by the consequences of acts displeasing to family, friends, and the
law. Chapter 5 explores the nature and sources of such self-control,
locating it largely in family child-rearing practices and using it as the
basis of a general theory of crime.

In Chapters 6–10, we apply our theory and the facts revealed by
our critical examination of the literature to the persistent problems of

criminology. Why are men, adolescents, and minorities more likely than their counterparts to commit criminal acts? What is the role of the school in the causation of delinquency? To what extent could crime be reduced by providing meaningful work? To what extent are children drawn into delinquency by their friends? Why do some societies have crime rates that are only a fraction of the crime rates of others? Does white-collar crime require its own theory? Is there such a thing as organized crime? In all cases, our theory provides answers that conflict with the conventional wisdom of academicians and criminal justice practitioners.

The last two chapters explore the implications of our theory for the study and control of crime. Contemporary criminology offers confused advice about how crime should be studied and about what policies might be adopted to reduce the crime rate. Here, too, our conclusions are at odds with prevailing views within and outside academia. We see little hope for important reductions in crime through modification of the criminal justice system. We see considerable hope in policies that would reduce the role of the state and return responsibility for crime control to ordinary citizens.

I

CRIME

1

Classical Theory and the Idea of Crime

Criminologists often complain that they do not control their own dependent variable, that the definition of crime is decided by political-legal acts rather than by scientific procedures. The state, not the scientist, determines the nature or definition of crime. After registering this complaint, the modern criminologist proceeds to define crime as "behavior in violation of law" and to study the phenomenon as defined by others. This book breaks with this tradition of passive compliance and attempts to construct a definition of crime consistent with the phenomenon itself and with the best available theory of criminal behavior. In doing so, it grants the basic thrust of the classical and of the positivist traditions, where the former focuses on the criminal act, or crime, and the latter on the properties of the actor, or criminal (see Matza 1964; Gottfredson and Hirschi 1987a: ch. 1).

The classical tradition began with a general theory of human behavior, then quickly narrowed its attention to government crime-control policy. In restricting its attention to "crime," this tradition eventually ignored many forms of behavior analogous to crime in terms of social reaction and identical to crime in terms of causation. The positivist tradition began with a general method of research, but without a theory of behavior that would define its dependent variable, it initially accepted the classical focus on crime. As positivism evolved, it eventually encompassed, under the term "deviance," the many forms of behavior left behind by the classical tradition. Lacking the classical theory of behavior, however, positivists have not been able to deal with the connections among the many acts that make up deviance and crime. Consequently, they have tended to develop be-havior-specific theories and to treat the relations between deviance and crime as cause and effect rather than as manifestations of a single cause. One purpose of this book is to reunite deviance and crime under a general theory of behavior.

To do so, it is necessary to reinterpret the classical tradition and emphasize its explanatory power. This chapter and the next attempt such a reinterpretation. As will be clear, we disavow the current construction of the classical view, especially the construction preva-lent in economics that would limit this tradition to concern about government-defined and -sanctioned behavior. In the theory that emerges, we also disavow the contemporary division between the classical and positivist traditions. We suggest that a properly concep-tualized classical view is fully consistent with the assumptions of modern positivism and with the facts produced by research.

A Modern Version of the Classical Conception of Crime

Force and fraud are ever-present possibilities in human affairs. Denial of this fact promotes the development of theories of crime that are misleading as guides to policy. Awareness of this fact allows the development of a theory of crime consistent with research and the needs of sound public policy. It has implications for how crime itself is construed, how it should be measured, the kind of people who are likely to engage in it, the institutional context within which it is con-trolled, and the most useful ways of studying it. One purpose of this book is to promote this view of crime.

People vary in their propensity to use force and fraud (criminality). This fact has implications for the way crime is measured, for the kinds of crimes that occur, for understanding the relation between crimes and social problems such as accidents and disease, for the proper design of research, and for the creation of useful public policies. Another purpose of this book is to promote explicit consideration of the propensity to crime as distinct from the commission of criminal acts.

These ideas about crime and criminality have been around a long time, surfacing again and again in academic criminology. Today, however, they are contrary to the views dominant in the field, where "crime" is seen as aberrant behavior and "criminality" as a distasteful relic of earlier modes of thought. In our view, the reason these views of crime and criminality come and go is that they have never been fully and systematically developed and defended. As the first step in such a systematic development and defense, we propose to trace the intellectual history of the ideas of crime and criminality.

This chapter deals with the concept of crime. The origins of the concept are found in the classical tradition, a tradition whose insights are badly neglected in modern criminological thought.

A conception of crime presupposes a conception of human nature. In the classical tradition, represented by Thomas Hobbes, Jeremy Bentham, and Cesare Beccaria, human nature was easily described: "Nature has placed mankind under the governance of two sovereign masters, *pain* and *pleasure*" (Bentham 1970 [1789]: 11). In this view, all human conduct can be understood as the self-interested pursuit of pleasure or the avoidance of pain. By definition, therefore, crimes too are merely acts designed to satisfy some combination of these basic tendencies. The idea that criminal acts are an expression of fundamental human tendencies has straightforward and profound implications. It tells us that crime is not unique with respect to the motives or desires it is intended to satisfy. It tells us that crime presupposes no particular skills or abilities, that it is within the reach of everyone without specialized learning. It tells us that all crimes are alike in that they satisfy ordinary and universal desires. It tells us that people behave rationally when they commit crimes and when they do not. It tells us that people are free to choose their course of conduct, whether it be legal or illegal. And it tells us that people think of and act first for themselves, that they are not naturally inclined to subordinate their interests to the interests of others.

Sanction Systems

Since crimes will be committed whenever the pleasures produced by them exceed the pain attendant on their commission, it follows that crime is caused or prevented by constellations of pleasurable and painful *consequences*. In the original classical formulation, there were many sources, or kinds, of "sanctions" for criminal acts.[1] In his justly famous exposition, Bentham described four general sources of pleasure and pain, or sanction systems: physical, political, moral, and religious. As indicated, sources of pleasure and pain are also sources

---

[1] Bentham traced the origin of the word "sanctions" to the latin *sanctio*, which "was used to signify the *act of binding*, and, by a common grammatical transition, *any thing which serves to bind a man*: to wit, to the observance of such or such a mode of conduct" (1970: 34). In modern usage, sanctions have come to denote rewards and especially punishments provided by the state or some other recognized authority. This shift of course follows the path of classical theory from a general theory of behavior to a special theory of the effects of state punishment on the crime rate.

of crime. Bentham thus introduced in 1789 a general theory of crime composed of these four sanction elements.

Physical sanctions. In keeping with the intellectual traditions of his day, Bentham distinguished between causes of human behavior that flow from purposeful intervention and those given by nature without human or divine assistance. Physical sanctions are thus those consequences of behavior that follow automatically from it and require no active intervention by others. It turns out that many criminal or deviant acts are sufficiently risky or inherently difficult that they are, at least to some extent, naturally limited. Many appear to have within themselves the potential to cause long-range suffering by their "perpetrators." Such consequences of course tend to deter people from committing the acts in question. For example, intravenous drug use apparently produces great pleasure, but it also carries with it a large increase in the risk of accident, infection, permanent physiological damage, and death. Promiscuous sexual activity apparently produces great pleasure, but it also increases the risk of disease, unintended pregnancy, and death. Gaining one's way through physical aggression (such as by threatening someone with a blunt instrument) may sometimes secure the intended result, yet it also increases the risk of bodily injury and even death. (All crimes involving force entail the risk of victim retaliation or defense. Making illegitimate demands involves the risk that they will be met with physical force, a risk apparently much appreciated by those making them, since they tend to minimize such risk by carrying weapons or outnumbering their victims.)

Even ordinary property crimes are to some extent controlled by natural "sanctions": small electrical appliances are more likely to be stolen than refrigerators; helicopters and airplanes are rarely stolen by people who do not know how to fly them; and dwellings beyond the walking range of young people are seldom burglarized.

In the classical view, then, crime is to some extent naturally restrained. Although natural controls on crime are, in principle, no different from those operating on other pleasure-producing activities, they appear to be stronger and more numerous than those operating on noncriminal behavior, especially if we take as natural the response of the victim. In fact, this asymmetry is the motive behind the social contract: in a state of nature, the physical sanctions attendant on force and fraud make life nasty, brutish, and short. In society, the physical sanctions attendant on lawful behavior are typically acceptable to a prudent person.

Still, physical and physiological controls ultimately limit the pursuit of noncriminal pleasures as well. Food and drink are pleasurable, up to a point; beyond this point their consumption is automatically controlled. And so for all activities, legitimate and illegitimate. None can be pursued without limit, without running into the pain of repetition or the demands of the body for rest and recuperation. (Knowledge of the operation of such natural limits would seem to be a good starting point for a theory of crime: How much crime would there be if no [other] limits were imposed?)

Religious sanctions. Writing in the eighteenth century, Bentham assumed that human behavior was to some degree restrained by religious belief and scruple. The extent of this restraint relative to other sanctions was not addressed, and it is hard to know how much influence Bentham attributed to religious sanctions. ("The best ideas we can obtain of such pains and pleasures are altogether unliquidated in point of quality" [1970: 36–37].) Still, it was common in the classical tradition to note that, because religious sanctions can be delivered in this life and in a life to come, they are a potentially powerful influence on behavior.[2]

Moral sanctions. In Bentham's time, the distinction between social and legal sanctions had not been clearly drawn. He therefore referred to the power of "popular sanction" as a reward or punishment for behavior. Bentham's central purpose in *An Introduction to the Principles of Morals and Legislation* was to outline a foundation for political sanctions, and he did not therefore elaborate on the other types. Clearly, however, Bentham saw the actions of neighbors and the community as the most important sources of pleasure and pain to the individual (1970: 141). Modern criminologists with direct ties to the classical tradition, particularly economists (Becker 1974), tend to ignore moral sanctions or to minimize their importance (see also Wilson 1975). The social control and social disorganization traditions within sociology tend, in contrast, to rank moral sanctions above political sanctions in their effects on crime (Hirschi 1969; Kornhauser 1978).[3]

Political sanctions. As indicated, Bentham's *Introduction* was written

---

[2] In their zeal to distinguish scientific criminology from prescientific or classical thought, the positivists eschewed religious influence on behavior. Thus the classical tendency to grant religion at least some potential effect on behavior was lost to positivist thought until recently (Hirschi and Stark 1969).

[3] As we will show, the classical theory is not dependent on any given classification of what Bentham called "sanctions." It does not prejudge the pleasures and pains of people, making them a matter of observation. Other theories assume that some pleasures and pains are more important than others. This is especially true of social theories, which tend to select a particular pleasure (e.g., money) as the goal of criminal behavior. Other theories prejudge sanctions on some vague but strongly held notion that only some actions are possible or appropriate for the state, a selection criterion even less cogent than that employed by the social theorist.

as a foundation for reforms of the criminal law. Bentham wished to use the principles of utility (the pleasure/pain theory of human behavior) to justify state sanctions of individual behavior and to describe how these sanctions might have optimum effect. Bentham's approach thus typifies the tendency of the classical school to use its general theory of behavior as a theory of crime and as a guide to public crime-control policy. Given this tendency, political sanctions assume a central role in the theory as applied to crime (Hobbes 1957 [1651]; Beccaria 1963 [1764]; Becker 1974).

Bentham described dimensions of sanctions relevant to their ability to modify behavior. Several of his dimensions survive to the present day, with much current research built around assessments of the effectiveness of the *certainty, severity* (that is, duration or intensity), and *celerity* of punishment in deterring crime. Other distinctions introduced by Bentham have proved less useful for social policy and crime theory (for example, fecundity and purity) and are no longer encountered. As originally described, these qualities applied to all sanctions, whether physical, political, moral, or religious. Interesting enough, they are today also found as factors in general learning theories of criminal behavior (see, e.g., Burgess and Akers 1966; Sutherland and Cressey 1978). (Sanctions, it should be recalled, are constellations of pleasures and pains, whatever their source. Current theories often consider pleasures [rewards] to be more effective than pains [punishments] in controlling behavior, and therefore many theories typically advocate the use of rewards. It is not clear that this conclusion is justified by a theory that focuses on the *mix* of the two properties or, as will be shown, by research.)

Eventually, Bentham focused exclusively on political sanctions, and his work as well as that of the classical school as a whole came down to us as political science rather than behavioral science, as a theory of government rather than a theory of the causes of crime.[4] As we shall see, this narrow interpretation of Bentham and of the classical school as dealing largely with political sanctions has had unfortunate consequences for criminology.

Crime, Deviation, Sin, and Recklessness

If we stay with Bentham's complete theory, we derive a conception of crime that does not restrict interest to a single type of sanction. At

---

[4]The justification for this treatment of the classical school is perhaps clearest in Beccaria's *On Crimes and Punishments* (1963 [1764]), where the utilitarian perspective is used almost exclusively to limit the authority of the state rather than to describe the sources of conduct.

its most general level, Bentham's theory does not distinguish between "criminal" and "noncriminal" acts. Behavior is governed by pleasure and pain, whether the behavior be criminal or noncriminal. At this level, the theory also does not distinguish sin from crime, immorality from accident, or bad manners from bad judgment. With the introduction of specific sanction systems, distinctions between types of behavior automatically follow. If the sanctioning body is political, we have the distinction between crime and noncrime. If the sanctioning body is the social system, the theory distinguishes between conformity and deviation. If the sanctioning body is religious, the theory distinguishes between sin and rectitude. And if the sanctions are physical, the theory distinguishes between prudent and imprudent or careful and reckless behavior.

The sanctioning system is important only with respect to a descriptive characterization of the behavior in question. It is not important with respect to the causal mechanisms thought to produce the behavior. The theory of sin is also a theory of crime and of immorality and of accident. In other words, the sanctioning system determines whether the behavior is criminal or noncriminal, moral or immoral, but this is merely a matter of description or system reference, not a matter of causation.[5] If it defines the behavior as criminal or immoral or sinful, the tendency of those sanctioning systems under human control will be to increase the cost of the behavior proportionate to their own displeasure (or sufficient to reduce its frequency to acceptable levels). (The strength of these tendencies is a measure of the gravity or value accorded the behavior by the sanctioning system. Obviously, this too is descriptive of the values of the sanctioning system and is not necessarily suggestive of causal processes unique to serious and trivial behavior.) If the behavior is defined by the relevant sanctioning body as noncriminal or moral or correct, it will normally assume that no action is required to perpetuate the behavior. Because the existence of any item of behavior is *prima facie* evidence that its benefits exceed its costs, this assumption is consistent with the theory. Virtue is its own reward. (This asymmetry accounts for the oft-noted imbalance between the resources devoted to the punishment of crime and those devoted to the reward of virtue, such as the otherwise perplexing observation that a year in prison costs as much as a year at Harvard.)[6]

[5]In practice, the various sanctioning systems will tend to operate in the same direction—that is, they will tend to reward and punish the same kinds of behavior. Specifically, all systems will tend to oppose the use of force and fraud.

[6]This asymmetry also helps to explain the difficulty that behavioral psychologists have had in discovering the positive impact of treatment programs based on positive reinforcement of desirable behavior.

At the most general level of the theory, then, crime is not a separate or distinct type of behavior. Crime, like noncrime, satisfies universal human desires. It is, in terms of causation, indistinguishable from all other behavior. Crime was eventually distinguished from other forms of behavior by introducing the notion of political sanctions: pleasures and pains manipulated by the state. By introducing and then focusing on state sanctions, the early classicists identified the behavior that eventually became the subject matter of the discipline of criminology.

Deviant behavior was distinguished from other forms of behavior by introducing the notion of group sanctions or social control: pleasures and pains manipulated by public opinion. By introducing group sanctions, the early classicists identified the behavior that eventually became the subject matter of the discipline of sociology.

Sinful behavior was distinguished from other forms of behavior by introducing the notion of religious sanctions: pleasures and pains controlled by supernatural forces. Because the supernatural by definition does not exist in positivistic thought, sinful behavior did not become the focus of a positivistic discipline.

Reckless or imprudent behavior was distinguished from other forms of behavior by introducing the notion of natural harm or physical sanctions. This large class of behavior is not systematically incorporated into any modern discipline but is partitioned among problem-oriented researchers in a variety of disciplines. For example, work on the causes of accidents, injuries, and illnesses and on the physical consequences of certain foods, drugs, and activity patterns is carried out by a multitude of researchers without any notion of the common element in these phenomena.

In our view, the common element in crime, deviant behavior, sin, and accident is so overriding that the tendency to treat them as distinct phenomena subject to distinct causes is one of the major intellectual errors of positive thought and is a major cost of the tendency to divide intellectual problems among academic disciplines. We identify and explicate this common element in the chapters that follow.

Of the major disciplines, sociology was best positioned to follow the classical school. If we follow the logic spelled out by Bentham, it is easy to identify sociology as the modern discipline focusing on moral rather than on political sanctions. Had it remained true to classical logic, sociology would have developed broad theories of *deviant behavior* (theories to include crime, sin, and recklessness) using the general principles of "hedonic calculus," where the important sanctioning bodies are the social groups to which the individual belongs. In other words, following classical logic would have led sociology to theories of social control, theories in which crimes differ from other forms of deviant behavior only because in their case the state is interested in adding sanctions to those operating at the group level. But sociology has tended to reject hedonic calculus in favor of the positivistic view that people are naturally social and must therefore be compelled to commit deviant or criminal acts by forces over which they have no control. Thus sociology has not capitalized on its naturally favored position to exploit the classical logic without concern for the particular source of sanctions governing behavior.

Such limited vision is not unique to sociology; it is inherent in the positivistic frame of reference. In positivistic thought, the definition of a phenomenon is distinct from its explanation or causes. The motives or desires of those committing criminal acts may be different from the motives or desires of those committing immoral or physically harmful acts. Thus in positivistic thought the only thing possibly common to diverse acts is that they may be effects of the same causes.

In the classical tradition, the qualities of acts are implicated in their own causation. Thus acts are fun, worthwhile, enjoyable, easy, and exciting, or they are painful, boring, and difficult. The classical theory of causation combines its explanation of an act with its conception of the nature of the act. The acts that a theory explains therefore have more in common than the explanation of them, and the theory itself will not contain the means of making distinctions among them.

Theories that do not implicate acts in their own causation tend eventually to forget why they were put together in the first place, and naturally enough when acts are seen to be different there is an inclination to produce different explanations for each of them. Having separated the definition of crime from the causes of crime, the positivists have had no way to see the similarities among criminal acts beyond the fact that they are violations of the law. This deficiency in the conceptual apparatus of positivism eventually produces radical empiricism, which attempts to discover distinct types of causes for distinct types of offenses. That is, radical empiricism attempts to locate homogeneous offense clusters, meaningful sequences of criminal events, and causally important distinctions between "serious" and "trivial" offenses. Clearly, in the classical view just described none of these issues is worthy of attention.

Because the classical view contains a conception of the substantive nature of crime, we can proceed directly to a description of criminal acts in terms relevant to an explanation of them. Note that in the classical image crimes are first of all pleasurable. By itself, this image does little to limit the choices available to the actor or to rule out much in the way of behavior. After all, within the terms of the theory, noncrimes are also pleasurable. But note too that in the classical conception the actor chooses between criminal and noncriminal acts. On what grounds is the choice made? Obviously, the actor chooses between crime and noncrime on the basis of the pleasures they provide. It follows that some acts produce more pleasure than others and that the characteristics of pleasure-producing acts can be described.

The general dimensions of acts that enhance pleasure were introduced earlier to describe the characteristics of effective legal sanctions: certainty, severity, and celerity. Clearly, these dimensions are applicable to all sanctions, whatever their source.

Thus, other things being equal, acts that have immediate consequences will tend to be more pleasurable than those whose consequences are delayed. For example, smoking marijuana after school, which provides immediate benefit, is more pleasurable than doing one's homework, the benefit of which is delayed. Similarly, acts that are mentally and physically easy are more pleasurable than acts that require mental and physical exertion. For example, walking into an unlocked house and taking the coins from the dresser is more pleasurable than earning the same amount of money by selling newspapers. Swindling a government bureaucracy by submitting excessive Medicaid claims is more pleasurable than earning the same amount of money by treating recalcitrant patients. And finally, risky or exciting acts are more pleasurable than routine or dull acts. Driving fast is more pleasurable than driving within the speed limit.

Note that all qualities of criminal acts may be found in acts that are not crimes; note too that noncriminal acts vary among themselves in their "proximity" to crime. For example, riding a motorcycle is more exciting than driving a car; the benefits from smoking a cigarette are more immediate than the benefits from homework; sexual activity is more pleasurable than abstinence; and cursing the boss is more fun than suffering in silence. In addition, the use of force or fraud is often easier, simpler, faster, more exciting, and more certain than other means of securing one's ends. In this sense, then, the use of force or fraud (crime) enhances the pleasure of self-interested pursuit.

Given these properties, the nature of criminal acts is fully predicted: they will tend, on the whole, to require little foresight, planning, or effort. Between the thought and the deed, little time will elapse. Thus the carefully planned and executed crime will be extremely rare. The tendency of crime to take place at little remove from the present also implies that crimes will tend to take place at little remove from the offender's usual location. The time and space boundaries of criminal acts will be highly circumscribed. The preference for simplicity over complexity implies that potential targets will be selected based on the ease with which they can be victimized. The same considerations lead to the conclusion that targets that provide immediate benefits will be selected over targets that occasion delay. The spontaneity of criminal acts further implies that they will, on the whole, produce little in the way of profit. Targets that pose little risk of detection and little risk of resistance will be chosen over those with greater risks.[7]

All of the choices listed have both short-term and long-term consequences. As described, the criminal act is governed primarily by short-term pleasures and only secondarily—if at all—by the threat of long-term pains. The fact that pleasures and pains are time-discounted in such calculations is of enormous importance for the effectiveness of sanctioning systems, especially those constrained by considerations of procedural fairness. The fact that they are differentially discounted depending on the current situation of individuals is of enormous importance to the etiology of crime.

In the classical view, the state should be able to control crime by adjusting the certainty, severity, and celerity of the sanctions at its disposal. In the positivist view, the penalties of the criminal law should have little effect because the offender's behavior is *caused* by forces operating independent of the sanction system. Our position is that the classical view presupposes the ready availability of draconian penalties inconsistent with the values of liberal democratic societies (societies that owe much of their character to acceptance of the political philosophy of the classical school) and misapprehends the nature of people with high crime potential. As a result, the penalties available to the state are largely redundant, acting mainly on potential offenders already deterred by previous learning and social sanctions.

In our view, the positivist position on sanctions is equally misin-

---

[7]These properties of criminal acts, we believe, may be deduced from the classical perspective outlined above. Others have reached similar conclusions starting from different premises. For example, Michael Hindelang, Michael Gottfredson, and James Garofalo state: "For a personal victimization to occur, several conditions must be met. First, the prime actors—the offender and the victim—must have occasion to intersect in time and space. Second, some source of dispute or claim must arise between the actors in which the victim is perceived by the offender as an appropriate object of the victimization. Third, the offender must be willing and able to threaten or use force (or stealth) in order to achieve the desired end. Fourth, the circumstances must be such that the offender views it as advantageous to use or threaten force (or stealth) to achieve the desired end" (1978: 250). Similar ideas are expressed by Lawrence Cohen and Marcus Felson (1979).

formed, assuming as it does that failure to document a strong effect of legal sanctions is evidence that sanctions in general do not operate to restrict criminal behavior. As we will describe in detail, the evidence is fully consistent with the view that criminal, deviant, sinful, and reckless behavior flourish in the absence of negative consequences or in the absence of social control.

It is not hard to show that these predictions about the properties of criminal acts are confirmed by research. We defer this demonstration to Chapter 2, where a variety of specific criminal acts are described in these terms.

Conclusions

Criminology once had an idea of crime, an idea it lost with the development of the scientific perspective. This idea of crime derived from the classical theory of human behavior, which asserted that people pursue self-interest by avoiding pain and seeking pleasure. In this conception, crimes too are events that satisfy self-interest. Criminal events can be explained using principles that explain all other human conduct. Moreover, the classical conception of crime dictated the properties of criminal as opposed to noncriminal acts. Criminal acts will tend to be short lived, immediately gratifying, easy, simple, and exciting. In subsequent chapters it will become clear that the properties of criminal acts are closely connected to the characteristics of people likely to engage in them—that is, the description of crimes cannot be separated from the description of criminals.

In current criminology, the idea of crime survives only as an event, a count of acts that may be used to estimate the propensities of the offender. Different acts and different constellations of acts are thought to imply different propensities. Virtually no attention is paid to the general qualities of criminal acts, to their connection to analogous noncriminal acts, or to the qualities of the targets involved in them.[8] Instead, attention focuses almost entirely on offenders, ironically even within those disciplines that derive from the classical school. In the chapter to follow, we attempt to correct this imbalance by paying specific attention to the nature of crime.

[8] Significant exceptions to this generalization involve the various criminal-opportunity perspectives (Mayhew et al. 1976; Sparks, Genn, and Dodd 1977; Clarke 1983; Cornish and Clarke 1986). David Matza (1964) also called attention to the tendency of positivistic criminology to abandon crime in favor of focusing on the criminal.

2

The Nature of Crime

We have defined crimes as acts of force or fraud undertaken in pursuit of self-interest. Because a definition of crime automatically undermines theories inconsistent with it, theorists typically
avoid prior definitions in favor of definitions derived from their theories of crime. The usual approach in contemporary criminology begins with the background or motives of the offender, asking in effect
what causes him or her to commit criminal acts. The nature of crime
is thus inferred from the characteristics of offenders or from a theory
of crime causation.

Every intellectual enterprise must start somewhere, and in principle we are free to begin by explaining *or* by defining crime. We are
also obligated, however, to reconsider and modify our starting point
in light of its consistency with fact and its consequences for research
and policy. Such reconsideration and modification of theories is rarely
seen. Theories of crime typically start from the presuppositions of
disciplines and are often in effect tested by their consistency with
these presuppositions rather than by the phenomenon they were
ostensibly designed to explain. Put another way, modern criminology
pays little attention to the nature of crime and rarely modifies its
theories of crime as a result of observation or analysis of the phenomenon that is its object.

We wish to reverse this tendency; we want to understand and
appreciate the nature of crime. Such a task is not easy.[1] Many of our

[1]Note the inability to focus on crime in a recent, thoughtful work on the topic: "A
crime is any act committed in violation of a law that prohibits it and authorizes punishment for its commission. If we propose to confine our attention chiefly to *persons who*

questions will tend to lead us down the path of explanation and theory. Because our ultimate purpose is a theory- and policy-relevant description of crime, such a temptation must be temporarily resisted in favor of such questions as: What are the formal properties of crimes? What are the conditions necessary for their occurrence? What happens when people attempt to pursue their self-interest through the use of force or fraud? What pleasures and gratifications are achieved through crime? What is the proper conceptualization of crime—that is, what does crime tell us about the criminal? And, what distinctions, if any, ought to be made among crimes?

The Characteristics of Ordinary Crime

It is easy to be misled about the nature of crime in American society. All one has to do is read the newspaper, where the unusual, bizarre, or uncharacteristic crime is routinely portrayed. The fact of the matter is that the vast majority of criminal acts are trivial and mundane affairs that result in little loss and less gain. These are events whose temporal and spatial distributions are highly predictable, that require little preparation, leave few lasting consequences, and often do not produce the result intended by the offender. We begin by summarizing the space and time dimensions of common offenses.

Spatial and Temporal Correlates of Crime

According to police records and victim survey data, crimes of personal violence, such as rape, assault, and robbery, occur disproportionately late at night and early in the morning (i.e., between 1:00 and 2:00 A.M.). Automobiles tend to be stolen at night as well, whereas personal larceny (taking property without force or threat of force) tends to happen during the day. Burglary occurs about half the time during the day and about half the time at night (Hindelang 1976; Hindelang, Gottfredson, and Garofalo 1978; Rand, Klaus, and Taylor 1983).

Violent crimes generally take place outside the home. According to victim data, 70 percent of robberies and 50 percent of assaults occur in the streets or in other public places. Official data on robbery, assault, and rape also indicate that the great portion of these events occur

---

commit serious crimes at high rates, then we must specify what we mean by 'serious.' The arguments we shall make and the evidence we shall cite in this book will chiefly refer to aggressive, violent, or larcenous behavior" (Wilson and Herrnstein 1985: 22; emphasis added).

away from the home, particularly on the street (Hindelang, Gottfredson, and Garofalo 1978).

In both official and victim survey data, most violent crimes (except homicide) are committed by strangers and only rarely by relatives (7 percent of nonhomicide violent crime is committed by relatives). According to victim survey data, 80 percent of all personal crimes involve strangers. For theft, the proportion is higher yet (Hindelang 1976).

All crime data, whether for victims or offenders, consistently show high crime rates for large cities and much variation across areas of cities. As household income goes up, the rate of crime in an area declines (Gottfredson 1986).

The victims of personal crime tend overwhelmingly to be male, young, disproportionately minority, and of low income. It turns out that victims and offenders tend to share all or nearly all social and personal characteristics. Indeed, the correlation between self-reported offending and self-reported victimization is, by social science standards, very high.

These characteristics of crime have significance for etiological questions. They show a pattern of crime consistent with the recreational patterns of youth and inconsistent with the vocational patterns of adults; they show a disinclination to expend effort in pursuit of crime; they show that accessibility increases the risk of potential victims; and they show that avoiding detection is part of the calculation of the offender.

The Requirements of a Criminal Act

Available data are consistent with the view that ordinary crime requires little in the way of effort, planning, preparation, or skill. Most crime in fact occurs in close proximity to the offender's residence (Suttles 1968; Turner 1969; Reiss 1976): the burglar typically walks to the scene of the crime; the robber victimizes available targets on the street; the embezzler steals from his own cash register; and the car thief drives away cars with keys left in the ignition.

What planning does take place in burglary, for example, seems designed to minimize the momentary probability of detection and to minimize the effort required to complete the crime. Thus the burglar searches for an unlocked door or an open window in an unoccupied, single-story house. Once inside, he concentrates on easily portable goods of interest to himself without concern for potential value in a larger market.

The robber prefers to avoid direct confrontation with the victim and, when confrontation cannot be avoided, tends to select targets incapable of, or unlikely to offer, resistance. The occasional use of weapons is designed to minimize the likelihood of resistance. Commercial targets, too, are selected largely on the basis of accessibility. It is no accident that "convenience" stores and gas stations are common targets or that businesses located along major thoroughfares and at freeway offramps are especially attractive.

The skill required to complete the general run of crime is minimal. Consider crimes of personal violence, assault, rape, and homicide. The major requirement for successful completion of these crimes is the appearance of superior strength or the command of instruments of force. A gun, a club, or a knife is often sufficient. Property crimes may require physical strength or dexterity, but in most cases no more than is necessary for the ordinary activities of life.

The Benefits of Crime to the Offender

Many crimes do not produce the results intended by those committing them. One reason for this high rate of failure is that crimes are, by definition, opposed by their would-be victims. Potential victims seek to protect themselves from the inclinations of others. They therefore lock doors, hide valuables, watch strangers, move in groups, carry weapons, travel during the day, avoid provocation, and resist assaults. As a result, the intention to commit a crime does not in itself assure a successful result. Indeed, according to victim surveys, most crimes are attempts to commit crime (Hindelang, Gottfredson, and Garofalo 1978; Hough 1987). Because these reported crimes are by definition known to the potential victims, we must assume that many more attempted crimes are known only to the would-be offender. For example, would-be burglars may try many doors before finding one that is unlocked.

Among crimes completed, the average loss is remarkably small. For example, according to victim reports, the median loss for robbery is less than $50, whereas the median loss for burglary is something like $100 (McGarrell and Flanagan 1985: 312). Trustworthy figures are not available, but the average shoplifting appears to involve items of trivial value, items whose loss must be discounted by the items often purchased to cover the crime. Even fraud does not typically involve large sums, and embezzlements rarely make the offender wealthy (it is hard to get rich stealing from the till of a fast-food restaurant or service station). Auto theft would appear to be an exception, but most stolen automobiles are soon abandoned, and the ratio of attempted to completed auto thefts is very large indeed.

Of course the ramifications of crime must include not only the money and goods for the offender but also the personal suffering and physical injury of the victim. Here too, however, it is easy to be misled by popular accounts about the true level of loss. According to the National Crime Survey—a large, nationally representative sample of adults—many victims elect not to inform the police of criminal events because they consider those events to be too trivial or to be an inappropriate concern of the criminal justice system. And this is true even for offenses that bear such labels as rape, aggravated assault, robbery, and burglary. Indeed, in 1982 (National Crime Survey results are remarkably consistent from one year to the next), 39 percent of aggravated assaults, 42 percent of robberies, 45 percent of rapes, and 49 percent of burglaries were not reported to the police (McGarrell and Flanagan 1985: 273).

Most assaults result in little if any physical injury to the victim. Many assaults and homicides involve disputes between people previously known to each other where it is difficult to distinguish victim from offender in terms of provocation or responsibility. (Although the consequences of such ambiguous events may be serious, it remains true that the benefits to the offender from such acts have little or no connection to their "seriousness" and are in any event typically difficult to ascertain.)

Large exceptions to these generalizations are sometimes inferred from disciplinary paradigms. Organized crime, for example, and white-collar crime, in particular, are said by sociologists and economists to cost the nation billions of dollars annually, to undermine the normative foundations of civilization, and to produce huge profits for those involved. The credible evidence on these issues appears to suggest otherwise. For example, Peter Reuter (1983) shows that illegal gambling, loan-sharking, and prostitution tend to be local affairs with limited profits, largely because they are illegal activities operated by people with few business skills and strong tendencies to engage in activities detrimental to the long-term profitability of their own enterprises. The same can be said for drug-dealing, where the popular (law enforcement) conception is especially misleading.

None of this is to deny that offenders occasionally make big scores, that purses sometimes contain large amounts of money, that the burgled house or business may have a large amount of cash, jewelry, or precious metals, that a corporate executive may embezzle a significant sum of money, or that victims are sometimes killed. Rather, it is to stress that such events are exceptional and that the image of crime created by them is grossly misleading. Even such apparent "successes" do not necessarily ultimately produce large benefit to the offender. The ordinary offender has little use for expensive jewelry or even for expensive cars, and he has little knowledge of how to dispose of them to obtain their true value. The benefits of murder are notoriously difficult to detect. (The next morning the offender is often unable to recall what prompted the act.)

Even crimes producing relatively large sums of cash turn out to provide the offender only short-term benefits as compared to alternative sources of cash income. Consider, for example, the benefit of what by any estimate would be a "successful" robbery ($500) as compared with the gains from a minimum-wage job. The robbery cannot be repeated for any period of time with reasonable expectation of success, whereas the minimum-wage job can be a continuous source of income. Seen in this context, even the extremely rare big scores of criminal activity are at best only supplemental sources of income and must therefore be interpreted as sources of short-term gratification only.

The white-collar offender is not exempt from this problem. Embezzlement and fraud are difficult to carry out successfully over a long period. The larger the embezzlement or fraud, the more remote the likelihood of long-term success. As a result, white-collar crime too tends to provide relatively small or short-term benefit as compared to stable and honest employment.

On inspection, crimes of personal violence, such as rape, assault, and homicide, are by their nature incapable of providing more than short-term gratification for the offender. The homicide-for-hire career may seem to be an exception. However, it too is consistent with our view of crimes as short-term, limited-benefit activities rather than realistic long-term alternatives to stable employment. Hired killers, it turns out, can be had for not much money, a fact suggesting that the alternative criminal careers available to this segment of the labor force are not all that lucrative. When the hired killer takes the money and does not make the hit, his behavior is consistent with the nature of criminal employment. One such "score" would be possible, but two would be difficult, and it would be extremely difficult to make a career of failing to fulfill one's contractual obligations.

Obviously, the long-term or lasting benefits of crime are profoundly limited. As a result, the volume of crime is heavily constrained by the nature of criminal activities, by the hazards they entail, by the effort they require, and by the limited gains they produce.

Political sanctions are also a constituent element of crime. In principle, political sanctions work to reduce further the net benefits of criminal activities. Given the features of crime thus far discussed, how effective would we expect political sanctions to be? The risk of apprehension and punishment should effectively interfere with projects involving long-term planning and a considerable commitment. After all, such projects presuppose a reasonable expectation of success. What effect would we expect the risk of apprehension and punishment to have on projects where little objective gain can be established and no planning or commitment is in evidence? Obviously, very little. The evidence, however charitably it may be construed (see, e.g., Blumstein, Cohen, and Nagin 1978), is consistent with this expectation. The criminal justice system has little effect on the volume of crime (see Chapter 12).

Although it may be more glamorous and profitable for law enforcement to portray an image of crime as a highly profitable alternative to legal work, a valid theory of crime must see it as it is: largely petty, typically not completed, and usually of little lasting or substantial benefit to the offender.

Connections Among Crimes

Recall the classical definition of crime as an event involving force or fraud that satisfies self-interest. This tradition evinces little interest in connections among crimes. Whatever connections exist are merely definitional. However, the classical view would certainly assume that acts promoting self-interest in some meaningful or substantial way would tend to be repeated. And this, of course, is the basic, straightforward, and eminently reasonable assumption of modern learning theories of crime. Nevertheless, the evidence shows that specific crimes, regardless of their outcome, do not tend to be repeated. That is, burglary, even "successful" burglary, does not tend to be followed by burglary, *even in the short run*. Robbery is not followed by robbery with any more likelihood than by some other short-term pleasure, a pleasure that may well be inconsistent with another robbery (such as rape, drug use, or assault).

The reason for all of this interchangeability among crimes must be that these diverse events provide benefits with similar qualities, such qualities as immediacy, brevity of obligation, and effortlessness. (By definition, it is possible to engage in large numbers of such events in a short period of time. Given such potential frequencies, there are many possible counts of crime, and exclusive reliance on any one of them may be highly problematic.)

Many other benefits of particular criminal acts are not essential parts of the definition of crime. As a result, pursuit of such benefits is not predictive of subsequent criminal activity. For example, pecuniary gain is not essential to crime and cannot therefore be used to predict the nature of subsequent activity. (The burglary that produces pecuniary gain may be followed by drug use that entails considerable pecuniary loss.) Thus distinctions among crimes based on the mixture of pecuniary and nonpecuniary gains they produce are likely to be of little value. The same is true of distinctions between serious and petty offenses, between instrumental and expressive crimes, between person and property crimes, between crimes of passion and crimes of premeditation, between crimes *mala prohibita* and crimes *mala in se*, between status offenses and delinquent acts, between vice or victimless crimes and crimes with victims, and so on. All of these distinctions are without import. In fact, such distinctions mislead more than they inform, create needless analytical difficulties, and invite questions (such as, does shoplifting lead to burglary?)—the pursuit of which is a waste of time. The evidence is clear that the offender by his behavior and by his reports recognizes none of these distinctions; his behavior is governed by properties of crime not included in statutory distinctions, in developmental theories of crime, or, indeed, in any of the many distinctions among crimes found in positive criminology.

Conditions Necessary for Criminal Acts to Occur

Recent years have seen several attempts to specify the conditions necessary for crimes to occur. These efforts go under such names as the "routine activity approach" (Cohen and Felson 1979), the "opportunity perspective" (Cornish and Clarke 1986; Mayhew et al. 1976), and the "lifestyle opportunity" perspective (Hindelang, Gottfredson, and Garofalo 1978). In all cases, the authors attempt to specify the minimal elements necessary (and collectively sufficient) for a crime to occur and to focus research attention on elements of crime independent of the offender, elements such as characteristics of situations, targets, or victims.

At first glance, this "necessary conditions" approach to crime appears to represent a return to classical thought. For one thing, it focuses on the crime and tries to ignore the criminal; for another, it seems to deny the idea that the actions of the offender are determined by prior events, appearing instead to envision a rational, calculating actor; further, it appears to emphasize or embrace the rational, deductive approach to explanation that was replaced by the empirical, inductive approaches favored by positivists. In our view, such apparent contrast actually reveals the basic potential complementarity of the classical and positivist traditions (Gottfredson ahd Hirschi 1987a). On inspection, the two approaches turn out to contain no inherently contradictory assumptions. In fact, assertions that crimes are a product of the criminality of the actor and assertions that environmental conditions are necessary for crimes to occur are not necessarily inconsistent.[2]

There is every reason to believe that the necessary conditions strategy of opportunity theory is compatible with the idea of criminality, although the connection between the two is far from straightforward and has been largely neglected by both sides. As a result, one of our major initial tasks is to spell out the implications of opportunity theory for the concept of criminality, and vice versa. Our approach involves a detailed examination of the idea of crime, from which we are able to deduce the nature of individuals or the specific properties of individuals who are likely to fit the opportunity model of crime—that is, who are likely to engage in the crimes that the model describes. It is important to take this step for several reasons. First, we take it as axiomatic that theories of crime and theories of criminality must be consistent. Second, no theory of criminality has taken as its starting point a thorough examination of the concept of crime. Third, because existing theories of criminality rarely attend to this issue, they can be tested by their compatibility with the idea of crime. In other words, our approach allows us to judge the validity of theories of criminality

---

[2]Nor, for that matter, do these assertions differ in methodological assumption to the degree historically suggested by disputes between their advocates. Search for the necessary conditions for crime is perfectly compatible with search for the causes of crime. The causes of crime may be seen as operational indicators of the necessary conditions for crime (or the necessary conditions may be seen as abstract [theoretical] summaries of the causes of crime). For example, the number of cars in a community is predictive of the volume of auto theft. "Number of cars" is then a *cause* of crime. At the same time, the presence of automobiles in a community is a necessary condition for auto theft. These two facts, one empirical and one logical, can presumably be inferred from one another. The traditional positivistic empiricist searched for correlates or causes of crime and rarely, if ever, stopped to conceptualize them—that is, to translate them into necessary conditions. Opportunity theorists sometimes start from an examination of the correlates of crime or victimization (see, e.g., Hindelang, Gottfredson, and Garofalo 1978), but they as often start from an *a priori* or deductive list of conditions necessary for crime and go on to examine trends in the crime rates or correlates of crime consistent with these lists (Cohen and Felson 1979).

based on the consistency between their notions of criminality and opportunity theories of crime.[3]

The following chapters will thus address the concept of criminality, taking as their point of departure the features of crime described in this and the preceding chapter. For now, we extend the necessary conditions approach to common crimes, where its value in revealing the necessary characteristics of the offender can be readily seen.

To begin, we take the conditions necessary for crimes in general as commonly stated in opportunity theory. For example, in the version advanced by Lawrence Cohen and Marcus Felson (1979), crime requires a motivated offender, the absence of a capable guardian, and a suitable target. Extension or modification of definitions of crime must begin with one or another of these three elements. Normally, one would think that theories interested in the offender would concentrate on the first element. Indeed, most theories of criminality take the second and third elements as irrelevant and develop accounts of offender motivation. In fact, in our view, this is the fundamental mistake of modern theory. If we begin to construct our picture of the offender after first understanding the role of guardians and targets, he does not resemble the picture painted by current theories of criminality.

A good example is provided by Michael Hough (1987), who extends and refines the concept of a suitable target by noting that burglars base their judgment of suitability on proximity, accessibility, and reward. Hough's concept of accessibility includes ideas of defense against victimization, and his concept of reward incorporates the idea of potential yield (i.e., return for effort expended).

Hough's extension of the opportunity perspective shows that greater precision and hence predictability may be achieved by incorporating notions of offender characteristics into the definition of the criminal act, characteristics originally inferred from the nature of the act itself. Here, the burglar is seen to prefer easily available targets that offer prospects for success. Expansion of this insight leads directly to difficulty for some theories of criminality, since many would require burglary by people who tend toward criminality regardless of their assessment of the target.

A good place to look for the nature of criminality is in crimes actually committed. With this thought in mind, let us review the

---

[3] Ironically, one of the etiological theories most *in*compatible with opportunity explanations of crime is that of Richard Cloward and Lloyd Ohlin (1960). Because it is sometimes called an "opportunity" theory, some scholars put these oppositional perspectives in the same class. For an excellent discussion of the compatibility of choice and opportunity perspectives, see Philip Cook (1986).

fundamental characteristics and general patterns of common crimes. Our list of crimes is based on considerations of structure, data availability, and relevance to the criminality issue.

Burglary

Burglary is the crime most often described (implicitly or explicitly) by opportunity theorists. The reasons are not hard to find. In burglary, the "target" is, in effect, a physical object that plays no active role in its own victimization; in burglary, the offender is clearly where he should not be doing something he should not be doing. There is thus little question about whether his or her behavior is criminal. Burglary involves a physical structure or access to a physical space, all of which suggests the ability to control the crime by modification of the environment. Finally, burglary is one of the most common felonies. In fact, according to the National Crime Survey, about 7–8 percent of the households in the United States are victimized annually. According to the same survey, about half of these burglaries are reported to the police.

Pat Mayhew (1987) reports that about half of burglaries occur during the daytime, when houses are empty. Michael Hindelang (1976: 292) has shown that vacant or unoccupied houses are at greater risk than occupied houses. Lawrence Cohen and David Cantor (1981) indirectly illustrate the impact of occupancy by establishing a correlation between burglary rates and female labor force participation. Others have done so directly: Stuart Winchester and Hilary Jackson (1982: 16) report that "the most striking characteristic of burglary is that it usually takes place in houses that have been left unoccupied. . . . 80% took place in dwellings where there was nobody in the house at the time."

According to Hough (1987), the majority of *successful* burglaries are carried out in empty homes, whereas a high proportion of *attempted* burglaries take place when victims are present. Physical accessibility is also a predictor of burglary risk. Houses at the ends of rows of houses, which have greater access from the street, have higher burglary rates. Hough shows that, in England, physical accessibility to the rear of property is also important.

According to police records and the reports of those arrested for burglary (Reppetto 1974), burglars use unsophisticated methods to gain entry. If the door or window is locked, the term "break in" is apt; police reports indicate that more than half of burglaries involve forcible entry. However, according to the National Crime Survey (based on the reports of victims whether or not they called the police), less than one-third of burglaries actually involve forcible entry.

Items most frequently stolen are relatively light electronic goods. Cash is of course taken, if it is present, but credit cards and check books are typically ignored (Reppetto 1974). The National Crime Survey reveals that, in 1983, two-thirds of the burglaries resulted in less than a $250 loss, a figure that includes damages to doors, windows, and the like. Hough and Mayhew (1985: 28) report from the 1984 British Crime Survey that the value of theft losses in Britain for burglaries was less than £100 in 65 percent of the cases.

The net income to offenders from burglaries is much less than the losses to victims, since offenders gain no pecuniary benefit from damaged doors or broken windows and since they must sell the goods they steal for much less than the value their owners place on them.[4] In many cases, offenders may intend simply to appropriate the property for their own use, an intention consistent with the theft of items of recreational value to young people. Such use of stolen items is, however, inconsistent with the notion that burglary is a source of employment-like income, since offenders cannot make a living on portable radios or VCRs.

According to interviews with offenders, the major deterrents are "a house being occupied, dogs, poor back access, visibility to neighbors and passers-by, and poor escape routes; conventional security is claimed by [incarcerated] burglars to be of little importance" (Mayhew 1984: 34). Research has also shown that burglars do not travel far to offend. Paul and Patricia Brantingham say that "burglars [select] their targets from within a narrow personal 'activity space,' that is, from areas they pass through in daily journeys from home to work or school and to the principal social and shopping locations they [frequent] in the evenings or on weekends" (1984: 79). Put another way, offenders burglarize "in areas close to major activity areas and along major traffic arteries" (ibid.).

People arrested for burglary tend to be male (about 95 percent), young (median age about 17), and disproportionately nonwhite (about one-third). Although young, they are likely to have prior records of offending (for a variety of offenses). They are also highly likely to be arrested subsequently, again for a variety of offenses.

[4]The cash value of stolen goods varies from 100 percent (for cash) of original cost to practically zero. Police sting operators report being able to buy stolen goods for seven cents on the dollar, but this is considered by some scholars to be more than the goods are worth (see Klockars 1988). An average of ten cents on the dollar is also frequently reported (see, e.g., Hindelang 1976: 312).

The Typical or Standard Burglary

In the standard burglary, a young male (or group of males; see Reiss 1988) knocks on a door not far from where he lives. Finding no one home, he tests the door to see if it is open. If it is open (as it often is), he walks in and looks to see if the dwelling contains anything of interest that he can quickly consume or easily haul away. In most cases, the only items that appeal to these mid-teen boys are cash, booze, and entertainment equipment. In most cases, the proceeds of the burglary are quickly consumed, used up, given away, or discarded. The crime provides, then, immediate, easy, short-term gratification. And nothing more. Obviously, not all burglaries fit this pattern. The police and the media portray an image of burglary that makes it more exotic, more worthwhile, more difficult, and more taxing of police skills in its detection. The events that seem to fit the police/media image are so rare that the same ones must be used repeatedly; they are also sufficiently rare that they are strongly misleading about the causes and control of burglary.

The Logical Structure of Burglary

For burglary to occur, several conditions must be present. There must be, first of all, a building or dwelling. This building or dwelling must be capable of entry by someone who does not have permission to do so. Second, the building or dwelling must have contents that are apparently attractive to the offender and capable of being removed from the premises. Third, the building or dwelling must not be monitored by someone able to observe the burglary and interfere with its completion. Finally, burglary requires an actor insufficiently restrained from taking advantage of these conditions.

Burglary can therefore be prevented in a variety of ways. In principle, buildings and dwellings could be constructed such that they cannot be entered by persons who do not have permission to do so.[5] The value or portability of the contents of buildings and dwellings can be reduced below the point of attractiveness to the offender. Buildings can be monitored by those interested and capable of intervening in the act. And, burglary can be prevented by putting sufficient restraints on people who encounter attractive opportunities for burglary.

[5]This discussion is predicated on the technical definition of burglary. As will be described in subsequent chapters, we are aware that a considerable amount of theft that takes place within buildings or dwellings is performed by people who have permission to be there. Our notion of criminality does not preclude the possibility that likely offenders are willing to victimize people close to them.

Such an analysis has obvious implications for the relative merits of various explanations of crime and notions of criminality. If criminality is as we will describe it (see Chapter 5), burglary can be efficiently prevented by several of the devices listed. (According to our scheme, other devices will be relatively less efficient.) Recall that crime implies interest in immediate, easy gratification of short-term desires. If this view of crime is correct, nearly any obstacle placed in the path of the offender is likely to have some consequence for the likelihood that a given dwelling will be burglarized and for the likelihood that a burglary will take place at all. Thus a locked door will prevent some burglary. A locked door that cannot be smashed without mechanical aid will prevent more. A residence that appears to be observed by neighbors will be less vulnerable than a residence that cannot be seen by people living in the area.

On the other hand, given the immediate, easy, short-term needs that most offenders seek to gratify, the prevention benefits of reducing target attractiveness are extremely limited. When a few coins and a bottle of liquor are the attractive objects, the burglary rate cannot be controlled by greater use of safety deposit boxes and credit cards. (The loss from any given burglary can, however, be reduced by such means.) Given the large number of potential targets that satisfy the attractiveness threshold of people who tend toward criminality, marked reduction of the burglary rate by intentional efforts to increase the monitoring of interested parties is unlikely. Finally, given the temporary nature of the burglar's interest in burglary and the concentration of these interests in the mid-teen years (see the age distribution of burglary in Chapter 6), greater restraint on potential burglars is likely to produce a lower burglary rate than greater restraint on those already convicted of burglary. Finally, of course, long-term reductions in burglary rates might be effected by reduction in the level of criminality in the population. Since this approach would have an impact on all forms of crime, we will treat it at some length in Chapter 12.

In all of these respects, our scheme has empirical implications very different from those derived from standard criminological theories or from atheoretical policy advice based on the assumption of an "active offender" or a "criminal career" (Blumstein et al. 1986). Fortunately for our scheme, its empirical implications seem to be borne out by the research on burglary.

Robbery

Robbery is defined by the FBI as taking or attempting to take something from someone by the use of force or the threat of force. Rates of robbery in the United States are high as compared to those in other countries, with seven people per thousand aged twelve or older reporting being victimized in any given year (according to the National Crime Survey). This rate is more than three times the rate in England and Wales (Hough and Mayhew 1985: 62). The U.S. rate is much higher in central cities than in other regions of the country. In fact, Wesley Skogan (1979) reports that two-thirds of the reported robberies in the United States in 1970 were concentrated in 32 cities that housed only 16 percent of the nation's population.

In popular conception, robbery is the ultimate street crime. About seven in ten personal robberies take place on the street (Reiss 1967: 22; Conklin 1972: 81; Hindelang 1976: 206). Losses from robbery tend to be modest. According to victim estimates derived from the National Crime Survey for 1982, 55 percent of robberies resulted in less than a $50 loss; 80 percent resulted in losses of less than $250. About half of robberies involve weapons, with guns appearing about one-fifth of the time (Hindelang 1976: 213). The presence of a gun reduces the likelihood of injury to the victim (Hindelang, Gottfredson, and Garofalo 1978). Hindelang (1976) has shown that about 95 percent of personal theft crimes involve a lone victim. In contrast, in more than 60 percent of such incidents there are multiple offenders; in fact, there are three or more offenders in 33 percent of all robberies.

Robbers, like burglars, tend to be young; in recent years the median age has been nineteen. The robbers tend be male (about 95 percent) and disproportionately nonwhite (a majority). Arrestees tend to have prior records, with no evidence of specialization; they are also highly likely to be arrested again, for a variety of offenses.

Interviews with offenders incarcerated for robbery document the fact that they do not specialize in robbery (Petersilia 1980; Feeney 1986). Data confirm the conclusion that persons reporting robbery are more likely to report all other offenses as well (see, e.g., Hindelang, Hirschi, and Weis 1981). Although robbers tend to claim a monetary motive for their acts, many robberies seem to be incidental to other activities (Feeney 1986). High proportions of robbers report alcohol and drug use prior to or during the offense (Petersilia 1980; Feeney 1986), and there is little evidence of advance planning or fear of apprehension. Indeed, planning appears to be more a matter of convenience than anything else. Floyd Feeney's Oakland, California, robbers explain their choice of targets: "Just where we happened to be, I guess"; "Nothing else open at 2:00 A.M. Had been there before"; "We thought it would be quickest, you know, it's a small donut shop" (1986: 62). Feeney summarizes the issue:

The impulsive, spur-of-the-moment nature of many of these robberies is well illustrated by two adult robbers who said they had passengers in their cars who had no idea that they planned a robbery. One passenger, who thought his friend was buying root beer and cigarets, found out the hard way what had happened. A clerk chased his robber-friend out the door and fired a shotgun blast through the windshield of the passenger's car. [Ibid.: 60]

There is substantial evidence that most robbers attack victims close to where they live. Andre Normandeau (1968) reports that in Philadelphia the median distance from the residence of the offender to the robbery was about one mile (see also Feeney 1986). In fact, the age-race-gender profile of victims of robbery closely parallels the profile of offenders—indicating a strong tendency for robbers to rob people like themselves.

The Typical or Standard Robbery

In the ordinary robbery, a young male in his late teens or a group of young males in their middle teens approaches a solitary person on the street and, either through stealth (purse snatching) or intimidation gained by size or numerical advantage (but sometimes with a weapon), demands valuables. Once the transaction is completed, the offender runs from the scene and the victim begins to search for means of calling the police.

The ordinary commercial robbery also involves a young man, sometimes two young men, also in possession of an advantage gained through possession of a weapon (or the claim of such possession), who demands cash from the register of a convenience store or gas station. Once the transaction is completed, the offender runs from the store and the clerk calls the police.

The Logical Structure of Robbery

The structure of robbery differs from the structure of burglary in several important respects. For one thing, there is a direct confrontation between the victim and the offender. For another, in a robbery the offender typically has the "right" to be where he is, and there is no physical device that can stop him from being there. But let us describe the necessary elements of robbery. First, there must be an attractive target, such as a person with goods potentially attractive to the offender (a purse, a wallet, a lunch pail or lunch money) or a commercial establishment that deals in cash or that carries expensive portable goods (e.g., jewelry). Second, the offender must have an advantage over the target in terms of power or apparent force. And third, the offender must be a person insufficiently restrained from taking advantage of the opportunity.

Robbery can be prevented by eliminating interaction between potential robbers and potential victims and by increasing the apparent power of targets relative to that of potential offenders. It can also be reduced, in principle, by reducing the attractiveness of potential targets. Finally, of course, robbery can be reduced by increasing the restraints on people who tend toward criminality.

Again, in our view, not all of these logical possibilities are equally likely to be effective in preventing robbery. Altering the attractiveness of potential targets can have some impact (witness the effectiveness of "we carry no cash" programs), but the gratifications the offender seeks are often so modest that many limitations become impractical. Altering the balance of power can be effective, but given the offender's probable lack of attention to subtle clues and abstract probabilities, such power must be readily visible. So far as preventing robbery is concerned, moving in groups is therefore more effective than carrying a concealed weapon, and not carrying a purse is more effective than carrying a purse containing mace.

Mechanical devices may prevent robbery by separating potential victims from potential robbers such that the physical control over the victim necessary to complete the robbery is impossible to obtain. Partitions in taxis, cages in liquor stores, and locked doors in automobiles are examples of such devices.

Given the age distribution of offending (see Chapter 6) and the temporal and spatial characteristics of robbery, an effective curfew would do much to restrain potential offenders and eliminate potential targets; so too would greater supervision of young people going to and from school. By the same token, it is unlikely that any conceivable increase in police patrolling could have an impact on the robbery rate.

Homicide

Despite popular and scholarly opinion to the contrary, homicide is perhaps the most mundane and, in our view, most easily explainable crime. First, some facts. The homicide rate in the United States in 1987 was about eight per 100,000 people per year, though it was as high as ten in 1980 and as low as five in the early 1960's. Nearly 60 percent of murders are committed with firearms. Poisoning is extremely rare, and about 20 percent of murders are committed with a knife. About 15 percent of the time, the offender beats the victim to death.

About 20 percent of homicides in which the relationship between the victim and the offender is known involve family members. About the same proportion involve strangers. The remainder involve people known to each other with a degree of intimacy ranging from recognition (such as a fellow patron of a bar) to boyfriend or girlfriend. Seventy-five percent of the victims of homicide are males. Forty percent of the victims are black.

Homicides involving family members or acquaintances may appear to be crimes of passion, but they occur with considerable predictability and regularity. They most often take place on weekends, at night, indoors, and in front of an audience. Frequently, the victim, the offender, or both are using alcohol or drugs at the time of the offense. James Wilson and Richard Herrnstein report that "there have, in fact, been at least 28 separate studies of alcohol involvement in murder; fourteen of these found alcohol present in at least 60 percent of the cases, and the great majority found it present in a third or more of the cases" (1985: 356). As is widely reported, there is often difficulty in establishing the distinction between victim and offender—that is, in knowing where the primary blame for the offense resides. Furthermore, both victim and offender tend to have relatively high rates of prior involvement in crimes and delinquencies.

A second common pattern of homicide involves the so-called felony homicides, in which a victim is killed in the course of a lesser crime such as burglary, robbery, or rape. These events tend to occur among strangers and tend not to take place inside residences. Indeed, in these respects they generally follow the pattern of the lesser crimes from which they derive.

Again, offenders and victims bear remarkable similarity to each other. Offenders tend overwhelmingly to be young (in 1983 the peak age of homicide arrestees was nineteen), male (87 percent), and disproportionately nonwhite (about 51 percent). Homicide arrestees have records similar to those of other offenders—that is, there is considerable versatility in the types of offenses. The recidivism records of persons arrested for murder tend to show fewer subsequent arrests than ordinary offenders, but these differences are attributable to differences in length of imprisonment. (Murderers are not the "good risks" sometimes claimed.)

Homicide is the classic example given by opponents of hedonistic explanations of crime. By definition, they say, crimes of passion are not crimes of rational gain. Impulse, the argument goes, cannot be reasoned, cannot be governed by considerations of costs and benefits. Such an argument is not germane to a theory built on the idea that crime is governed by its short-term, immediate benefits, without consideration of long-term cost. In this view, homicide is precisely the kind of behavior produced by high levels of criminality, where serious crimes are committed for trivial reasons. Many homicides in fact seem to have little to do with "pleasure" and much to do with the reduction of "pain." The pain suffered by the offender is not great by usual standards; often the only benefit to the offender is the removal of a temporary source of irritation or an obstacle to the achievement of some immediate end, such as a successful burglary. In other words, the benefits of homicide are not large, profound, or serious. They are, on the contrary, benefits of the moment, and the effect of alcohol or drugs may be found precisely in their tendency to reduce the time-horizon of the offender to the here and now. A consideration of the logical structure of homicide will make this clear.

The Typical or Standard Homicide

Homicide comes in two basic varieties. In one version, people who are known to one another argue over some trivial matter, as they have argued frequently in the past. In fact, in the past their argument has on occasion led to physical violence, sometimes on the part of the offender, sometimes on the part of the victim. In the present instance, one of them decides that he has had enough, and he hits a little harder or with what turns out to be a lethal instrument. Often, of course, the offender simply ends the dispute with a gun.

In the other version, the standard robbery described above becomes a homicide when for some reason (sometimes because the victim resists, sometimes for no apparent reason at all) the offender fires his gun at the clerk or store owner. Or, occasionally, there is a miscalculation during a burglary and the house turns out to be occupied. Again sometimes because the victim resists and sometimes for no apparent reason the offender clubs, knifes, or shoots the resident.

The Logical Structure of Homicide

In law, criminal homicide is the willful killing of one human being by another without excuse or defense. In order for criminal homicide to occur: there must be an offender and a victim in interaction with each other; the offender must possess the means of taking the life of another; the offender must be insufficiently restrained to prevent the crime; the victim must lack the opportunity or inclination to remove himself from the threat posed by the offender; and no life-saving third-party intervention is available to the victim.

Criminal homicide differs from other crimes more in the complexity of its structure than in the depth or seriousness of its motives. The difference between homicide and assault may simply be the intervention of a bystander, the accuracy of a gun, the weight of a frying pan, the speed of an ambulance, or the availability of a trauma center. The difference between robbery and felony murder may simply be the resistance offered by a store clerk. The difference between burglary and felony murder may be whether the occupant of the dwelling returns home during the crime.

Complex crimes are more easily controlled than simple crimes because interference with any of the necessary elements is sufficient to prevent the crime. So, for example, homicide may be prevented by eliminating interaction between victims and offenders, by removing lethal weapons from offenders, by increasing the availability of bystanders and the probability of their intervention, by decreasing the resistance of victims of lesser crimes, and by decreasing the use of alcohol and drugs. Homicide can also be prevented by reducing the number of people who tend toward criminality.

Evidence for the short-term, immediate nature of the motive for homicide is found in the fact that victims of attempted homicide or aggravated assault rarely require police protection following the crime. In fact, the evidence suggests that most victims of such acts resume their prior relation with the offender or their prior activity pattern (Sherman and Berk 1984).

Auto Theft

Auto theft is theft or attempted theft of a motor vehicle. Rates of auto theft in the United States in 1985 ranged from about eight to twenty thefts per 1,000 vehicles per year. There is considerable variability in the risk of automobile theft depending on the brand of car, its age, and its accessibility. Thus, for example, station wagons are less likely to be stolen than two-door coupes. New cars are at greater risk than old cars; cars parked in public places and cars driven frequently are more likely to be stolen. Cars with antitheft devices, such as steering-column locks, are relatively unlikely to be stolen (Mayhew et al. 1976). Unlocked cars, cars with keys in the ignition, and cars left unattended with the motor running are especially vulnerable to theft.

About 70 percent of car thefts occur at night, and about 80 percent of stolen cars are recovered (Hindelang 1976: 302, 308). The common police assertion that cars are stolen for parts is discredited by Carl

Klockars (1988), who notes that the market for used auto parts is not sufficiently active to sustain auto theft. The auto junk yards surrounding U.S. cities provide an ample supply of cheap carburetors and used wheels. The fact that the owners of such yards do not disassemble wrecked vehicles until a specific part is requested suggests that auto thieves would also find prior disassembly unprofitable. The age of the typical auto thief (the age of arrestees peaks at age sixteen, and over half of arrestees are under eighteen) also casts doubt on the auto-theft-ring explanation of this offense. Once again the field of criminology (and the public) has been misled by rare but highly publicized events.

For the record, persons arrested for auto theft tend to be young (16–18), male (over 90 percent), and disproportionately nonwhite (about 33 percent).

The Typical or Standard Auto Theft

In the typical auto theft, a car left unlocked on a public street or in a public parking lot with the keys in the ignition or in plain view is entered by a sixteen-year-old male or group of males and is driven until it runs out of gas or until the offenders must attend to other obligations.

The Logical Structure of Auto Theft

Auto theft is an especially complex crime. In order for a car theft to occur, there must be an automobile that is accessible, drivable, and attractive. There must also be an offender who is both capable of driving and insufficiently restrained. For auto theft, as opposed to joyriding, it is also necessary that the offender possess the means to maintain and store the vehicle. As a result of this last condition, joyriding is much more common than other forms of auto theft, and thus the recovery rate for stolen vehicles is high and the thief is rarely caught. In recent years, undercover police officers have acted as potential buyers of stolen vehicles, but these sting operations, ironically, may well have increased the rate of auto theft (see Chapters 10 and 12).

Auto theft can therefore be prevented by reduction in the number of automobiles, by making access to automobiles more difficult, by making them more difficult to drive, and by making them less attractive to offenders. Auto theft can also be reduced by increasing restraints on people who tend toward criminality, perhaps by making eighteen the minimum age for a driver's license.

Rape

According to the National Crime Survey, there are about 140 rapes or attempted rapes per 100,000 females age twelve and older per year. According to the *Uniform Crime Reports* (U.S. Department of Justice 1985), about 70 rapes and attempted rapes per 100,000 females were reported to the police in 1983. According to victim surveys and police data, rapes occur disproportionately in the evening or at night and on weekends (see Hindelang, Gottfredson, and Garofalo 1978). According to victim survey data, most rapes do not occur in the home of the victim, and fewer than 20 percent involve weapons. About 60 percent of rapes reported in victim surveys involve strangers (the proportion of strangers in rapes reported to the police is slightly lower than in victim surveys).

Persons arrested for rape tend to be young (the peak age of arrest is 21) and disproportionately nonwhite (about 51 percent in 1983). They tend to have prior records of arrest for a variety of crimes, and their recidivism records resemble those of offenders arrested for burglary or robbery—that is, they are generalists, likely to be arrested again for a crime other than rape. Victims of rape also tend to be young (the peak age of victimization was 16–19 in 1982) and members of minority groups.

The Standard or Typical Rape

Few crimes are as misunderstood in the popular conception as forcible rape. The common contemporary image, influenced by media depictions of atypical events, involves one of the following scenarios: (1) A family member or close personal friend forces himself on the victim. The victim reacts to the violence and humiliation without invoking the criminal justice system. This scenario is variously labeled, in the popular literature, "family violence" or "date rape." (2) A woman is attacked by a group of males, in a public place, and suffers serious physical injuries in addition to those inflicted by the rape itself. Such "gang" rapes evoke an official response.

According to the data, both of these scenarios are relatively rare. Family members and close friends apparently rarely jeopardize long-term relations by committing or reporting rape. And single offenders overwhelmingly predominate in rape statistics.

A statistically more common scenario begins with a public encounter at night between strangers. The woman is alone and out of public view. A lone offender either lies in wait or follows and attacks her.

The attack may take place on the spot or after the victim has been forced to a more remote setting.

In nonstranger victimizations, the contemporary literature overstates the extent of prior relationship between the rape victim and her attacker. In the typical "nonstranger" rape, the offender and the victim, who know one another only slightly, are in a vulnerable setting by mutual consent, such as in a car or an apartment, and the offender forces the victim to submit. In this situation, the victim often does not call the police.

One final scenario involves a woman asleep alone in her home who is awakened by a lone offender who has entered through an unlocked door or open window. After he leaves she calls the police.

The Logical Structure of Rape

More so than for any other form of crime, it is difficult to discuss objectively the properties of rape. The crime, and the criminal justice system response to it, are so emotionally charged that objective descriptions are often seen as reflecting a lack of sensitivity. Nevertheless, much of the contemporary image of rape is erroneous and misleading, and it should be evaluated through careful assessment of the best available data and careful attention to the logical structure of the crime.

In order for rape to occur, several conditions are necessary. First, there must be a victim who is attractive to an offender, available to the offender, unwilling to engage in sexual activity, and unable to resist the offender's advances. Second, there must be an offender who is insufficiently restrained.

For almost every crime, sensible prevention methods can be designed around the concept of target hardening. Thus, we can make cars less vulnerable with locks and homes less vulnerable with good lighting. Such prevention measures take advantage of the logical structure of the crime and of the characteristics of the target that make it attractive to potential offenders. The emotions evoked by rape, by the trauma suffered by its victims, and by the inadequacy of the criminal justice system response make efforts to offer similar suggestions vulnerable to the charge of blaming the victim. Offering advice to car owners not to leave keys in the ignition because it makes the car more attractive on opportunity grounds is widely seen as sensible advice; however, offering advice to young women not to travel alone at night in public places, particularly near bars or other places where alcohol is consumed, is seen by many as insensitive because it limits the freedom of women. Obviously, and regrettably, good advice in the crime area often reduces the liberty of potential victims.

Nevertheless, the logical structure of a crime produces recommendations for prevention and predicts the variables that cause the crime. According to the data, rape is more likely when young men and women can encounter each other alone in public places, particularly at night. Reduction of such opportunities would be expected to reduce the incidence of rape. Rape can also be prevented by exercising caution in entering vulnerable settings with strangers (including casual acquaintances). Rape can also be prevented by locking doors and windows, especially for women who live alone. Rape can be prevented by increasing the ability of women to resist (such as by providing companions, visible weapons, and whistles). Finally, of course, rape can also be prevented by reducing the number of men who tend toward criminality.

White-Collar Crime

The concept of white-collar crime raises difficult theoretical issues that have not been given sufficient attention by academicians or criminal justice functionaries. However, as it turns out, the white-collar crime area provides a useful explication of the central ideas of this book. This explication is only suggested here. We reserve full treatment of the topic to Chapter 9.

There is no legal definition of white-collar crime because there is no crime that goes by that name. In fact, the term white-collar crime was invented by the sociologist Edwin Sutherland to refer to crimes committed by people of respectability and high standing in the community. The idea that such people have crimes unique to them is directly contrary to the idea of crime used throughout this book. If crime involves immediate, easy gratification of short-term desires, it seems unlikely that crime would appeal to persons of high social status who must, by definition, attend to the long-term consequences of their acts. The existence of white-collar crimes in fact turns out to support rather than to undermine our conception of the nature of criminal acts, as the following discussion of a specific crime associated with white-collar employment will demonstrate.

Embezzlement

Embezzlement is the misappropriation or misapplication of money or property entrusted to one's care, custody, or control. Arrest rates for embezzlement are low. In 1983, there were 7,600 arrests for embezzlement in the United States, as compared to 400,000 for burglary, 30,000 for forcible rape, and 18,000 for murder. Contrary to the popular image, the rate of embezzlement is highest among young people, males, and minority groups.

The Standard or Ordinary Embezzlement

As the demographic profile suggests, in the ordinary embezzlement a young man recently hired steals money from his employer's cash register or goods from the store. Little or no skill is required, the benefits are obvious and immediate, and the opportunity is given in the position itself. Clearly there are embezzlements of large amounts by older employees in trusted positions, but the rarity of these acts is an important datum in itself and should not be allowed to obscure the unremarkable nature of most embezzlements.

The Logical Structure of Embezzlement

In an influential study devoted exclusively to embezzlement, Donald Cressey argues that three conditions are necessary for embezzlement:

1. The feeling that a personal financial problem is unshareable.
2. Knowledge of how to solve the problem in secret, by violating a position of financial trust.
3. Ability to find a formula that describes the act of embezzling in words that do not conflict with the image of oneself as a trusted person. [1986: 199]

In our terminology, the conditions necessary for embezzlement are as follows: there must be (1) money or goods that are attractive to the offender, available to the offender, and not rightfully the property of the offender, and (2) an offender insufficiently restrained.

The contrast between the logical structure of embezzlement we present and Cressey's differential association version of the same offense illustrates the contrast between theories that start from a concept of crime and those that start from a concept of the offender. Cressey obviously begins with a concept of the offender that makes the fruits of embezzlement appealing only to a select group of people and that makes embezzlement difficult to accomplish and hard to justify. We begin with a concept of the offense that makes the fruits of the crime attractive to everyone and that makes the crime easy to do, without the need for special justification. Both views predict a relatively low rate of embezzlement (see Chapter 9), but they have rather different views of causation and of effective prevention.

In Cressey's version, embezzlement can be prevented by removing the motive to offend, by reducing the opportunity to do so, and by changing the values of the business world. In our version, embezzlement can be prevented by reducing opportunity and by hiring employees or managers who have been adequately socialized to generally accepted values both inside and outside the business world that forbid stealing. A major difference in the theories is found in their assumptions about the nature of white-collar offenders: Cressey's theory assumes that embezzlers are a representative sample of white-collar workers; our theory assumes that embezzlers will turn out to have been involved in other crimes as well. Full explication of this issue must await our discussion of low self-control in Chapter 5.

Drugs and Alcohol

The correlation between the use of drugs, alcohol, or tobacco and the commission of delinquent and criminal acts is well established. According to Ronald Akers, "compared to the abstaining teenager, the drinking, smoking, and drug taking teen is much more likely to be getting into fights, stealing, hurting other people, and committing other delinquencies" (1984: 41; see also Hirschi 1969; Kandel 1978; Johnston, Bachman, and O'Malley 1978; Hindelang, Hirschi, and Weis 1981). It is also established that national trends in drug use parallel those for all other crimes. Thus rates of drug use peaked in about 1980 and have held steady or declined subsequently, a pattern describing the crime rate as well.

Despite this decline, the use of some drugs remains widespread in American society. For example, among high school seniors of both sexes graduating in 1983, 69 percent reported using alcohol in the previous 30 days; 30 percent reported having smoked cigarettes; 27 percent reported using marijuana; and 5 percent reported using cocaine (Johnston, O'Malley, and Bachman 1984).

Drug and alcohol use account for much of the activity of the criminal justice system. In the early 1980's, there were annually more than one million arrests for drunkenness, one and a half million arrests for driving under the influence, half a million arrests for drug abuse, and nearly half a million arrests for liquor law violations. Not included in this compilation are arrests for more serious offenses where the offender had been consuming drugs or alcohol prior to or during the offense.

Drug and alcohol use peaks in the early twenties and then declines. Rates of drug use are higher among males than females, but there has been a tendency toward convergence in recent years, and the differences in use (as opposed to abuse) by gender are not large.

Drug and alcohol use are not universally proscribed by law. Some drugs are, however, proscribed for everyone, and all drugs are proscribed for some people, such as children. The proscription of drugs, it is generally agreed, drives up their price and reduces the rate at which they are consumed. The increase in price that comes with proscription is generally thought to make the sale of drugs an attractive source of income for offenders, and it is thought to cause income-producing crimes by addicts otherwise unable to support their drug habits. Thus the general view in the field has come to be that drugs and crime are related through some economic or cash nexus: because of their high price, drugs cause criminal acts by addicts and are themselves a direct cause of crime as an attractive source of (illegal) income. An additional source of the connection between drugs and crimes alleged in current criminology is found in the idea that they have a common cause in peer pressure or adolescent values.

In the first view, the connection between drugs and crime would disappear were drugs legal and (therefore) cheap. In the second view, there is also no *inherent* connection between drugs and crime; in fact, this relation may in some circumstances be positive and in others negative—for example, some criminal subcultures may forbid drug use (compare Cloward and Ohlin 1960 with Elliott, Huizinga, and Ageton 1985). In our view, both of these perspectives are wrong. Crime and drug use are connected because they share features that satisfy the tendencies of criminality. Both provide immediate, easy, and certain short-term pleasure. An additional source of the connection may well be the immediate effect of alcohol on inhibitions that control responses to momentary irritation (Aschaffenberg 1913: 85–86).

Evidence to support our contention is found in the correlation between the use of cheap drugs, such as alcohol and tobacco, and crime (Schoff 1915; Hirschi 1969; Ferri 1897: 117). Our view is also supported by the connection between crime and drugs that do not affect mood or behavior sufficient to cause crime (such as tobacco).

Typical Drug Offenses

In one typical drug offense, a young man consumes a large quantity of alcohol at a friend's house and is stopped on the way home for erratic driving. He is cited for driving under the influence. Typical drug *use* is, however, a different matter. Some drugs are used repeatedly on a daily basis. For example, it is not unusual for smokers to consume 40 or more cigarettes a day, and alcohol and marijuana consumption can occur on a daily basis for heavy users. *Abuse* that occasions calls for wars on drugs is yet another matter. In this context, the drug problem centers on addiction to "hard" drugs by people who must steal or sell drugs to novice users to support their habit.

The Logical Structure of Drug Use

The necessary conditions for drug use are easily identified. There must be a drug that is both attractive and available to the offender, and there must be an offender who is insufficiently restrained. In order to prevent the use of a particular drug, it is necessary to reduce its attractiveness by increasing its economic cost, by reducing its quality, or by increasing awareness of its impact on health. Alternatively, the availability of the drug may be affected by interfering with its production, sale, or distribution. Finally, drug use may be prevented by reducing the number of people who tend toward criminality.

Events Theoretically Equivalent to Crime

Crimes result from the pursuit of immediate, certain, easy benefits. Some noncriminal events appear to result from pursuit of the same kinds of benefits. As a result, these noncriminal events are correlated with crime, and examination of them can help elucidate the nature of crime and criminality.

One class of events analogous to crimes is accidents. Accidents are not ordinarily seen as producing benefits. On the contrary, they are by definition costly, and their long-term costs may be substantial. However, examination of the correlates of accidents and the circumstances under which they occur suggests that they have much in common with crimes. For example, motor vehicle accidents tend to be associated with speed, drinking, tail-gating, inattention, risk-taking, defective equipment, and young males. House fires tend to be associated with smoking, drinking, number of children, and defective equipment.

Distinctions Among Crimes

There is nothing more deeply ingrained in the common sense of criminology than the idea that not all crimes are alike. This common-sense criminology distinguishes between trivial and serious crimes (e.g., Elliott, Huizinga, and Ageton 1985; Wilson and Herrnstein 1985), between instrumental and expressive crimes (Chambliss 1969), between status offenses and delinquency, between victim and victimless crimes (Morris and Hawkins 1970), between crimes *mala in se* and crimes *mala prohibita*, and, most important, between person and property crimes. As should be clear by now, our theory regards all of these distinctions as irrelevant or misleading. Let us briefly examine trivial versus serious crimes here.

Criminologists operate as though there must be a difference in etiology between trivial crimes and serious crimes, but drawing the distinction between these events (and/or people) is difficult, as the following quotation illustrates:

> By looking mainly at serious crimes, we escape the problem of comparing persons who park by a fire hydrant to persons who rob banks. . . . If we propose to confine our attention to persons who commit serious crimes at high rates, then we must specify what we mean by 'serious.' . . . [T]his book will chiefly refer to aggressive, violent, or larcenous behavior; [the arguments] will be, for the most part, about persons who hit, rape, murder, steal, and threaten. . . . But there is an advantage to this emphasis on predatory crime. Such behavior . . . is condemned, in all societies and in all historical periods, by ancient tradition, moral sentiments, and formal law. . . . By drawing on empirical studies of behaviors that are universally regarded as wrong . . . we can be confident that we are in fact theorizing about *crime* and human nature and not about actions that people may or may not think are wrong. [Wilson and Herrnstein 1985: 21–23]

Inspection of this statement reveals that it does several things. First, it implies that it is somehow useful to study bank robbers separately from parking violators, a theoretical assertion that is problematic and empirically doubtful. (After all, it is at least arguable that persons who park illegally in front of fire hydrants may share characteristics with people who rob banks, such as a lack of concern for the interest of others and a disregard for the consequences of one's acts.)

Second, it implies that serious criminal acts somehow require causes of commensurate seriousness, that dastardly acts tell us more about human nature (or, for other theorists, about the structure of society) than acts of little consequence. As we have shown, there is no justification for this assumption in logic or fact. Murder may be among the least motivated, least deliberate, and least consequential (for the offender) crime. Shoplifting may be among the most.

Third, it implies specialization among offenders that does not exist. The idea of specialization in serious or petty crime is perhaps the least defensible of all specialization theories.

Fourth, it implies that there is something of etiological significance in the distinction between crimes that are fully executed and those that are not. Reasons that serious crimes go awry include poor aim (of the gun meant to kill the clerk), mistaking baking soda for cocaine, being beaten up by the person assaulted, stealing $49 instead of $51, and so on.

These distinctions are of obvious importance for the criminal law, which must draw the line between a sheep and a lamb in order to promote marginal deterrence, but they are of little importance to a theory of etiology. That is, the law seeks to persuade would-be armed robbers not to carry a gun by reducing penalties for unarmed robbery. But the criminal law assumes that the same theory (deterrence) applies equally to armed and unarmed robbery. Put another way, the law does not see different causes operating on events depending on their legal seriousness. In this respect, the criminal law is far ahead of crime theories that classify criminal events in terms of adventitious or extraneous properties.

On reflection, all of the distinctions between crimes listed above have been covered in our discussion of specific crimes recognized by the criminal law. We have examined person and property crimes, crimes *mala in se* and *mala prohibita*, victim and victimless crimes, status offenses and delinquencies, and instrumental and expressive crimes. In no case have we found it theoretically necessary or useful to classify a particular criminal event in these terms. As will be evident, these distinctions fare even worse when we focus on the offender rather than on the offense.

II

CRIMINALITY

3

Biological Positivism

The classical conception of human behavior, with its emphasis on choice in the service of self-interest, eventually gave way to a positivist conception of human behavior, with an emphasis on difference and determinism. The positivist revolution was greeted with great optimism and enthusiasm, and its methods were soon applied to almost everything, including crime. This chapter traces the positivist revolution from its origins in biology to the current state of biological criminology. Along the way, we attempt to identify some of the problems that stem from strict application of positivistic conceptions to the study of crime and criminality.

The Origins of Biological Positivism

Charles Darwin's *The Origin of Species*, published in 1859, and his *The Descent of Man*, first published in 1871, are widely held to mark the end of the "prescientific" (classical) thinking about the causes of human behavior described in Chapter 1. Prior to Darwin, so the story goes, humans were assumed to be a species distinct from the rest of the animal kingdom. They were assumed to have free will, to be able to choose a course of action depending on their assessment of the pleasures and pains that various alternatives were likely to provide. With the advent of Darwin's theory of evolution, such views were seen by many as no longer tenable. According to evolutionary biology, humans are animals subject to laws of nature like all other animals. Human behavior, like any animal trait, must therefore be governed by the laws of nature rather than by free will and choice. It remained for scientists interested in behavior to isolate or identify those causal forces producing the criminal behavior of humans. It is not surprising that the first place they looked for such forces was in the biology of the offender.

The origins of scientific criminology are usually traced to the work of Cesare Lombroso (1835–1909), a physician employed in the Italian penal system. Lombroso saw himself as a scientist in tune with the biology of his day. He tells us that the science of criminology actually began with his discovery of an anomaly in a robber's skull, but the connection between Lombroso's theory of crime (i.e., criminals are throwbacks to an earlier stage of evolution) and Darwin's theory of evolution is so direct we must conclude that Lombroso's theory was at first deductive rather than inductive—that it was derived from general *substantive* principles and preceded observation rather than vice versa.[1]

As a positivist, however, Lombroso could not long restrict his attention to the differences between criminals and noncriminals that might be derived from the theory of evolution. On the contrary, as a positivist, he had to seek all of the correlates of crime and to try somehow to make sense of them. The statistics of Lombroso's day did not allow conclusions about the relative importance of the many potential differences between criminals and noncriminals, and Lombroso did not have a general theory of crime that would organize them in a meaningful way. He therefore sorted the correlates of crime into clusters or groups based on traditional divisions of the physical and social world. These clusters or groups of variables are strangely akin to modern "disciplines." In fact, the table of contents of later editions of Lombroso's major work (1918 [1899]) looks much like a university catalog, with sections on meteorological, geological, anthropological, demographic, educational, economic, religious, genetic, and political causes of crime.

The importance and generality of this fact should not escape no-

[1] This is not meant to take anything away from Lombroso. In our view, he has been unjustly maligned by contemporary social scientists, most of whom appear to have read little of his work. Although it may be true that he is the father of biological determinism in criminology, his more important contribution perhaps comes from his advocacy of positivism and the principle of multiple causation. The first words in his famous *Crime: Its Causes and Remedies* address these issues: "Every crime has its origin in a multiplicity of causes, often intertwined and confused, each of which we must, in obedience to the necessities of thought and speech, investigate singly. This multiplicity is generally the rule with human phenomena, to which one can almost never assign a single cause unrelated to the others" (1918: 1). In fact, the 1918 version of his book includes twelve chapters on causation, and it anticipates virtually every concern of contemporary criminology, from white-collar crime to sex offenses, from differential association to poverty theory.

tice: in its search for meaning in nature, positivism clusters independent variables and thereby creates disciplines. But positivism has no
device for ranking "disciplinary" clusters of independent variables
according to their relevance to a given problem (dependent variable).
It must, therefore, put each problem up for grabs and hope that its
various disciplines can resolve their competing claims and in the process somehow discover meaningful solutions to the problem at issue.

Put another way, the methods of positivism automatically produce
multiple-factor conclusions whatever the "disciplinary" orientation of
the particular positivist using them. These methods therefore lead
automatically to disciplinary disputes that they cannot themselves
settle. The result is a "science" much concerned with allocating
"findings" to its constituent disciplines and not so concerned with
understanding nature. In this regard, Lombroso's fate is instructive.
Although he began with a biological theory of crime, he soon included variables from other disciplines and came eventually to see his
own theory as accounting for a minority of criminals. That he is today
regarded as the father of biological positivism and ignored by sociologists and psychologists attests to the tendency of modern discipli-
narians to confuse positivism as a method with positivism as a theory
of human behavior. In any event, Lombroso is as much the father of
sociological or psychological as of biological positivism.

The biological positivists did not have a conception of crime derived from a general theory of behavior. They were therefore forced
to accept the criminals provided them by the state: "A criminal is a
man who violates laws decreed by the State to regulate the relations
between its citizens" (Ferraro 1972 [1911]: 3). Crimes were then
merely acts in violation of the law. The biological positivist's problem
seemed simple enough. All one had to do was locate the differences
among people that produce differences in their tendencies to commit
acts in violation of the law. Starting with the assumption that offenders differ from nonoffenders, positivism soon discovered that offenders also appeared to differ among themselves. It was obvious that
offenders committed different kinds of crimes. Moreover, offenders
committing the same kind of crime were not homogeneous on important characteristics.

Lombroso thus started with a theory of crime, a theory in which
physical anomalies with hereditary origins distinguish those with a
propensity to commit crime from those without such a propensity.
Almost immediately he encountered cases that did not fit the theory—that is, offenders were not all alike nor did they differ in the
same ways from nonoffenders. The solution to this problem adopted

by Lombroso (at the urging of his student Enrico Ferri) was to sub-
divide the criminal population into types, each of which was meant to
be internally homogeneous with respect to the causes of crime and
different from other types on the same dimensions. As Ferri wrote:

The work of Lombroso set out with two original faults: the mistake of having
given undue importance, at any rate apparently, to the data of craniology and
anthropometry, rather than to those of psychology; and, secondly, that of
having mixed up in the first two editions, all criminals in a single class. In
later editions these defects were eliminated, Lombroso having adopted the
observation which I made in the first instance, as to the various anthropological categories of criminals. [1897:11, referring to Lombroso's *L'Uomo de-
linquente* (1876)]

Thus to Lombroso's born criminal Ferri added occasional criminals
(those "who do not exhibit, or who exhibit in slighter degrees, the
anatomical, physiological, and psychological characteristics which
constitute the type described by Lombroso as the 'criminal man'"),
pseudo-criminals ("normal human beings who commit involuntary
offenses, or offenses which do not spring from perversity, and do not
hurt society, though they are punishable by law"), political criminals,
epileptic criminals, criminals by passion, incorrigible criminals, and
homosexual offenders, to name only some.

   Absent a conception of crime, the positivist has no choice but to
elaborate types of offenders. These typologies may be based on the
frequency of offending, the seriousness of the offense, the object of
the offense, the characteristics of the offender, or the nature of prior
and subsequent offenses, but whatever their dimensions, they lead to
complication rather than simplicity, to confusion rather than clarity.
Apparently little or no progress has been made on this point. Modern
typologies—such as those based on sociological (Clinard and Quinney 1973) or psychological (Megargee and Bohn 1979) constructs, or
on empirical clustering of criminal careers (Blumstein et al. 1986; Farrington, Ohlin, and Wilson 1986), or on the number of offenses committed (National Institute of Mental Health 1982)—all derive from the
positivist problem that itself stems from the absence of an idea of
crime, and none seems to solve the problem of internal diversity.
Absent a conception of crime, the positivistic method leads ineluctably to typologizing without end.

   Lombroso's criminal anthropology quickly became the subject of
considerable controversy. The first tests of his theory naturally focused on its claims about the peculiar physiognomy of the offender.
As early as 1913, these claims were vigorously disputed by Charles
Goring. Goring's conclusions are widely misstated by criminologists,

many of whom perhaps attend more to the tone of his remarks about Lombroso than to the actual results of his research. The famous statistician Karl Pearson (who assisted Goring in much of his work) summarizes that portion of Goring's findings dealing with Lombroso's view that the offender has a peculiar physiognomy:

It is not too much to say that in the early chapters of Goring's work he clears out of the way for ever the tangled and exuberant growths of the Lombrosian School. He then turns to the constructive side of his work, and using precisely the same methods of investigation, tells us of the English criminal as he really is, not absolutely differentiated by numerous anomalies from the general population, but relatively differentiated from the mean or population type, because on the average he is selected from the physically poorer and mentally feebler portion of the general population. The criminal is not a *random* sample of the general population, either physically or mentally. He is, rather, a sample of the less fit moiety of it. [Pearson, in Goring 1913: xii]

It would be easy to conclude that Goring actually found substantial empirical support for the central contention of Lombroso's biological positivism—that the criminal is differentiated from the noncriminal in terms of biological or genetic characteristics. Whatever the details of their disagreement about the biological traits associated with crime, this disagreement is clearly within a context of fundamental agreement on the idea that crime is the product of biological deficiency. Where Lombroso saw physical anomalies as central, Goring disagreed: "No evidence has emerged confirming the existence of a physical criminal type, such as Lombroso and his disciples have described. . . . In fact, both with regard to measurements and the presence of physical anomalies in criminals, our statistics present a startling conformity with similar statistics of the law-abiding classes" (Goring 1919: 96–97). But with respect to physical stature and physique, Goring reported differences:

All English criminals, with the exception of those technically convicted of fraud, are markedly differentiated from the general population in stature and body-weight; in addition, offenders convicted of violence to the person are characterized by an average degree of strength and of constitutional soundness considerably above the average of other criminals and of the law-abiding community; finally, thieves and burglars (who constitute, it must be borne in mind, 90 per cent of all criminals) and also incendiaries, as well as being inferior in stature and weight, are also, relatively to other criminals and the population at large, puny in their general bodily habit. [1919: 121]

Goring also found differences between the criminal and noncriminal populations with respect to "alcoholism, epilepsy, and sexual profligacy," but he concluded "that the one vital mental constitutional factor in the etiology of crime is defective intelligence" (ibid.: 184).

So, in the end, Goring and Lombroso disagreed on the important biological differences between criminals and noncriminals, not on the idea that such differences were present. Working with inferior samples, measures, and statistical techniques, Lombroso was able only to speculate about differences, and naturally he focused on potential sources of differences that could be readily observed. Working with highly sophisticated statistics, Goring's findings naturally diverged in detail from those of Lombroso. They did not, however, dispute the general thrust of Lombroso's argument or the tenets of biological positivism (as is so widely assumed). Instead, the findings offered support for the expectation of important biological differences between offenders and nonoffenders, support for the multiple-factor approach, for rigorous empirical research, and for further differentiation of the offender population as required by causal analysis.

Goring examined the relations among the causes of crime he uncovered, and he asked himself what they might have in common:

To resume: defective physique, extreme forms of alcoholism, epilepsy, insanity, sexual profligacy, and weak-mindedness—these are the constitutional conditions, and the only ones, which so far have emerged as significantly associated with the committing of crime in this country. An interesting question that arises is to what extent are these conditions several manifestations of one and the same thing? The correlation with criminality of alcoholism is .39, of epilepsy is .26, of sexual profligacy is .31, and of mental deficiency is .64. From the high value of the last coefficient we would presume that, if reducible to one condition, it is mental defectiveness which would most likely prove to be the common antecedent of the alcoholism, epilepsy, insanity, and sexual profligacy. [1919: 183]

Goring's logic is revealing. He began by asking what the various correlates of crime may have in common, suggesting a search for a concept of criminality. But the search for commonality was limited to the causes of crime, and the question quickly focused on the possibility that one of the putative independent variables causes the others. Absent a conception of the dependent variable, Goring had nothing to guide his conceptualization of the independent variables, and he ended up treating all but one of them as conceptually equivalent to crime. That is, everything may be a consequence of the variable with the largest correlation with crime, mental deficiency.

Goring's reliance on an ill-defined empirical solution to his conceptual problem illustrates another characteristic of criminological positivism that survives to the present day. Modern criminologists often note intercorrelations among "crime types" as a platform for asking which causes which. It remains rare, however, for modern criminologists to suspect that various types of behavior—some criminal, some noncriminal—may have enough in common to justify treating them as the same thing. Goring glimpsed this solution to his conceptual problem, but the instinct of positivism to seek homogeneity through differentiation rather than abstraction was too strong to allow him to adopt it.

With the publication of Goring's work, biological positivism reached its natural limits. Without a concept of crime or of criminality, biological positivism is reduced to endless examination of lists of possible physiological, anatomical, and constitutional variables that may or may not be correlated with behavior defined as crime by contemporary political sanctions (see, e.g., Herrnstein 1983). Advances in the field must await improvements in sampling, measurement, or statistical procedures. Without a concept of crime, biological positivism, like any branch of positivism, has no way of ascribing importance to its independent variables, no way of understanding the relations among them, and, ultimately, no way of assessing the importance of its own findings. Furthermore, the separation of independent and dependent variables becomes problematic, resulting in frequent confusion of the two.

Contemporary Biological Positivism

These assertions are easily illustrated by contemporary biological positivism, the principle achievements of which have been to improve research design by the use of twin and adoption studies and to use measurement procedures more sophisticated than those previously available, such as measures of skin conductance and chromosomal abnormalities.

One of the most celebrated findings of modern biological positivism is that reported by Sarnoff Mednick and his colleagues from a large-scale study of a Danish adoption cohort, a study said to be confirmed by work in Sweden and Iowa. As Mednick summarizes the situation, these studies "irrefutably support the influence of heritable factors in the etiology of some forms of antisocial acts. Because we can only inherit biological predispositions, the genetic evidence conclusively admits biological factors among the important agents influencing some forms of criminal behavior" (1987: 6). The conclusiveness of adoption studies apparently derives from the persuasiveness of their design: "Of all nonexperimental designs, properly executed adoption

TABLE 1

*Percentage of Adopted Sons Who Are Registered Criminals,
by Background of Biological and Adoptive Fathers*

| | | Is biological father criminal? | |
		Yes	No
Is adoptive father criminal?	Yes	36.2% (of 58)	11.5% (of 52)
	No	22% (of 219)	10.5% (of 333)

SOURCE: Hutchings and Mednick 1977: 137.

NOTE: Tables 1–4 are to be read as follows: 36.2 percent of the 58 adopted sons whose biological and adoptive fathers both had a criminal record were also registered criminals themselves.

studies constitute an extremely powerful design for isolating significant amounts of the influence of genetic factors from all conceivable environmental factors. . . . The reason for their power is that they actually approach a controlled experiment" (Ellis 1982: 52).

In a pilot study, Barry Hutchings and Sarnoff Mednick (1977) used a Copenhagen sample to examine the effects on the criminality of adopted boys of criminality in their biological and adoptive fathers. The results of this initial study are reproduced in Table 1.

Hutchings and Mednick note that the differences in Table 1 do not reach statistical significance, "but the direction of the difference favors the strength of the biological father's criminality" over that of the adoptive father's criminality (1977: 137). The clear implication is that, were a larger sample of cases available, these impressive percentage point differences would reach conventional levels of statistical significance. With statistical significance, such differences would provide evidence for a strong genetic influence on crime as defined by the state of Denmark.

In pursuit of such evidence, Mednick and his colleagues expanded their study to encompass all nonfamilial adoptions in Denmark between 1924 and 1947. The results of this study are presented in Table 2.

This table appears to confirm the results of Table 1 on a much larger sample. According to Mednick, Gabrielli, and Hutchings:

In summary, in a population of adoptions a relation was found between biological parent criminal convictions and criminal convictions in their adoptee children. . . . A number of potentially confounding variables were considered; none proved sufficient to explain the genetic relation. We conclude that some factor transmitted by criminal parents increases the likelihood that their children will engage in criminal behavior. [1984: 893]

Table 2 differs from Table 1 in several respects, each of which would seem to bear on the interpretation of the results. First, the

TABLE 2

*Percentage of Adopted Sons Who Have Been Convicted
of Criminal Law Offenses, by Background of
Biological and Adoptive Parents*

| | | Are biological parents criminal? | |
		Yes	No
Are adoptive parents criminal?	Yes	25.5% (of 143)	14.7% (of 204)
	No	20.0% (of 1,226)	13.5% (of 2,492)

SOURCE: Wilson and Herrnstein 1985: 96. See also Mednick, Gabrielli, and Hutchings 1984: 892, 1987: 79.

measure of criminality among adoptees appears to have shifted from "registered criminality" to "court convictions." Second, the criminality of biological and adoptive *fathers*, the independent variable in the pilot study, has changed to criminality of the biological and adoptive *parents* in the final study. Third, the numbers in the final study are much larger than in the pilot study, representing 4,065 adoptees in the final study as compared to 662 in the pilot study. Fourth, the final study is based on the population of "a small northern European nation" (Mednick, Gabrielli, and Hutchings 1984: 891), whereas the pilot study was restricted to "the city and county of Copenhagen" (Hutchings and Mednick 1977: 128). Fifth, the crime rate for the adoptee sample as a whole has declined from 16.6 percent in the pilot study to 15.9 percent in the final study. Finally, the differences in criminality between adoptees whose biological parents were criminal and those whose biological parents were not criminal are smaller in the final study than in the pilot study. In the final study, the differences are 9.8 percentage points when adoptive parents are criminal and 6.5 percentage points when adoptive parents are noncriminal. In the pilot study, these percentage differences were 24.7 and 11.5, respectively. In other words, in the final study the crucial differences for the biological effect hypothesis have declined to 40 percent and 56 percent of their original value.

As noted, the original (1977) adoptee study was defined as a pilot study. The subsequent study (reported in *Science* in 1984) would normally be defined as a replication study, an attempt to determine whether the results of the pilot study could be confirmed. Traditionally, such replications are independent—that is, they follow the same procedure on a different sample of cases from the same population. Independence of samples is essential to the interpretation of replication research.

TABLE 3

The Joint Effects of Biological Parents' and Adoptive Parents'
Criminality on the Criminality of Adopted Sons,
Denmark Other Than Copenhagen, 1924–47

| | | Are biological parents criminal? | |
		Yes	No
Are adoptive parents criminal?	Yes	16.5% (85)	15.8% (152)
	No	19.6% (1,007)	15.3% (2,159)

Is the final 1984 sample independent of the initial or pilot study, or are the cases in the original study included in the final sample? The conclusions one draws about a genetic effect on crime are utterly dependent on the answer to this question.[2]

Table 3 is created under the assumption that the cases in the pilot study were included in the final study and that other differences between the two studies can be safely ignored. Under this assumption, we subtract the cases in Table 1 from the cases in Table 2 and compute the percentage of adoptees who are criminal in each of the cells of the replication sample.

Clearly, Table 3 shows no effect of the criminality of the biological parents on the criminality of their adopted sons. The differences are in the direction suggested by the genetic hypothesis, but they are at best insubstantial. On the basis of Table 3 we would be forced to reject the genetic hypothesis, to conclude that we are dealing here with a failure to replicate the findings reported in the first or pilot study. In order to reach this conclusion, however, we must consider in a systematic way the several differences between the two studies noted earlier.

First, could change in the criterion of criminality negate our conclusion? In the report of the second study in *Science*, Mednick and his colleagues do not directly compare the results of their two studies. However, the second study emphasizes the fact that the criterion of crime is a "court conviction" (see also Wilson and Herrnstein 1985), whereas the pilot study uses the terms "criminal record" and "registered criminality." These latter terms are defined as follows: "A separate criminal record (*Personalia Blad*) is kept on all persons who

[2]Mednick and his colleagues clearly do not share our concern with this issue. Apparently, they see the initial or pilot study as a "subsample of [the] adoption cohort" (Mednick, Gabrielli, and Hutchings 1983: 21) or as "a large subsample of this population" (Mednick et al. 1987: 89) and the final study as an "extension" of the original study. Although they occasionally note similarities in the results of the two studies (see Mednick et al. 1983: 21; Mednick et al. 1984: 893), so far as we have been able to determine they nowhere address the differences in results between them.

have at any time been convicted of offenses treated as *statsadvokat-sager*. These correspond very closely to indictable offenses in British justice and can be contrasted with *politisager* (summary offenses). . . . The distinction corresponds very roughly to the difference between felonies and misdemeanors in the United States" (Hutchings and Mednick 1977: 129). Apparently, therefore, the criterion of conviction is used in both the pilot and the final study. (If the measure of the dependent variable actually changed from one study to the next, it would still be necessary to exclude the pilot study cases from the replication analysis. Otherwise, the differences in the final study could still be entirely due to differences in the pilot study, differences not in question.)

Second, Mednick and his colleagues shift from criminality of the *father* to criminality of the *parents* as the measure of the independent variable. They report that "in all our analyses, the relation between biological mother conviction and adoptee conviction is significantly stronger than that between biological father and adoptee convictions" (1984: 893). In other words, changing the measure of the independent variable by adding mothers strengthened the apparent genetic effect over that shown in the pilot study (making the failure to replicate all the more dramatic). It did so by adding cases to those cells with small numbers and by adding "criminals" to the ranks of adoptees with criminal biological parents. (We estimate that mothers added about 200 cases to the criminal biological parent category in the final sample. Mednick et al. do not indicate whether this adjustment was applied to the pilot study cases and, if so, what effect it had on the conclusions for that sample.)

Recall that the major problem with the pilot study was that it lacked sufficient cases (in the criminal biological father category) to allow confident conclusions. Although the "replication" study was able to find 3,403 additional cases, the increase in the number of cases in the crucial category was from 58 to 85, and this increase included the children of criminal biological *mothers*. Given the virtual absence of a relation between parent criminality and the criminality of the son in the replication study, however, its numbers are sufficient to reduce rather than increase our confidence in the findings of the pilot study.

The shift in the sample from the city and county of Copenhagen to the entire country of Denmark could be interpreted as a critical difference between the replication and the pilot study. One possibility is that the record-keeping on convictions differs between Copenhagen and the rest of Denmark such that the genetic effect is obscured by poor record-keeping in the country or enhanced by poor record-

TABLE 4

*Cross-Fostering Data in a Swedish Study of Male Adoptees:
Percentage Committing "Petty Crimes" by
Biological Predisposition*

		Congenital predisposition	
		Low	High
Postnatal predisposition	Low	2.9% (666)	12.1% (66)
	High	6.7% (120)	40.0% (10)

SOURCE: Cloninger and Gottesman 1987: 105.

keeping in the city. In this situation, combining the samples from the two locations is ill advised. A second possibility is that the genetic effect differs between the city and county of Copenhagen and the balance of Denmark. Neither of these hypotheses, in our judgment, has any merit.

In our view, the shift in the overall crime rate from the pilot to the final sample (from 16.6 to 15.9 percent) is evidence that the decline in the genetic effect between the two studies cannot be accounted for by the shift in the criterion. The small decline observed is consistent with what would be expected were an urban sample combined with a sample drawn from nonurban areas, areas with a typically lower crime rate.

In our judgment, then, the proper interpretation of the Mednick et al. "cross-fostering" research is that their second, larger study failed to replicate the finding of a genetic effect from their pilot study. Such failure to replicate is common in behavioral research, particularly when the initial findings suggest effects out of line with those normally encountered in the research area. We would not be surprised to learn that the true genetic effect on the likelihood of criminal behavior is *somewhere between zero and the results finally reported by Mednick, Gabrielli, and Hutchings*. That is, we suspect that the magnitude of this effect is minimal.

The Mednick et al. results are often reported to be consistent with other research. According to Wilson and Herrnstein (1985: 99), "a large Swedish study has confirmed and extended much of these Danish findings." The cross-fostering data for males from the Swedish study are therefore reproduced in Table 4.

The cases in this table were assembled by Robert Cloninger and Irving Gottesman (1987) from a Stockholm adoption study. According to the authors, in this analysis "congenital" refers to variables about biological parents, whereas "postnatal" refers to variables about adoptive placements. Several aspects of Table 4 merit comment. First, the total number of subjects with records for petty crimes was relatively small (39). The research project began with 108 convicted offenders. Second, note the greater likelihood of postnatal as opposed to congenital predisposition, a "finding" out of line with usual cross-fostering data (see Tables 1–3, above). The data suggest that Swedish procedures place 15 percent of adoptees in environments of "high" predisposition to petty crime, whereas the genetic makeup of the same adoptees puts only 9 percent of them at such risk. Third, the cell of most interest in this "large Swedish study" contains ten cases, four of which are classified as "petty criminals." Fourth, consider the classification "predisposition to petty crime." According to Cloninger and Gottesman, this classification "depends on whether the background variables are more like the average characteristics of adoptees with petty crime only (classified as high) than like those of adoptees with no crime and/or alcohol abuse (classified as low) (1987: 105).

In other words, Cloninger and Gottesman devised a "cross-fostering" table based on variables known to predict petty criminality in their own sample *and* said by them to reflect the *environmental* conditions of the biological parents (congenital) and of the adoptive parents (postnatal). Consequently, this aspect of their study has no bearing on the heritability question. Even if it were possible to overlook the constructed nature of the results, it would not be possible to overlook their *ex post facto* nature. How these results could be construed as supportive of the Danish research finding is entirely unclear. In fact, these results seem to support our reinterpretation of the Danish cross-fostering analysis. Also consistent with our view is this statement by Cloninger and Gottesman: "In the same Swedish population, Bohman [1972] found no excess of deliquency before the age of 12 years in adopted-away children from criminal biological parents" (1987: 104).

The third study cited in support of the Danish adoption research is based on 52 adoptees born during a 31-year period in Iowa (Crowe 1975). Raymond Crowe identified female offenders in prison whose children had been adopted. (Some of these mothers contributed more than one child to the sample.) These adoptees were matched with a second set of adoptees on age, sex, and race. Comparison of subsequent records of criminality revealed seven arrests among the 37 children of prisoners and two arrests among the 37 adoptees in the control group for whom records were available. This difference is reported by Crowe to be significant at the .076 level (1975: 98).

There is no need to quibble about this confidence level. The Crowe

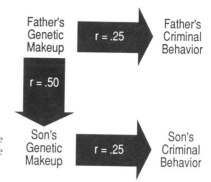

Fig. 1.   Correlations Necessary to Produce an Observed Correlation of .03 Between the Criminal Behavior of Fathers and Sons.

study is so far from minimal standards of scientific adequacy that it deserves only minimal comment. For one thing, no information was collected concerning the biological parents of the control group. They may have been less, equally, or more criminal that the biological parents of the prison adoptees. For another, no information is supplied about the arrest records of other relevant comparison groups. The Crowe study, best characterized as a "one-shot case study" (the control group is for all intents and purposes hypothetical), therefore provides no basis for the conclusion that crime is inherited in Iowa.

We began this section with a statement from Lee Ellis (1982) to the effect that adoption studies provide the strongest basis for inference concerning the heritability of criminal behavior. There is little disagreement about the strength of the adoption design: "The most convincing evidence for genetic influence on antisocial behavior comes from studies of adopted children who were separated at birth from their criminal biological parents" (Rowe and Osgood 1984: 535). We agree that these studies are convincing. They provide strong evidence that the inheritance of criminality is *minimal*. We must therefore disagree with Wilson and Herrnstein, who conclude on the basis of this same body of empirical data: "All told, this small sample, like the much larger Danish and Swedish ones, suggests a strong biological resemblance between a parent and a child given up for adoption in some trait or traits that predispose people toward trouble with the law" (1985: 100). On the contrary, we conclude that the magnitude of the "genetic effect," as determined by adoption studies, is near zero.

This result should not be surprising, and it should not be interpreted as showing that biology has nothing to do with crime. In our view, the best guess about the magnitude of a genetic effect would be derived as follows:

Take the correlation between the father's biology (i.e., genetic makeup) and his own criminal behavior, and multiply it by the correlation between his biology and his child's biology. Multiply the result by the correlation between his child's biology and his child's criminal behavior. (This path diagram is shown in Figure 1.)

To put the case for heritability in its strongest possible terms, assume an observed correlations of .25 between biology and crime in both generations, and a correlation of .5 between the biology of the father and the biology of his sons. These correlations would yield a correlation between father's and son's crimes of .031, a correlation that would require very large samples to reach statistical significance, and a correlation that if statistically significant would be substantively trivial.[3]

Conclusions

Biological positivism accepted the state's definition of crime as a violation of law and of the criminal as someone arrested, convicted, and sentenced for a crime. This decision allowed comparison of "criminals" and "noncriminals," subdivision of the "criminal" population by type of offense (e.g., property), and discussion of the possibility of a heritable "predisposition" to crime. The idea of predisposition suggests a theory or explanation of crime. It stems directly from the positivistic view that crime is caused by factors beyond the control of the criminal. Thus the idea of causation, meant to embody the neutrality of science, in fact brought with it a substantive theory of crime, a theory according to which people committing criminal acts are required or forced to do so by constellations of antecedent factors.

Acceptance of the state's definition of crime, science's presumed view of causation, and the substantive variables assigned to it by the disciplinary division of labor did not lead biological positivism to an idea of crime. On the contrary, they led it to search for the *biological causes of state-defined* crime, an ostensibly empirical enterprise that was actually massively constrained by *a priori* principles. As a result, biological positivism has produced little in the way of meaningful or

[3] These correlation coefficients translate into a "heritability coefficient" of .177, which may be described as the theoretical upper limit of the correlation between father's criminality and son's criminality given our assumptions. We would not argue that this result proves the irrelevance of biology to crime. We would argue, however, that it shows the need for greater attention to conceptual matters by those interested in the connection between biology and crime.

interpretable research. Instead, as we have seen, it has produced a series of "findings" (e.g., physiognomy, feeblemindedness, XYY, inheritance of criminality) that survived only so long as was necessary to subject them to replication or to straightforward critical analysis.

Apparently, improvements in statistics, measurement, and sampling by themselves cannot overcome problems inherent in biological positivism. More than 100 years after Lombroso initiated this line of inquiry, the major contribution of biological research would appear to be data suggesting that biological variables *may* be correlated with crime. Unfortunately, this evidence is often so suspect that scholars friendly to the idea of biological causation are left wondering why this discipline has so much trouble contributing "acceptable" facts to the field of criminology.

The reasons for the absence of influence from biology are, in our view, not hard to find. The discipline proceeds without a concept of crime and without a concept of criminality. As a result, the Mednick et al. research is not unique in terms of its contribution to criminology. We discuss it at length because it illustrates the general problems of biological positivism. The history of XYY chromosome research tells a similar story: extraordinary effort expended to document the possible existence of a small effect, the significance of which is unclear even to those pursuing it (Witkin et al. 1977).

There is another tendency in this research with even greater implications for the ultimate contribution of biological positivism. Researchers in this tradition adopt in near serial fashion one dependent variable after another, suggesting that each is individually important in its own right (see the Mednick et al. shift from "registered criminality" to "court convictions") and paying no attention to the possible conceptual overlap among them. Thus the sample used by Mednick and his colleagues to study "crime" was originally collected to allow study of the genetic transmission of mental illness. The sample has also been used to study the genetic transmission of alcoholism, and it could be (if it has not been) used to study the genetic transmission of many other forms of behavior (such as smoking, obesity, truancy, or accidents). What escapes the notice of biological positivists is that such samples could also document the "genetic transmission" of illegitimate parenthood, unstable job performance, broken marriages, poor child-rearing practices, and being late for school. If these behaviors seem disconnected, it is because the behavioral sciences share with biological positivism the view that the study of concrete acts or items of behavior is scientific while study of abstract concepts is not. Recall that a major tenet of positivism is the view that acts have causes. All too frequently, the idea that acts have causes is translated via the research literature into the idea that specific acts have specific causes. For biological positivism, this leads to the search for a genetic component to account for variation in specific acts. (And leads, not surprisingly, to focus on "important" or "serious" acts—as though they can be explained independently of "trivial" acts in the same domain.) As we will see, these problems are not unique to the biological branch of positivism.

4

Psychological, Economic, and Sociological Positivism

Contemporary criminology is highly skeptical of the contributions of biological positivism. Much of this skepticism can be traced to disciplinary rivalries or concerns. Sociologists, psychologists, and economists are naturally concerned with the possibility that biology could leave them with little to explain. But the concern for biology goes beyond academic rivalry to worries about social policies based on notions of heredity or biological defect. In fact, the latter concerns are so pronounced that their expression often serves to conceal the basic similarity between biological positivism and its social and behavioral science counterparts. In this chapter, we show that the strategies and premises of positivism limit the conception of crime and the criminal in all disciplines, whatever their apparent distance from the biological perspective. We begin with biology's nearest neighbor in the study of crime.

Psychological Positivism

Psychology should have been able to avoid the problems inherent in accepting a political definition of crime. Psychologists define their subject matter as the study of behavior, and modern psychological positivists eschew the study of crime and criminality in favor of a focus on "aggression," "psychopathology," "violence," or "sexuality," dimensions of behavior that can be identified without the assistance of the state. Modern psychological positivists also assume that behavior is in large part shaped by contingencies of reinforcement, a view directly compatible with Bentham's classical theory of behavior.

In fact, the student of aggression or violence is interested in a broad range of criminal and noncriminal acts, and the psychopathologist is typically interested in behavioral manifestations of underlying pathology whether or not they bring the person into conflict with the law. Indeed, psychological positivism explicitly attends to concepts like "predisposition," "trait," or "personality," concepts that presuppose relatively stable characteristics of people relevant to their involvement in criminal acts. For that matter, the most popular theory of crime at any given time is likely to take for granted the currently most attractive psychological theory of learning (Bandura 1973; Akers 1973; Wilson and Herrnstein 1985). On all counts, then, psychological positivism would appear to have avoided the problem of dependence on the specific act as the object of explanation and to have an explanatory mechanism compatible with a concept of crime. Unlike biology, psychology seems to have the requisite conceptual tools to think about crime and produce meaningful research on it. The lack of influence within criminology of psychological positivism is therefore something of a puzzle—until we consider its treatment of its major concepts, such as aggression.[1]

The Theoretical Import of the Concept of Aggression

From a positivistic point of view, the concept of aggression has several desirable properties. For one, it suggests without elaboration an active animal, an animal possessing its own driving force or motive for behavior. For another, aggression seems applicable to behavior in a broad range of settings, from the playing field to the boardroom, and even to a broad range of species, from birds to humans. Further, aggression appears to be compatible with the conceptual schemes of all the disciplines, suggesting frustration to the sociologist, testosterone to the biologist, and imitation to the psychologist. Finally, aggression seems uniquely relevant to the explanation of crime, suggesting as it does the source of differences among people in their inclination to resort to force in pursuit of private interests.

Unfortunately, the concept of aggression does not square with the concept of crime. Its continued unexamined use is therefore further evidence of the tendency of positivistic presuppositions and disciplinary interests to dominate the study of crime even when they are demonstrably misguided and inappropriate.

[1]Our discussion of aggression is meant to illustrate the conceptual problems of psychological positivism. Other concepts, such as psychopathy, could serve as well. In fact, we avoid psychopathy partly for the reason that it has been so extensively criticized.

Evidence of inconsistency between aggression and crime is not hard to find, although at first glance they may appear to be simply different words for the same behavior. Operational definitions of aggression typically include such things as hitting and hurting, pushing and shoving, injuring and irritating (Eron 1987), unprovoked physical aggression (starting a fight), and mildly provoked verbal aggression (sassing a teacher) (Olweus 1979), all acts that can be seen as behavioral equivalents of crime. Apparently such behavior can be measured with a high degree of reliability (Huesmann et al. 1984; Eron 1987). Apparently, too, individual differences in aggressiveness are highly stable over time (Olweus 1979; Huesmann et al. 1984). So far, so good. We have items of behavior akin to crime that can be reliably measured without reference to the operations of the criminal justice system.

Do measures of aggression predict state-defined criminal behavior? They certainly do. In fact, in studying the stability of aggression over the life course, researchers often use standard crime counts (e.g., "criminal justice convictions," "seriousness of criminal acts," "driving while intoxicated") as measures of aggression during the adult years (Farrington 1978; Huesmann et al. 1984: 1124). Given such long-term predictability, short-term predictability would be expected to be excellent. In fact, Sheldon and Eleanor Glueck (1950: 149–153) report that "characteristics of attacking behavior" such as disobedience, disorderliness, stubbornness, defiance, impudence, rudeness, quarrelsomeness, cruelty, bullying, and destruction of materials were reported significantly more often for delinquents than nondelinquents in the school setting.

It is generally agreed that the validity of concepts is determined by empirical relations between their measures and measures of cognate concepts. Given this standard, the correlation between (or identity of) measures of aggression and measures of criminality would seem to establish at least provisionally the validity of the idea of aggression. Unfortunately, this conclusion requires that we ignore the content of the concepts in question. If aggression means anything, then highly aggressive people should be more likely to attack than withdraw, more likely to use force than stealth, more likely to be active than passive, and more likely to be bold than timid. But criminality does not connote activity, force, or violence any more than it connotes passivity, fraud, or deceit. Criminality is all these things at once. Criminality can thus absorb "aggression," but a concept of aggression that is synonymous with "a tendency to commit criminal acts" is practically meaningless. A strong correlation between aggression and ordinary measures of crime thus challenges the meaning of the concept of aggression.

Recall the Gluecks' finding that delinquents were more likely than nondelinquents to exhibit *attacking* behavior. Consistent with our conclusion, the Gluecks found that delinquents in the same sample were also more likely than nondelinquents to exhibit *withdrawing* behavior (lack of interest, inattention, easy discouragement, unhappiness, depression, and unsociability)!

The Gluecks faced the fact that delinquents tend to be aggressive *and* nonaggressive. The solution they came up with was standard positivism: there are two types of delinquents, those who tend to attack and those who tend to withdraw. It complicates matters that the two types tend to be found in the same people, but such a condition may be assumed to be inherently unstable. Indeed, a tendency to specialize in attack or withdrawal may be reasonably assumed: "One form of reaction usually becomes dominant over the other in that the greater portion of an individual's evasions of social requirements are expressed in one or the other fashion" (1950: 153).[2]

It is in fact traditional to "explain" the relation between aggression and crime by introducing a distinction between passivity and activity, or between attack and withdrawal. By this device Robert Merton (1938) separated innovators (criminals) from retreatists (drug users); by the same device Talcott Parsons (1957) doubles his several "directions of deviant orientations"; and, of course, economists such as Isaac Ehrlich (1974) use the same distinction in positing the existence of risk preferrers and risk avoiders. These solutions share a common problem: they are not consistent with the evidence. Offenders do not specialize or even tend to specialize in aggressive or nonaggressive ("retreatist") behavior. In fact, they do not tend to specialize in any particular type of crime.

At least the Gluecks and other typologists realize that they have a conceptual problem. It is more common that students of aggression seem oblivious to the consequences of equating aggression and criminality. In fact, once they discover that aggression predicts criminality, they typically simply expand the definition of aggression to include crime. For example, in what is perhaps the best-known study of the stability of aggression, L. Rowell Huesmann et al. (1984) define aggression as:

an act that injures or irritates another person. This definition excludes self-hurt . . . but makes no distinction between accidental and instrumental aggression or between socially acceptable and antisocial aggression. The as-

---

[2] The Gluecks are quoting E. K. Wickman, *Children's Behavior and Teachers' Attitudes* (New York: Norton, 1937). Obviously, Wickman had also discovered that attacking and withdrawing behaviors tend to be found together in the same people.

sumption is that there is a response class, aggression, that can include a variety of behaviors, exhibited in numerous situations, all of which result in injury or irritation to another person. Thus, this category includes both hitting and hurting behaviors, whether or not these behaviors are reinforced by pain cues from the victim or target person. This category also includes *injury to or theft of property*. [in Eron 1987: 435; emphasis added]

Such definitions would exclude nothing found in ordinary definitions of crime and delinquency. This is puzzling (to say the least), since the "dependent variable" in studies of aggression is often some form of ordinary crime, as measured by convictions for criminal offenses in a court of law

Psychological positivism thus creates what researchers regard as a new or distinct concept, one that embodies the major premises of the discipline itself (a stable individual personality trait or predisposition). It then goes about measuring and explaining this concept without regard to the fact that the same concept exists in other disciplines, such as sociology. It is hard to see what is gained by this exercise. It is, however, easy to see what has been lost: students of aggression cannot attend to the research literature on crime and delinquency. If they did, they would discover that their findings have been found many times before (compare, for example, the findings about parental behavior toward the child in Eron [1987] with the parental behavior described in Glueck and Glueck [1950] and McCord and McCord [1959]). They would also find that their conceptual and theoretical efforts have been anticipated many times by more than one well-developed theory of crime and delinquency. And, they would have to grant that there is currently no reason to believe that there is something in this world called "aggression" that requires specific public or scientific attention.

To illustrate how a surplus term creates problems, consider the television-violence-causes-aggression debate. In this debate, both sides assume that in principle aggressive responses may be learned independently of other forms of deviant behavior. Commenting on the correlation between the frequency of viewing television at age eight and criminal convictions 22 years later, Leonard Eron writes:

What was probably important were the attitudes and behavioral norms inculcated by continued watching of those and similar programs. In this regard, we can consider continued television violence viewing as rehearsal of aggressive sequences. Thus, one who watches more aggressive sequences on television should respond more aggressively when presented with similar or relevant cues. From an information-processing perspective, sociocultural norms, reinforced by continual displays in the broadcast media, play an important role by providing standards and values against which the child can compare his or her own behavior and the behavior of others to judge whether they are appropriate. [1987: 440]

This explanation appears in a different light when it is recalled that television-viewing at age eight would (given the operational definition of aggression used in this research) equally well predict theft, motor-vehicle accidents, trivial nonviolent offending, drug consumption, and employment instability, behaviors hard to attribute to the number of shootings or fistfights watched on television twenty years previously. In fact, Eron tells us that "aggression at age 8 predicted social failure, psychopathology, aggression, and low educational and occupational success" 22 years later (ibid.). Put another way, if researchers treat aggression as a general concept that includes accidents, theft, withdrawal, lack of ambition, and drug use, they cannot at the same time treat it as a specific concept centered on physical assault. Since it behaves as a general tendency, it seems unlikely that television-viewing at age eight was independent of this tendency at age eight. It therefore seems unlikely that the specific content of television programming viewed at age eight could contribute independently to subsequent levels of "aggression."

The relative lack of influence of psychology in the study of crime, despite an impressive literature on obviously relevant topics, illustrates a fundamental weakness of positivism as a whole. Because it starts from a multiple factor methodology, where all correlates and all disciplines are *a priori* equal, it lacks the tools to resolve disciplinary disputes. Early in its history, sociology claimed to possess a concept of crime and to own criminology. This left psychology as an interloper, a discipline without any real disciplinary interest in the subject.

In Goring's time, the impact of psychology was substantial. This discipline had begun the systematic development of standardized tests of mental ability, and researchers working with such tests immediately discovered that criminals performed worse on them than noncriminals. Indeed, from Goring (1919) and Goddard (1914) to Eysenck (1977) and Herrnstein (1983), the assumption of IQ differences between offenders and nonoffenders has been a staple of psychological positivism. The assumption within psychology— that offenders differ from nonoffenders—extends to many other individual-level properties as well.[3]

---

[3] From the point of view of criminologists, finding a robust individual-level correlate of crime was extremely important (because most such correlates tend to come and go). From the point of view of psychologists, finding a robust individual-level correlate of IQ was not particularly important, since the number of such correlates seemed virtually unlimited. Thus, when criminologists in general and sociologists in particular rejected

For most of the same period, however, criminology has assumed that all of the important variation in crime is at the group level (e.g., class, ethnicity, neighborhood, community) and that individual-level correlates are artifactual. How did this happen?

It happened that one of the positivistic disciplines was based on assumptions opposite to those underlying classical thought. Whereas Bentham saw "crime" as behavior in pursuit of self-interest, the distinguishing feature of which was that it was sanctioned (i.e., punished) socially, politically, or religiously, sociology rejected the notion that self-interest is the basis of human behavior, arguing instead that human behavior is naturally social. Crime, then, must also have a social, or group, basis. If crime is social behavior, it seemed to follow that it must have social rather than psychological causes: "Although crime and criminality are by definition social phenomena, people have for centuries entertained the notion that they are products of nonsocial causes" (Sutherland and Cressey 1978: 118).[4]

In other words, sociology possessed a conceptual scheme that explicitly denied the claims of all other disciplines potentially interested in crime. From the open multiple-factor criminology of Lombroso, criminology became a field closed to the possibility that disciplines other than sociology might have something to contribute. Since psychological positivists had no special concern for the dependent variable of criminology, they were disinclined to put up a struggle at this level. By failing to mount a defense of their own position, psychologists effectively removed themselves from direct involvement in mainstream criminological issues.

Ironically, however, psychological learning theories have exercised considerable influence on explanations of crime. Indeed, both within criminology (Sutherland 1939; Burgess and Akers 1966; Akers 1973) and in general psychology (Skinner 1953; Bandura 1986), learning theories of crime have for the last half-century predominated. And these theories continue to enjoy considerable popularity (e.g., Elliott, Huizinga, and Ageton 1985; Wilson and Herrnstein 1985).

As indicated above, the essential features of learning theories of

the IQ-crime relation, there was little in the way of resistance on the part of psychologists. And the same pattern may be found with respect to other individual-level correlates of crime. Criminology, which came to be dominated by sociology, eventually saw the destruction of individual-level correlates as a prerequisite to "truly social" theorizing, and no psychologist devoted to crime came forward to defend the interests of that discipline.

[4]Sociologists make much of Bentham's observation that sanctioning systems decide what to sanction. But where Bentham assumed that all societies sanction particular behaviors in order to assure their own survival, sociologists tend to assume that the choice of behaviors to sanction is arbitrary and highly variable.

crime are consistent with the classical model. They assume that behavior is governed by its consequences. Behavior that is rewarded has an increased probability of repetition, whereas behavior that is punished has a decreased probability of repetition. This basic duality suggests that it is possible to build two distinct but compatible learning theories of crime. In one, the theorist emphasizes the rewards of criminal behavior, seeking those factors that serve to increase the probability of crime. (Common sources of such rewards in criminological theories are the appreciation of the group to which one belongs and material goods generally valued in the larger society.) In the other, the theorist emphasizes the pains of criminal behavior, seeking those factors that serve to reduce the probability of crime. (Common sources of such pain are the disapproval of significant others, criminal justice sanctions, and the pangs of conscience.) Although the form or logic of both of these theories is consistent with classical thought, only one of them is consistent with the *content* of the classical view. In the classical view of human nature, positive learning theories of crime are redundant or superfluous because they seek to explain something unproblematic—that is, the benefits of crime.

Not accidentally, psychological learning theories of crime are exclusively positive or reward versions of learning theory. This circumstance is inherent in the logic of positivistic thought. In the reaction against the classical view, positivists emphasized the notion that scientific explanations of behavior are themselves "positive"; that is, the assumption that behavior is caused or determined by directly observable factors leads to the search for causes that by definition actually produce (rather than allow or inhibit) the behavior in question.[5]

Thus positivism again produced a brand of criminology consistent with its own peculiar preconceptions. This criminology accepts one

[5]The fact that learning theorists sometimes include references to "negative reinforcement" does not contradict our assertion about the tendency of modern learning theories. Thus Ronald Akers distinguishes between his social learning theory and classical or social control theory: "The person with weakened or broken bonds is less affected by the rewards and punishments of the groups. I pointed out that this is where control theory usually stops, namely that the failure of controls sets the stage for deviance. The social learning connection allows for the process to be extended. Failure of conventional social control may be enough by itself for deviant behavior, but: 'the person may also gravitate to other groups or may encounter situations in which the controls operate positively to reinforce his deviant behavior. Thus, the person whose ties with conformity have been broken may remain just a candidate for deviance; whether he becomes a deviant depends on further social or other rewards. Social control is still functioning when the individual's behavior comes under the influence of the sanctions of deviant subcultures or other groups, only the direction of that control is deviant by the standards of the conventional groups with which he has broken'" (1987, quoting Akers 1973: 292).

brand of psychological learning theory, rejects the idea of individual differences as causes of crime, and rejects the idea of personality as a stable influence on criminal behavior.

Economic Positivism

According to Richard Posner, "Economics, the science of human choice in a world in which resources are limited in relation to human wants, explores and tests the implications of assuming that man is a rational maximizer of his ends in life, his satisfactions—what we shall call his 'self interest'" (1977: 3). Or, as Gary Becker puts it: "A useful theory of criminal behavior can dispense with special theories of anomie, psychological inadequacies, or inheritance of special traits, and simply extend the economist's usual analysis of choice" (1974: 2).

At first glance, the modern economic approach to crime appears identical to the classical model of Bentham and Beccaria. The economic model and the classical model agree on the nature of human nature, on the idea that all behavior (criminal and noncriminal) can be understood as the rational pursuit of self-interest. As with the classical school, the modern economist's pursuit of a general theory leads to (in our view, proper) disregard for distinctions among types of crime (e.g., the theory applies to white-collar crime as well as burglary) and to disregard for distinctions among types of offenders (all are assumed to behave according to principles of hedonism and self-interest). The economic positivists express little doubt about the power of their perspective:

Whatever its deficiencies, the economic theory of law appears to be the most promising positive theory of law extant. While anthropologists, sociologists, psychologists, political scientists, and other social scientists besides economists also make positive analyses of the legal system, their work is thus far insufficiently rich in theoretical and empirical content to afford serious competition to the economists. [Posner 1977: 21; see also Becker 1974; Ehrlich 1974: 68–69][6]

To criminologists, many of whom have read Beccaria and Bentham, the theoretical contribution of the new economic positivism is not as impressive as it is to its authors. On the contrary, many criminologists, including ourselves, see the new economic positivism as merely repeating Beccaria and Bentham (especially the latter) to the point that it reaffirms the strengths of the basic perspective and re-

---

[6] Posner goes on to write: "The reader is challenged to adduce evidence contradicting this presumptuous, sweeping, and perhaps uninformed judgment" (1977: 21). What follows in the text may be taken as a humble response to this challenge.

peats the misguided emphasis on legal (or, in Bentham's terms, political) sanctions.

Classical scholars, such as Bentham and especially Beccaria, focused on political sanctions for good reason. They were interested in the reform of legal systems they considered barbaric or irrational, and in providing legitimation to state power. Bentham did not denigrate the importance of nonpolitical sanctions; rather, he saw such sanctions as being actually more important than those controlled by the state. Bentham reached this correct conclusion without having at his disposal a substantial body of empirical criminology documenting the power of moral and social sanctions on crime (e.g., Glueck and Glueck 1950; Hirschi 1969), something that cannot be said for contemporary economists. What can be said about them is that they have apparently fallen victim to the major errors of positivism: the tendency to define research issues so as to maximize their apparent policy relevance, and the tendency to confuse the interests of one's discipline with the interests of scientific explanation.

In Becker's famous essay, "Crime and Punishment: An Economic Approach" (1974), he says that he:

uses economic analysis to develop optimal public and private policies to combat illegal behavior. The public's decision variables are its expenditures on police, courts, etc., which help determine the probability (p) that an offense is discovered and the offender apprehended and convicted, the size of the punishment for those convicted (f), and the form of the punishment: imprisonment, probation, fine, etc. . . . . "Optimal" decisions are interpreted to mean decisions that minimize the social loss in income from offenses. This loss is the sum of damages, costs of apprehension and conviction, and costs of carrying out the punishments imposed. [p. 43]

Research on the deterrent effect of law enforcement activities shows the extremely limited value of economic analyses for policy purposes (see, e.g., Blumstein, Cohen, and Nagin 1978), and such analyses are by design irrelevant to the understanding of crime causation. Furthermore, by ignoring the concept of *crime*, the economist is led to empirical predictions consistently contrary to the nature of criminal behavior. For example, Becker sees the opportunity for collusion as adding strength and profit to illegal enterprises, specifically to "syndicate" control of narcotics, gambling, and prostitution (1974: 43). Empirical research casts doubt on this portrait, suggesting that the character of crime works against collusion and organization (Reuter 1983), since crime requires quick profits and momentary opportunities, and criminal propensities work against stable long-term relationships.

But perhaps the most general failing of economic analysis is its unexamined tendency to regard crime as "work," as the illegitimate equivalent of labor-force participation. This fundamental misconception of crime leads to the view that the decision to engage in crime has the same properties as the decision to engage in any other income-producing occupation, that it has career characteristics (e.g., specialization), that it can be a realistic source of lasting income, that its pursuit is compatible with the pursuit of legitimate activities, and that its participants respond to fluctuations in risk created by crime-control bureaucrats. For example, Ehrlich, whose analysis in his own words "goes beyond that of Becker and other previous contributions" (1974: 69), described a typology of offenders dependent on their attitudes toward risk:

A risk-neutral offender will spend more time in illegitimate activity relative to a risk avoider, and a risk preferrer will spend more time there relative to both. Moreover [under certain conditions], offenders who are risk preferrers would necessarily specialize in illegitimate activity. . . . In contrast, offenders who are risk avoiders are likely to combine a relatively safe legitimate activity with their illegitimate activity to hedge against the relatively greater risk involved in a full-time pursuit of the latter. Whether offenders are likely to specialize in illegitimate activity thus becomes an aspect of their attitudes toward risk, as well as their relative opportunities in alternative legitimate and illegitimate activities. [1974: 76]

The data on property crime cannot be reconciled with the view of crime derived from economic models of work. The modal age for burglars is about seventeen, and the rate of burglary declines rapidly with age (Hirschi and Gottfredson 1983). The most likely "pecuniary" outcome for a burglar is *no* gain, and his next offense is likely to be something other than burglary. Shoplifting of something he does not need and cannot use is high on the list of probabilities, or an offense likely to terminate his legitimate and illegitimate careers—such as rape, assault, or homicide—for (again) no pecuniary gain is also highly probable. In the unlikely event that he is legitimately employed, his most likely victim will be his employer, an act difficult to reconcile with maximization of long-term utility or the equation of legitimate work with risk avoidance. Because research shows that offenders are versatile (Wolfgang, Figlio, and Sellin 1972; Hindelang, Hirschi, and Weis 1981; Klein 1984) our portrait of the burglar applies equally well to the white-collar offender, the organized-crime offender, the dope dealer, and the assaulter; they are, after all, the *same* people.

Economic positivism begins with a fundamental compatibility with the classical notion of crime. Unfortunately, it follows the classical emphasis on political sanctions to the detriment of more powerful causal forces. Unfortunately, too, it makes another standard disciplinary mistake, which is to assume that crime reflects the major concept of the discipline studying it. Thus for the sociologist, crime is *social* behavior (when in fact it is the contrary); for the psychologist, crime is *learned* behavior (when in fact no learning is required); for the biologist, crime is an *inherited* trait (when in fact crime, like accidents, cannot be inherited); finally, for the economist, crime is *economic* behavior or labor-force participation (when in fact it is uneconomical behavior outside the labor force).

Economists will object to this characterization of their theory, pointing out that they include nonpecuniary (psychic) costs and benefits and "taste for risk" in their models. However, they discount such factors almost the moment they are introduced (almost as if the factors were "in the equation" to deflect criticism), and tests of economic theories focus exclusively on the pecuniary costs and benefits of state sanctions. In any event, if economic positivism is not as we have described it, it is hard to see how it goes beyond or is distinct from ordinary psychological or sociological positivism.

Sociological Positivism

Criminology is taught in American universities today mainly under the auspices of departments of sociology. This discipline has claimed criminology as a subfield for most of the twentieth century. Originally, the sociological version of criminology was indistinguishable from the multiple-factor criminology of early positivism (see, e.g., Parmelee 1918; Sutherland 1924), and one segment of the discipline (the social disorganization perspective) retained ties to the classical tradition. However, sociologists generally rejected social disorganization and the multiple-factor approach on the grounds that they were inconsistent with the central assumptions of the discipline. This rejection took one of two forms. One replaced the classical assumption of self-interested behavior with the assumption that people always act in the interest of the groups to which they belong (the cultural deviance tradition). The other replaced the assumption that self-interest is natural, universal, and requires no explanation with the assumption that social sources of motivation are required to account for crime (the strain tradition).

The Cultural Deviance Perspective

The foundation for cultural deviance theory came with the conclusion of Thorsten Sellin (1938) that crime is always relative to the norms of the group defining it as crime—therefore, it is a product of social definitions. As Ruth Kornhauser (1978: 29) describes it:

In cultural deviance models there is no such thing as deviance in the ordinary meaning of that word. If conformity is defined as obedience to the norms of one's culture and deviance as violation of those norms, then human beings apparently lack the capacity for deviance. Except for the idiot and the insane, who cannot know what they are about, the universal experience of mankind is conformity to the norms of the groups into which they have been socialized and to which they owe allegiance. People never violate the norms of their *own* groups, only the norms of other groups. What appears to be deviance is simply a label applied by an outgroup to the conforming behavior endorsed in one's own subculture.

For current purposes, two features of sociological relativism have important implications for the development of criminology. One is the assumption that socialization is always complete, that people do not violate the norms of the group to which they belong. The other is the assumption that group norms are infinitely variable, in principle and in fact.

The classical school assumed that socialization of the individual was never so "complete" that the possibility of crime could be ignored. The cultural deviance brand of sociological positivism assumes that socialization is always so complete that the possibility of acting contrary to "group" norms can be ignored. If the idea of human nature inherent in the classical school permits the idea of crime, the idea of human nature inherent in the cultural deviance theory is incompatible with the idea of crime. If all human conduct conforms to group norms, people must always act in the interest of the group. If self-interest cannot conflict with group interest, self-interest cannot be the cause of crime. At the most basic level, therefore, the classical school and cultural deviance models are incompatible. (In the conflict version of the cultural deviance view, the empirical existence of "crime" is evidence that the state, which defines crime, does not share the norms of all of its constituent groups. Crime is therefore literally created by the state, and its prosecution is evidence of state discrimination or bias.)

The cultural deviance idea is the intellectual foundation of perhaps the most influential criminological theories of the twentieth century, including differential association (Sutherland 1939), labeling (Tannenbaum 1938; Lemert 1951; Becker 1963), conflict (Turk 1969; Vold 1979), subcultural (Cohen 1955; Wolfgang and Ferracuti 1967), and social learning theories (Akers 1973; Elliott, Huizinga, and Ageton 1985). In none of these theories does one find an interest in individual differences in propensity to commit criminal acts. If these theorists address individual-level correlates of crime, it is only to show that they operate through their effects on group membership, not on crime itself. Thus, for example, these theorists argue that young people are more likely to commit criminal acts only because they are more likely to be exposed to peer groups that positively reward involvement in crime. School dropouts are more likely to engage in crime than those who stay in school only because they are more likely to be in contact with values conducive to crime. The children of offenders are more likely to be offenders themselves only because they live in a culture that fosters behavior that the larger culture deems criminal, not because they have tendencies to crime independent of the normative structure of their group.

Ironically, the criminal in cultural deviance theory is highly likely to continue committing criminal acts because such acts have external or social support (reinforcement). Thus a theory designed to contradict the notion of "criminality" ends up constructing an animal who follows crime as a way of life (see, e.g., Sutherland 1937; Cressey 1969.)

Given its commitment to the idea that crime is indistinguishable from other forms of behavior, the cultural deviance tradition has no means for recognizing similarity across criminal acts.[7] It thus leads directly to typologies of offenders and offenses and to concern about organized crime (Cressey 1969), white-collar crime (Sutherland 1940), delinquent gangs (Cohen 1955; Cloward and Ohlin 1960), drug users (Becker 1963), and violent offenders (Wolfgang and Ferracuti 1967), where each type of crime or "criminal" is assumed to have distinct group support.

For now it should be noted that the cultural deviance branch of sociological positivism is contrary to the tenets of the classical school on every count. It is inhospitable to the idea of crime and to the idea of criminality. At the same time, the cultural deviance branch of so-

---

[7]Most theories strive for and claim generality. The devices they use to achieve generality are, however, various. Our theory seeks generality by identifying features common to a wide variety of acts (such features as immediate, easy pleasure) and by assuming that individuals vary in their freedom to engage in such acts. Our theory thus identifies a large number of distinct acts and in effect ranks individuals in terms of the likelihood that they will engage in them. Other theories seek generality by identifying common causal processes in a variety of acts (such processes as strain reduction, group support, or labeling). These theories may be applied *seriatim* to many criminal and noncriminal acts, but the focus is on the distinct features of particular acts and of individuals that make them compatible with one another. These theories thus achieve generality at the expense of parsimony. They also achieve generality at the expense of empirical accuracy, since at least those theories listed end up predicting specialization in particular criminal acts, a prediction contrary to fact (see also Chapter 5).

ciological positivism is contrary to the tenets of criminological positivism, which explicitly endorses a multiple-factor, multidisciplinary view of crime causation.

The Strain Tradition

In 1938 Robert Merton advanced a theory of crime built explicitly on the major assumptions of the discipline of sociology. Merton had no interest in criminology and little interest in the nature of crime or its correlates. He explicitly disdained interest in prior research in the field, and he did not bother to summarize the evidence bearing on the empirical relation most important to his theory (the correlation between social class and crime). Instead, Merton's paper, "Social Structure and 'Anomie,'" was designed to be an exposition of general sociological principles as they applied to a wide variety of conduct.

Classical theory found in the concept of self-interest a plausible, general motive for crime and other forms of deviant behavior. Given the assumptions of sociological positivism, the classical view of motivation was no longer plausible. If humans are naturally social, self-interest cannot be taken as a general motive for their criminal conduct. Instead, the motive to crime must be created by unnatural circumstances. Since in the sociological view humans naturally conform, this motive must be produced by some "contradiction," "disjunction," or other "abnormality" in society.

In Merton's strain theory, the motivation to commit crime derives from a disjunction in American society between the universal aspiration to accumulate material wealth and the limitations imposed by the American system of stratification, where all are not given an equal chance to realize their aspirations. This inability to reach one's "culturally induced" goals is a source of intense frustration or strain. Under the pressure of culturally induced and structurally frustrated desire, people must do something to make life tolerable. One escape or "adaptation" is to *turn to crime* as an alternative means of attaining material success.

Although there are, in Merton's view, several adaptations to such stress, they are not equally available to everyone, and only one of them involves crime. In particular, some modes of adaptation are closed to some people because the behavior they require conflicts with their values, or socialization. Thus middle-class people have a hard time turning to crime because they have been socialized to be law-abiding. Not having been so socialized, lower-class people find crime a relatively easy or obvious route to a goal they would otherwise have no opportunity to achieve. (Why lower-class people, being poorly socialized, do not turn to crime in the absence of strain, Merton does not explain.)

Merton's strain theory, and variants on it, has become one of the most widely researched and advocated theories of sociological positivism. Its appeal stems from several sources. For now, we want to note two features of the theory that have general implications for the contribution of sociological positivism to criminology. First, the theory takes the *a priori* position that an "independent variable" central to a particular discipline is therefore a major cause of crime. For Merton, and for many sociologists after him, this variable is social class. Social class is to sociology what heritability is to biology, and there are striking parallels between sociology's search for the impact of social class (see Tittle, Villemez, and Smith 1978; Braithwaite 1981) and biology's search for evidence of the genetic transmission of crime. The second feature centers on the effort to identify and explain modes of specialization within crime or deviant behavior, in which the theory explicitly denies the idea of criminality as a general predisposition and therefore explicitly rejects the idea of versatility. Both of these features of the strain version of sociological positivism deserve further discussion.

Social Class

Controversy over the relation between social class and crime has occupied the sociological literature since the late 1950's. This debate was not occasioned by Merton's theory (which was written some twenty years earlier) but by the discovery in self-report research of no relation between social class and crime. An unresolved, 30-year empirical debate over one of its core propositions is not good news for a theory, but the issue was never the truth or falsity of Merton's theory (which one systematic review concludes is "disconfirmed" [Kornhauser 1978: 253]) but the truth or falsity of the discipline of sociology. Somehow, academic disciplines within the positive tradition have become isomorphic with theories of behavior, and they see the defense of such theories as defense of their own interests. For no good theoretical reason, then, the sociological journals swell with earnest summaries of the research literature on the class and crime issue, with potential corrections to previous deficiencies in the measurement of class or crime, with reports of high-order interactions between class and gender or class and age that "clarify" the class relationship, and even with charges of ideological blindness among those who cannot see a significant relation in the data.[8]

For that matter, the concept of social class is so factorially complex or ambiguous that an "empirical" relation would, if present, only serve as a starting point for theoretical speculation. Its central place in the strain branch of sociological positivism testifies to the continuing influence of disciplinary interests on the content of crime theory.

Modes of Adaptation

In our discussion of biological positivism, we described how the lack of a conception of crime led inevitably to subdivision of the domain of crime, to the creation of types of crime and types of offenders. In biological positivism, these types were created inductively, with each type commanding its own etiological theory (e.g., the born criminal and the habitual criminal). In the strain tradition of sociological positivism, which also lacks a conception of crime, such subdivision of the phenomenon of crime also takes place. In the strain approach, however, the typology is derived deductively from the general etiological theory. Given strain, the actor's responses are fixed and limited. Merton in fact deduced five possible "adaptations" to strain (although others have deduced many additional possibilities from Merton's discussion), only two of which are relevant to our discussion. One of these is the "innovator," a person who continues to pursue the cultural goal of financial success but who abandons legitimate means of doing so. The innovator is the criminal. The other is the "retreatist," a person who abandons the cultural goal of financial success and the legitimate means of attaining success. The retreatist is the drug user, the alcoholic, or the mentally ill. (These types surfaced again in the Richard Cloward and Lloyd Ohlin version of strain theory presented in *Delinquency and Opportunity* [1960]. In the Cloward and Ohlin theory, delinquent gangs specialize in crime *or* in drugs.)

The fact that the people who engage in crime also engage in drug use is incompatible with Merton's (and Cloward and Ohlin's) theory, as is the general connection among all forms of deviance. Following

[8]The most common device for "clinching" the argument about social class and crime invites the disputee to park his car in a slum area or to walk the streets of lower-class sections of town and compare the experience with a similar walk in affluent areas. As a rhetorical device, this argument is effective, but it is not necessarily accurate (graveyards also exude fear, although there is some question about whether the people in them are especially dangerous), and furthermore it is not clear how it bears on the assertion that the children of people who "work for a living" are no more or less criminal than the children of other members of the community.

the logic of the strain version of sociological positivism (and ignoring the results of prior research) thus leads to blunt inconsistency with the facts.

The Social Disorganization Tradition

The original American sociological perspective on crime shared much with the classical school. The ideas of social and personal disorganization, which dominated the study of social problems in the first half of the twentieth century, were perfectly compatible with the ideas of crime and criminality (see, e.g., Thomas 1923; Beeley 1954). These ideas, in turn, seemed to derive from positivistic research on the spatial distribution of crime.

The major assumption of the ecological school is that crime or "criminality" is not a property of persons but a property of the groups to which they belong. The foundation of this assumption was laid by the statisticians of the early nineteenth century. For example, the French statistician Adolphe Quetelet demonstrated that areal and demographic differences in crime rates were stable over long periods of time, and he concluded from these facts that some feature of the area or group must be responsible for its crime rate. Such data and interpretation became the foundation of social theories of crime. A hundred years later, such differences were reconfirmed by Clifford Shaw and Henry McKay in Chicago and interpreted as evidence of the social causation of crime.

In a series of studies, Shaw and McKay (1942) documented marked differences within the city of Chicago in rates of various community problems, including crime and delinquency, truancy, infant mortality, mental disorder, and tuberculosis. Shaw and McKay were able to show that areas with a high degree of such problems were also marked by low educational attainment, a high proportion of families on welfare, low rental value of property, a high percentage of the work force at low occupational levels, and poor community organization. They argued that these characteristics of areas remained relatively constant over time, whatever the particular groups dominant in them: "It appears to be established, then, that each racial, nativity, and nationality group in Chicago displays widely varying rates of delinquents; that rates for immigrant groups in particular show a wide historical fluctuation; [and] that diverse racial, nativity, and national groups possess relatively similar rates of delinquents in similar social areas" (Shaw and McKay, 1942: 162).

This finding is an important base of cultural deviance theories, which interpret such continuity as the transmission of values from one generation to the next. It is the basis of ecological criminology, which views the physical structure of communities as shaping the routine activities of inhabitants in ways that affect the likelihood of crime. The finding is also compatible with strain theory, which posits that stable areal differences reflect stable differences in poverty or lack of opportunity. Finally, differences in crime rates across areas of the city may reflect differences in social disorganization—that is, differences in the ability of community institutions to control the behavior of their members.

The social disorganization interpretation of crime-rate differences assumes that people will commit criminal acts when the surrounding "society" is unable to prevent them from doing so. It assumes that society must train or socialize individuals in the first instance and must continue to monitor their behavior if they are to remain law-abiding. Such assumptions are obviously those of the classical tradition, which means that the assumptions of the classical tradition are therefore compatible with (stable and unstable) variation in crime rates from one group to another, and that they are indeed compatible with all of the "findings" of sociological positivism.

So, in the beginning, sociological research and theory were compatible with or even identical to the classical concepts of crime and criminality. The fact that sociology now tends to deny this compatibility should not obscure the fact that sociological research can be easily interpreted within the classical conception of crime. There is no empirical or factual barrier to integration of the sociological and classical points of view. Since integration of diverse theories is a standard goal of positivistic criminology, the lack of progress in integrating the classical and sociological traditions is something of a puzzle.

Conclusions

Positivistic social science resists general conceptual schemes or theories. As a consequence, it proliferates concepts without concern for their distinctiveness or significance. This produces endless distinctions among behavioral categories and generates apparent interest in the countless permutations and combinations of units and their properties (e.g., internal labor markets of multinational firms devoted to extractive economies; male gang drug-related drive-by shootings; ideology and voting patterns among Southern workers in the 1930's). One way to produce *apparent* order out of such chaos is to divide the domain of science among "disciplines," giving each primary responsibility for the variables within its area. But disciplinary organization of scientific research does not solve the problem. On the contrary, by tending to grant proprietary rights to concepts, it creates petty jealousies and territorial disputes that restrict the growth and sharing of knowledge.

Another way to produce order out of chaos is to focus on the acts or behaviors of interest and ask what they might have in common. If commonality is discerned, this may lead to conclusions about causal mechanisms rather different from those generated by adherence to the notion that each item of behavior has unique causes to be found within the realm of the discipline owning it. In our view, examination of the acts that cluster together around crime and deviance reveals that they share a common structure and therefore the possibility of a common causation. In all cases, the behavior produces immediate, short-term pleasure or benefit to the actor; in all cases, the behavior tends to entail long-term cost. As Bentham (1970) pointed out, these costs may be physical, political, religious, or social, but they are costs nonetheless, and people pursuing such behavior must weigh current benefits against them. It follows that those pursuing such behaviors may therefore tend to have something in common, something that causes them to choose short-term advantage over long-term cost.

Many social scientists who regard themselves as scientists reject *a priori* the idea that choice can cause human behavior. They presumably do so because they find "choice" incompatible with or even contrary to the scientific notion of determinism. In psychology, this position surfaces in the conclusion that the principles of operant conditioning (according to which behavior is determined by its consequences) contradict the position of positivistic science that causes must precede their effects. In biology, it is encountered in the conclusion that the principles of evolution (according to which selection of traits is affected by their survival value) contradict the position of positivistic science according to which causes must precede their effects. In sociology, anti-choice sentiment favors the argument that to be fully social a theory must account for behavior without resort to the decisionmaking properties of individuals.

Obviously, the mechanism of crime causation is fair game for all disciplines and cannot reasonably be claimed to be the sole province of any of them. For example, family socialization practices may produce variation in concern about the costs of short-term hedonistic behavior (Hirschi 1969). By the same token, biological differences in physical size could reduce the costs of such behavior, thus increasing the probability that the actor will choose to engage in it. It is important to stress that the disciplinary source of such causes is irrelevant to the explanatory scheme and that there is in this scheme no distinction between choice theories and theories that rely on scientific notions of causal analysis. Indeed, the methods of positivism are fully applicable to such theories. All that is missing from them is the misguided notion that science favors particular substantive theories of human behavior and the equally misguided notion that specific causes belong to specific disciplines.

5

The Nature of Criminality:
Low Self-Control

Theories of crime lead naturally to interest in the propensities of individuals committing criminal acts. These propensities are often labeled "criminality." In pure classical theory, people committing criminal acts had no special propensities. They merely followed the universal tendency to enhance their own pleasure. If they differed from noncriminals, it was with respect to their location in or comprehension of relevant sanction systems. For example, the individual cut off from the community will suffer less than others from the ostracism that follows crime; the individual unaware of the natural or legal consequences of criminal behavior cannot be controlled by these consequences to the degree that people aware of them are controlled; the atheist will not be as concerned as the believer about penalties to be exacted in a life beyond death. Classical theories on the whole, then, are today called *control* theories, theories emphasizing the prevention of crime through consequences painful to the individual.

Although, for policy purposes, classical theorists emphasized legal consequences, the importance to them of moral sanctions is so obvious that their theories might well be called underdeveloped *social control* theories. In fact, Bentham's list of the major restraining motives—motives acting to prevent mischievous acts—begins with goodwill, love of reputation, and the desire for amity (1970: 134–36). He goes on to say that fear of detection prevents crime in large part because of detection's consequences for "reputation, and the desire for amity" (p. 138). Put another way, in Bentham's view, the restraining power of legal sanctions in large part stems from their connection to social sanctions.

If crime is evidence of the weakness of social motives, it follows that criminals are less social than noncriminals and that the extent of their asociality may be determined by the nature and number of their crimes. Calculation of the extent of an individual's mischievousness is a complex affair, but in general the more mischievous or depraved the offenses, and the greater their number, the more mischievous or depraved the offender (Bentham 1970: 134–42). (Classical theorists thus had reason to be interested in the seriousness of the offense. The relevance of seriousness to current theories of crime is not so clear.)

Because classical or control theories infer that offenders are not restrained by social motives, it is common to think of them as emphasizing an asocial human nature. Actually, such theories make people only as asocial as their acts require. Pure or consistent control theories do not add criminality (i.e., personality concepts or attributes such as "aggressiveness" or "extraversion") to individuals beyond that found in their criminal acts. As a result, control theories are suspicious of images of an antisocial, psychopathic, or career offender, or of an offender whose motives to crime are somehow larger than those given in the crimes themselves. Indeed, control theories are compatible with the view that the balance of the total control structure favors conformity, even among offenders:

For in every man, be his disposition ever so depraved, the social motives are those which . . . regulate and determine the general tenor of his life. . . . The general and standing bias of every man's nature is, therefore, towards that side to which the force of the social motives would determine him to adhere. This being the case, the force of the social motives tends continually to put an end to that of the dissocial ones; as, in natural bodies, the force of friction tends to put an end to that which is generated by impulse. Time, then, which wears away the force of the dissocial motives, adds to that of the social. [Bentham 1970: 141]

Positivism brought with it the idea that criminals differ from noncriminals in ways more radical than this, the idea that criminals carry within themselves properties peculiarly and positively conducive to crime. In Chapters 3 and 4, we examined the efforts of the major disciplines to identify these properties. Being friendly to both the classical and positivist traditions, we expected to end up with a list of individual properties reliably identified by competent research as useful in the description of "criminality"—such properties as aggressiveness, body build, activity level, and intelligence. We further expected that we would be able to connect these individual-level correlates of criminality directly to the classical idea of crime. As our review progressed, however, we were forced to conclude that we had overestimated the success of positivism in establishing important differences between "criminals" and "noncriminals" beyond their tendency to commit criminal acts. Stable individual differences in the tendency to commit criminal acts were clearly evident, but many or even most of the other differences between offenders and nonoffenders were not as clear or pronounced as our reading of the literature had led us to expect.[1]

If individual differences in the tendency to commit criminal acts (within an overall tendency for crime to decline with age) are at least potentially explicable within classical theory by reference to the social location of individuals and their comprehension of how the world works, the fact remains that classical theory cannot shed much light on the positivistic finding (denied by most positivistic theories, as pointed out in Chapters 3 and 4) that these differences *remain reasonably stable with change in the social location of individuals and change in their knowledge of the operation of sanction systems.* This is the problem of self-control, the differential tendency of people to avoid criminal acts whatever the circumstances in which they find themselves. Since this difference among people has attracted a variety of names, we begin by arguing the merits of the concept of self-control.

Self-Control and Alternative Concepts

Our decision to ascribe stable individual differences in criminal behavior to self-control was made only after considering several alternatives, one of which (criminality) we had used before (Hirschi and Gottfredson 1986). A major consideration was consistency between the classical conception of crime and our conception of the criminal. It seemed unwise to try to integrate a choice theory of crime with a deterministic image of the offender, especially when such integration was unnecessary. In fact, the compatibility of the classical view of crime and the idea that people differ in self-control is, in our view, remarkable. As we have seen, classical theory is a theory of social or external control, a theory based on the idea that the costs of crime depend on the individual's current location in or bond to society. What classical theory lacks is an explicit idea of self-control, the idea that people also differ in the extent to which they are vulnerable to the temptations of the moment. Combining the two ideas thus

[1] We do not mean to imply that stable individual differences between offenders and nonoffenders are nonexistent. The fact of the matter is, however, that substantial evidence documenting individual differences is not as clear to us as it appears to be to others. The evidence on intelligence is an exception. Here differences favoring nonoffenders have been abundantly documented (cf. Wilson and Herrnstein 1985).

merely recognizes the simultaneous existence of social and individual restraints on behavior.

An obvious alternative is the concept of criminality. The disadvantages of that concept, however, are numerous. First, it connotes causation or determinism, a positive tendency to crime that is contrary to the classical model and, in our view, contrary to the facts. Whereas self-control suggests that people differ in the extent to which they are restrained from criminal acts, criminality suggests that people differ in the extent to which they are compelled to crime. The concept of self-control is thus consistent with the observation that criminals do not require or need crime, and the concept of criminality is inconsistent with this observation. By the same token, the idea of low self-control is compatible with the observation that criminal acts require no special capabilities, needs, or motivation; they are, in this sense, available to everyone. In contrast, the idea of criminality as a special tendency suggests that criminal acts require special people for their performance and enjoyment. Finally, lack of restraint or low self-control allows almost any deviant, criminal, exciting, or dangerous act; in contrast, the idea of criminality covers only a narrow portion of the apparently diverse acts engaged in by people at one end of the dimension we are now discussing.

The concept of conscience comes closer than criminality to self-control, and is harder to distinguish from it. Unfortunately, that concept has connotations of compulsion (to conformity) not, strictly speaking, consistent with a choice model (or with the operation of conscience). It does not seem to cover the behaviors analogous to crime that appear to be controlled by natural sanctions rather than social or moral sanctions, and in the end it typically refers to how people feel about their acts rather than to the likelihood that they will or will not commit them. Thus accidents and employment instability are not usually seen as produced by failures of conscience, and writers in the conscience tradition do not typically make the connection between moral and prudent behavior. Finally, conscience is used primarily to summarize the results of learning via negative reinforcement, and even those favorably disposed to its use have little more to say about it (see, e.g., Eysenck 1977; Wilson and Herrnstein 1985).

We are now in position to describe the nature of self-control, the individual characteristic relevant to the commission of criminal acts. We assume that the nature of this characteristic can be derived directly from the nature of criminal acts. We thus infer from the nature of crime what people who refrain from criminal acts are like before they reach the age at which crime becomes a logical possibility. We then work back further to the factors producing their restraint, back to the causes of self-control. In our view, lack of self-control does not require crime and can be counteracted by situational conditions or other properties of the individual. At the same time, we suggest that high self-control effectively reduces the possibility of crime—that is, those possessing it will be substantially less likely at all periods of life to engage in criminal acts.

The Elements of Self-Control

Criminal acts provide *immediate* gratification of desires. A major characteristic of people with low self-control is therefore a tendency to respond to tangible stimuli in the immediate environment, to have a concrete "here and now" orientation. People with high self-control, in contrast, tend to defer gratification.

Criminal acts provide *easy or simple* gratification of desires. They provide money without work, sex without courtship, revenge without court delays. People lacking self-control also tend to lack diligence, tenacity, or persistence in a course of action.

Criminal acts are *exciting, risky, or thrilling*. They involve stealth, danger, speed, agility, deception, or power. People lacking self-control therefore tend to be adventuresome, active, and physical. Those with high levels of self-control tend to be cautious, cognitive, and verbal.

Crimes provide *few or meager long-term benefits*. They are not equivalent to a job or a career. On the contrary, crimes interfere with long-term commitments to jobs, marriages, family, or friends. People with low self-control thus tend to have unstable marriages, friendships, and job profiles. They tend to be little interested in and unprepared for long-term occupational pursuits.

Crimes require *little skill or planning*. The cognitive requirements for most crimes are minimal. It follows that people lacking self-control need not possess or value cognitive or academic skills. The manual skills required for most crimes are minimal. It follows that people lacking self-control need not possess manual skills that require training or apprenticeship.

Crimes often result in *pain or discomfort for the victim*. Property is lost, bodies are injured, privacy is violated, trust is broken. It follows that people with low self-control tend to be self-centered, indifferent, or insensitive to the suffering and needs of others. It does not follow, however, that people with low self-control are routinely unkind or antisocial. On the contrary, they may discover the immediate and easy rewards of charm and generosity.

Recall that crime involves the pursuit of immediate pleasure. It follows that people lacking self-control will also tend to pursue immediate pleasures that are *not* criminal: they will tend to smoke, drink, use drugs, gamble, have children out of wedlock, and engage in illicit sex.

Crimes require the interaction of an offender with people or their property. It does not follow that people lacking self-control will tend to be gregarious or social. However, it does follow that, other things being equal, gregarious or social people are more likely to be involved in criminal acts.

The major benefit of many crimes is not pleasure but relief from momentary irritation. The irritation caused by a crying child is often the stimulus for physical abuse. That caused by a taunting stranger in a bar is often the stimulus for aggravated assault. It follows that people with low self-control tend to have minimal tolerance for frustration and little ability to respond to conflict through verbal rather than physical means.

Crimes involve the risk of violence and physical injury, of pain and suffering on the part of the offender. It does not follow that people with low self-control will tend to be tolerant of physical pain or to be indifferent to physical discomfort. It does follow that people tolerant of physical pain or indifferent to physical discomfort will be more likely to engage in criminal acts whatever their level of self-control.

The risk of criminal penalty for any given criminal act is small, but this depends in part on the circumstances of the offense. Thus, for example, not all joyrides by teenagers are equally likely to result in arrest. A car stolen from a neighbor and returned unharmed before he notices its absence is less likely to result in official notice than is a car stolen from a shopping center parking lot and abandoned at the convenience of the offender. Drinking alcohol stolen from parents and consumed in the family garage is less likely to receive official notice than drinking in the parking lot outside a concert hall. It follows that offenses differ in their validity as measures of self-control: those offenses with large risk of public awareness are better measures than those with little risk.

In sum, people who lack self-control will tend to be impulsive, insensitive, physical (as opposed to mental), risk-taking, short-sighted, and nonverbal, and they will tend therefore to engage in criminal and analogous acts. Since these traits can be identified prior to the age of responsibility for crime, since there is considerable tendency for these traits to come together in the same people, and since the traits tend to persist through life, it seems reasonable to consider them as comprising a stable construct useful in the explanation of crime.

The Many Manifestations of Low Self-Control

Our image of the "offender" suggests that crime is not an automatic or necessary consequence of low self-control. It suggests that many noncriminal acts analogous to crime (such as accidents, smoking, and alcohol use) are also manifestations of low self-control. Our image therefore implies that no specific act, type of crime, or form of deviance is uniquely required by the absence of self-control.

Because both crime and analogous behaviors stem from low self-control (that is, both are manifestations of low self-control), they will all be engaged in at a relatively high rate by people with low self-control. Within the domain of crime, then, there will be much versatility among offenders in the criminal acts in which they engage.

Research on the versatility of deviant acts supports these predictions in the strongest possible way. The variety of manifestations of low self-control is immense. In spite of years of tireless research motivated by a belief in specialization, no credible evidence of specialization has been reported. In fact, the evidence of offender versatility is overwhelming (Hirschi 1969; Hindelang 1971; Wolfgang, Figlio, and Sellin 1972; Petersilia 1980; Hindelang, Hirschi, and Weis 1981; Rojek and Erickson 1982; Klein 1984).

By versatility we mean that offenders commit a wide variety of criminal acts, with no strong inclination to pursue a specific criminal act or a pattern of criminal acts to the exclusion of others. Most theories suggest that offenders tend to specialize, whereby such terms as robber, burglar, drug dealer, rapist, and murderer have predictive or descriptive import. In fact, some theories create offender specialization as part of their explanation of crime. For example, Cloward and Ohlin (1960) create distinctive subcultures of delinquency around particular forms of criminal behavior, identifying subcultures specializing in theft, violence, or drugs. In a related way, books are written about white-collar crime as though it were a clearly distinct specialty requiring a unique explanation. Research projects are undertaken for the study of drug use, or vandalism, or teen pregnancy (as though every study of delinquency were not a study of drug use and vandalism and teenage sexual behavior). Entire schools of criminology emerge to pursue patterning, sequencing, progression, escalation, onset, persistence, and desistance in the career of offenses or offenders. These efforts survive largely because their proponents fail to consider or acknowledge the clear evidence to the contrary. Other reasons for survival of such ideas may be found in the interest of politicians and members of the law enforcement community who see policy potential in criminal careers or "career criminals" (see, e.g., Blumstein et al. 1986).

Occasional reports of specialization seem to contradict this point, as do everyday observations of repetitive misbehavior by particular offenders. Some offenders rob the same store repeatedly over a period of years, or an offender commits several rapes over a (brief) period of time. Such offenders may be called "robbers" or "rapists." However, it should be noted that such labels are retrospective rather than predictive and that they typically ignore a large amount of delinquent or criminal behavior by the same offenders that is inconsistent with their alleged specialty. Thus, for example, the "rapist" will tend also to use drugs, to commit robberies and burglaries (often in concert with the rape), and to have a record for violent offenses other than rape. There is a perhaps natural tendency on the part of observers (and in official accounts) to focus on the most serious crimes in a series of events, but this tendency should not be confused with a tendency on the part of the offender to specialize in one kind of crime.

Recall that one of the defining features of crime is that it is simple and easy. Some apparent specialization will therefore occur because obvious opportunities for an easy score will tend to repeat themselves. An offender who lives next to a shopping area that is approached by pedestrians will have repeat opportunities for purse snatching, and this may show in his arrest record. But even here the specific "criminal career" will tend to quickly run its course and to be followed by offenses whose content and character is likewise determined by convenience and opportunity (which is the reason why some form of theft is always the best bet about what a person is likely to do next).

The evidence that offenders are likely to engage in noncriminal acts psychologically or theoretically equivalent to crime is, because of the relatively high rates of these "noncriminal" acts, even easier to document. Thieves are likely to smoke, drink, and skip school at considerably higher rates than nonthieves. Offenders are considerably more likely than nonoffenders to be involved in most types of accidents, including household fires, auto crashes, and unwanted pregnancies. They are also considerably more likely to die at an early age (see, e.g., Robins 1966; Eysenck 1977; Gottfredson 1984).

Good research on drug use and abuse routinely reveals that the correlates of delinquency and drug use are the same. As Akers (1984) has noted, "compared to the abstaining teenager, the drinking, smoking, and drug-taking teen is much more likely to be getting into fights, stealing, hurting other people, and committing other delinquencies." Akers goes on to say, "but the variation in the order in which they take up these things leaves little basis for proposing the causation of one by the other." In our view, the relation between drug use and delinquency is not a causal question. The correlates are the same because drug use and delinquency are both manifestations of an underlying tendency to pursue short-term, immediate pleasure. This underlying tendency (i.e., lack of self-control) has many manifestations, as listed by Harrison Gough (1948):

unconcern over the rights and privileges of others when recognizing them would interfere with personal satisfaction in any way; impulsive behavior, or apparent incongruity between the strength of the stimulus and the magnitude of the behavioral response; inability to form deep or persistent attachments to other persons or to identify in interpersonal relationships; poor judgment and planning in attaining defined goals; apparent lack of anxiety and distress over social maladjustment and unwillingness or inability to consider maladjustment qua maladjustment; a tendency to project blame onto others and to take no responsibility for failures; meaningless prevarication, often about trivial matters in situations where detection is inevitable; almost complete lack of dependability . . . and willingness to assume responsibility; and, finally, emotional poverty. [p. 362]

This combination of characteristics has been revealed in the life histories of the subjects in the famous studies by Lee Robins. Robins is one of the few researchers to focus on the varieties of deviance and the way they tend to go together in the lives of those she designates as having "antisocial personalities." In her words: "We refer to someone who fails to maintain close personal relationships with anyone else, [who] performs poorly on the job, who is involved in illegal behaviors (whether or not apprehended), who fails to support himself and his dependents without outside aid, and who is given to sudden changes of plan and loss of temper in response to what appear to others as minor frustrations" (1978: 255).

For 30 years Robins traced 524 children referred to a guidance clinic in St. Louis, Missouri, and she compared them to a control group matched on IQ, age, sex, and area of the city. She discovered that, in comparison to the control group, those people referred at an early age were more likely to be arrested as adults (for a wide variety of offenses), were less likely to get married, were more likely to be divorced, were more likely to marry a spouse with a behavior problem, were less likely to have children (but if they had children were likely to have more children), were more likely to have children with behavior problems, were more likely to be unemployed, had considerably more frequent job changes, were more likely to be on welfare, had fewer contacts with relatives, had fewer friends, were substantially less likely to attend church, were less likely to serve in the armed forces and more likely to be dishonorably discharged if they did serve, were more likely to exhibit physical evidence of excessive alcohol use, and were more likely to be hospitalized for psychiatric problems (1966: 42–73).

Note that these outcomes are consistent with four general elements of our notion of low self-control: basic stability of individual differences over a long period of time; great variability in the kinds of criminal acts engaged in; conceptual or causal equivalence of criminal and noncriminal acts; and inability to predict the specific forms of deviance engaged in, whether criminal or noncriminal. In our view, the idea of an antisocial personality defined by certain behavioral consequences is too positivistic or deterministic, suggesting that the offender must do certain things given his antisocial personality. Thus we would say only that the subjects in question are *more likely* to commit criminal acts (as the data indicate they are). We do not make commission of criminal acts part of the definition of the individual with low self-control.

Be this as it may, Robins's retrospective research shows that predictions derived from a concept of antisocial personality are highly consistent with the results of prospective longitudinal and cross-sectional research: offenders do not specialize; they tend to be involved in accidents, illness, and death at higher rates than the general population; they tend to have difficulty persisting in a job regardless of the particular characteristics of the job (no job will turn out to be a good job); they have difficulty acquiring and retaining friends; and they have difficulty meeting the demands of long-term financial commitments (such as mortgages or car payments) and the demands of parenting.

Seen in this light, the "costs" of low self-control for the individual may far exceed the costs of his criminal acts. In fact, it appears that crime is often among the least serious consequences of a lack of self-control in terms of the quality of life of those lacking it.

The Causes of Self-Control

We know better what deficiencies in self-control lead to than where they come from. One thing is, however, clear: low self-control is not produced by training, tutelage, or socialization. As a matter of fact, all of the characteristics associated with low self-control tend to show themselves in the absence of nurturance, discipline, or training. Given the classical appreciation of the causes of human behavior, the implications of this fact are straightforward: the causes of low self-control are negative rather than positive; self-control is unlikely in the absence of effort, intended or unintended, to create it. (This assumption separates the present theory from most modern theories of crime, where the offender is automatically seen as a product of positive forces, a creature of learning, particular pressures, or specific defect. We will return to this comparison once our theory has been fully explicated.)

At this point it would be easy to construct a theory of crime causation, according to which characteristics of potential offenders lead them ineluctably to the commission of criminal acts. Our task at this point would simply be to identify the likely sources of impulsiveness, intelligence, risk-taking, and the like. But to do so would be to follow the path that has proven so unproductive in the past, the path according to which criminals commit crimes irrespective of the characteristics of the setting or situation.

We can avoid this pitfall by recalling the elements inherent in the decision to commit a criminal act. The object of the offense is clearly pleasurable, and universally so. Engaging in the act, however, entails some risk of social, legal, and/or natural sanctions. Whereas the pleasure attained by the act is direct, obvious, and immediate, the pains risked by it are not obvious, or direct, and are in any event at greater remove from it. It follows that, though there will be little variability among people in their ability to see the pleasures of crime, there will be considerable variability in their ability to calculate potential pains. But the problem goes further than this: whereas the pleasures of crime are reasonably equally distributed over the population, this is not true for the pains. Everyone appreciates money; not everyone dreads parental anger or disappointment upon learning that the money was stolen.

So, the dimensions of self-control are, in our view, factors affecting calculation of the consequences of one's acts. The impulsive or short-sighted person fails to consider the negative or painful consequences of his acts; the insensitive person has fewer negative consequences to consider; the less intelligent person also has fewer negative consequences to consider (has less to lose).

No known social group, whether criminal or noncriminal, actively or purposefully attempts to reduce the self-control of its members.

Social life is not enhanced by low self-control and its consequences. On the contrary, the exhibition of these tendencies undermines harmonious group relations and the ability to achieve collective ends. These facts explicitly deny that a tendency to crime is a product of socialization, culture, or positive learning of any sort.

The traits composing low self-control are also not conducive to the achievement of long-term individual goals. On the contrary, they impede educational and occupational achievement, destroy interpersonal relations, and undermine physical health and economic well-being. Such facts explicitly deny the notion that criminality is an alternative route to the goals otherwise obtainable through legitimate avenues. It follows that people who care about the interpersonal skill, educational and occupational achievement, and physical and economic well-being of those in their care will seek to rid them of these traits.

Two general sources of variation are immediately apparent in this scheme. The first is the variation among children in the degree to which they manifest such traits to begin with. The second is the variation among caretakers in the degree to which they recognize low self-control and its consequences and the degree to which they are willing and able to correct it. Obviously, therefore, even at this threshold level the sources of low self-control are complex.

There is good evidence that some of the traits predicting subsequent involvement in crime appear as early as they can be reliably measured, including low intelligence, high activity level, physical strength, and adventuresomeness (Glueck and Glueck 1950; West and Farrington 1973). The evidence suggests that the connection between these traits and commission of criminal acts ranges from weak to moderate. Obviously, we do not suggest that people are born criminals, inherit a gene for criminality, or anything of the sort. In fact, we explicitly deny such notions (see Chapter 3). What we do suggest is that individual differences may have an impact on the prospects for effective socialization (or adequate control). Effective socialization is, however, always possible whatever the configuration of individual traits.

Other traits affecting crime appear later and seem to be largely products of ineffective or incomplete socialization. For example, differences in impulsivity and insensitivity become noticeable later in childhood when they are no longer common to all children. The ability and willingness to delay immediate gratification for some larger purpose may therefore be assumed to be a consequence of training. Much parental action is in fact geared toward suppression of impulsive behavior, toward making the child consider the long-range consequences of acts. Consistent sensitivity to the needs and feelings of others may also be assumed to be a consequence of training. Indeed, much parental behavior is directed toward teaching the child about the rights and feelings of others, and of how these rights and feelings ought to constrain the child's behavior. All of these points focus our attention on child-rearing.

Child-Rearing and Self-Control: The Family

The major "cause" of low self-control thus appears to be ineffective child-rearing. Put in positive terms, several conditions appear necessary to produce a socialized child. Perhaps the place to begin looking for these conditions is the research literature on the relation between family conditions and delinquency. This research (e.g., Glueck and Glueck 1950; McCord and McCord 1959) has examined the connection between many family factors and delinquency. It reports that discipline, supervision, and affection tend to be missing in the homes of delinquents, that the behavior of the parents is often "poor" (e.g., excessive drinking and poor supervision [Glueck and Glueck 1950: 110–11]); and that the parents of delinquents are unusually likely to have criminal records themselves. Indeed, according to Michael Rutter and Henri Giller, "of the parental characteristics associated with delinquency, criminality is the most striking and most consistent" 1984: 182).

Such information undermines the many explanations of crime that ignore the family, but in this form it does not represent much of an advance over the belief of the general public (and those who deal with offenders in the criminal justice system) that "defective upbringing" or "neglect" in the home is the primary cause of crime.

To put these standard research findings in perspective, we think it necessary to define the conditions necessary for adequate child-rearing to occur. The minimum conditions seem to be these: in order to teach the child self-control, someone must (1) monitor the child's behavior; (2) recognize deviant behavior when it occurs; and (3) punish such behavior. This seems simple and obvious enough. All that is required to activate the system is affection for *or* investment in the child. The person who cares for the child will watch his behavior, see him doing things he should not do, and correct him. The result may be a child more capable of delaying gratification, more sensitive to the interests and desires of others, more independent, more willing to accept restraints on his activity, and more unlikely to use force or violence to attain his ends.

When we seek the causes of low self-control, we ask where this system can go wrong. Obviously, parents do not prefer their children to be unsocialized in the terms described. We can therefore rule out in advance the possibility of positive socialization to unsocialized behavior (as cultural or subcultural deviance theories suggest). Still, the system can go wrong at any one of four places. First, the parents may not care for the child (in which case none of the other conditions would be met); second, the parents, even if they care, may not have the time or energy to monitor the child's behavior; third, the parents, even if they care *and* monitor, may not see anything wrong with the child's behavior; finally, even if everything else is in place, the parents may not have the inclination or the means to punish the child. So, what may appear at first glance to be nonproblematic turns out to be problematic indeed. Many things can go wrong. According to much research in crime and delinquency, in the homes of problem children many things have gone wrong: "Parents of stealers do not track ([they] do not interpret stealing . . . as 'deviant'); they do not punish; and they do not care" (Patterson 1980: 88–89; see also Glueck and Glueck 1950; McCord and McCord 1959; West and Farrington 1977).

Let us apply this scheme to some of the facts about the connection between child socialization and crime, beginning with the elements of the child-rearing model.

The Attachment of the Parent to the Child

Our model states that parental concern for the welfare or behavior of the child is a necessary condition for successful child-rearing. Because it is too often assumed that all parents are alike in their love for their children, the evidence directly on this point is not as good or extensive as it could be. However, what exists is clearly consistent with the model. Glueck and Glueck (1950: 125–28) report that, compared to the fathers of delinquents, fathers of nondelinquents were twice as likely to be warmly disposed toward their sons and one-fifth as likely to be hostile toward them. In the same sample, 28 percent of the mothers of delinquents were characterized as "indifferent or hostile" toward the child as compared to 4 percent of the mothers of nondelinquents. The evidence suggests that stepparents are especially unlikely to have feelings of affection toward their stepchildren (Burgess 1980), adding in contemporary society to the likelihood that children will be "reared" by people who do not especially care for them.

Parental Supervision

The connection between social control and self-control could not be more direct than in the case of parental supervision of the child. Such supervision presumably prevents criminal or analogous acts and at the same time trains the child to avoid them on his own. Consistent with this assumption, supervision tends to be a major predictor of delinquency, however supervision or delinquency is measured (Glueck and Glueck 1950; Hirschi 1969; West and Farrington 1977; Riley and Shaw 1985).

Our general theory in principle provides a method of separating supervision as external control from supervision as internal control. For one thing, offenses differ in the degree to which they can be prevented through monitoring; children at one age are monitored much more closely than children at other ages; girls are supervised more closely than boys. In some situations, monitoring is universal or nearly constant; in other situations monitoring for some offenses is virtually absent. In the present context, however, the concern is with the connection between supervision and self-control, a connection established by the stronger tendency of those poorly supervised when young to commit crimes as adults (McCord 1979).

Recognition of Deviant Behavior

In order for supervision to have an impact on self-control, the supervisor must perceive deviant behavior when it occurs. Remarkably, not all parents are adept at recognizing lack of self-control. Some parents allow the child to do pretty much as he pleases without interference. Extensive television-viewing is one modern example, as is the failure to require completion of homework, to prohibit smoking, to curtail the use of physical force, or to see to it that the child actually attends school. (As noted, truancy among second-graders presumably reflects on the adequacy of parental awareness of the child's misbehavior.) Again, the research is not as good as it should be, but evidence of "poor conduct standards" in the homes of delinquents is common.

Punishment of Deviant Acts

Control theories explicitly acknowledge the necessity of sanctions in preventing criminal behavior. They do not suggest that the major sanctions are legal or corporal. On the contrary, as we have seen, they suggest that disapproval by people one cares about is the most powerful of sanctions. Effective punishment by the parent or major caretaker therefore usually entails nothing more than explicit disapproval of unwanted behavior. The criticism of control theories that dwells on their alleged cruelty is therefore simply misguided or ill informed (see, e.g., Currie 1985).

Not all caretakers punish effectively. In fact, some are too harsh and some are too lenient (Glueck and Glueck 1950; McCord and McCord 1959; West and Farrington 1977; see generally Loeber and Stouthamer-Loeber 1986). Given our model, however, rewarding good behavior cannot compensate for failure to correct deviant behavior. (Recall that, in our view, deviant acts carry with them their own rewards [see Chapter 2].)

Given the consistency of the child-rearing model with our general theory and with the research literature, it should be possible to use it to explain other family correlates of criminal and otherwise deviant behavior.

Parental Criminality

Our theory focuses on the connection between the self-control of the parent and the subsequent self-control of the child. There is good reason to expect, and the data confirm, that people lacking self-control do not socialize their children well. According to Donald West and David Farrington, "the fact that delinquency is transmitted from one generation to the next is indisputable" (1977: 109; see also Robins 1966). Of course our theory does not allow transmission of criminality, genetic or otherwise. However, it does allow us to predict that some people are more likely than others to fail to socialize their children and that this will be a consequence of their own inadequate socialization. The extent of this connection between parent and child socialization is revealed by the fact that in the West and Farrington study fewer than 5 percent of the families accounted for almost half of the criminal convictions in the entire sample. (In our view, this finding is more important for the theory of crime, and for public policy, than the much better-known finding of Wolfgang and his colleagues [1972] that something like 6 percent of *individual* offenders account for about half of all criminal acts.) In order to achieve such concentration of crime in a small number of families, it is necessary that the parents and the brothers and sisters of offenders also be unusually likely to commit criminal acts.[2]

---

[2] It is commonly observed (in an unsystematic way) that in an otherwise law-abiding family individual children are seriously delinquent. This observation is taken as evi-

Why should the children of offenders be unusually vulnerable to crime? Recall that our theory assumes that criminality is not something the parents have to work to produce; on the contrary, it assumes that criminality is something they have to work to avoid. Consistent with this view, parents with criminal records do *not* encourage crime in their children and are in fact as disapproving of it as parents with no record of criminal involvement (West and Farrington 1977). Of course, not wanting criminal behavior in one's children and being upset when it occurs do not necessarily imply that great effort has been expended to prevent it. If criminal behavior is oriented toward short-term rewards, and if child-rearing is oriented toward long-term rewards, there is little reason to expect parents themselves lacking self-control to be particularly adept at instilling self-control in their children.

Consistent with this expectation, research consistently indicates that the supervision of delinquents in families where parents have criminal records tends to be "lax," "inadequate," or "poor." Punishment in these families also tends to be easy, short-term, and insensitive—that is, yelling and screaming, slapping and hitting, with threats that are not carried out.

Such facts do not, however, completely account for the concentration of criminality among some families. A major reason for this failure is probably that the most subtle element of child-rearing is not included in the analysis. This is the element of *recognition* of deviant behavior. According to Gerald Patterson (1980), many parents do not even recognize *criminal* behavior in their children, let alone the minor forms of deviance whose punishment is necessary for effective child-rearing. For example, when children steal outside the home, some parents discount reports that they have done so on the grounds that the charges are unproved and cannot therefore be used to justify punishment. By the same token, when children are suspended for misbehavior at school, some parents side with the child and blame the episode on prejudicial mistreatment by teachers. Obviously, parents who cannot see the misbehavior of their children are in no position to correct it, even if they are inclined to do so.

Given that recognition of deviant acts is a necessary component of the child-rearing model, research is needed on the question of what

---

dence against family or child-rearing explanations of crime. (If the parents reared most of their children properly, how can their child-rearing practices be responsible for their delinquent children as well?) Such observations do not dispute the strong tendencies toward consistency within families mentioned in the text. They do suggest that family child-rearing practices are not the only causes of crime.

parents should and should not recognize as deviant behavior if they are to prevent criminality. To the extent our theory is correct, parents need to know behaviors that reflect low self-control. That many parents are not now attentive to such behaviors should come as no surprise. The idea that criminal behavior is the product of deprivation or positive learning dominates modern theory. As a consequence, most influential social scientific theories of crime and delinquency ignore or deny the connection between crime and talking back, yelling, pushing and shoving, insisting on getting one's way, trouble in school, and poor school performance. Little wonder, then, that some parents do not see the significance of such acts. Research now makes it clear that parents differ in their reaction to these behaviors, with some parents attempting to correct behaviors that others ignore or even defend (Patterson 1980). Because social science in general sees little connection between these acts and crime, there has been little systematic integration of the child development and criminological literatures. Furthermore, because the conventional wisdom disputes the connection between child training and crime, public policy has not focused on it. We do not argue that crime is caused by these early misbehaviors. Instead, we argue that such behaviors indicate the presence of the major individual-level cause of crime, a cause that in principle may be attacked by punishing these early manifestations. Nor do we argue that criminal acts automatically follow early evidence of low self-control. Because crime requires more than low self-control, some parents are lucky and have children with low self-control who still manage to avoid acts that would bring them to the attention of the criminal justice system. It is less likely (in fact unlikely), however, that such children will avoid altogether behavior indicative of low self-control. Put another way, low self-control predicts low self-control better than it predicts any of its specific manifestations, such as crime.

Family Size

One of the most consistent findings of delinquency research is that the larger the number of children in the family, the greater the likelihood that each of them will be delinquent. This finding, too, is perfectly explicable from a child-rearing model. Affection for the individual child may be unaffected by numbers, and parents with large families may be as able as anyone else to recognize deviant behavior, but monitoring and punishment are probably more difficult the greater the number of children in the family. Greater numbers strain parental resources of time and energy. For this reason, the child in the large family is likely to spend more time with other children and less time with adults. Children are not as likely as adults to be effective trainers. They have less investment in the outcome, are more likely to be tolerant of deviant behavior, and do not have the power to enforce their edicts.

If the analysis of criminality of parents and size of family is sufficient to establish the plausibility of our child-rearing explanation, we can now attempt to apply it to some of the more problematic issues in the connection between the family and crime.

The Single-Parent Family

Such family measures as the percentage of the population divorced, the percentage of households headed by women, and the percentage of unattached individuals in the community are among the most powerful predictors of crime rates (Sampson 1987). Consistent with these findings, in most (but not all) studies that directly compare children living with both biological parents with children living in "broken" or reconstituted homes, the children from intact homes have lower rates of crime.

If the fact of a difference between single- and two-parent families is reasonably well established, the mechanisms by which it is produced are not adequately understood. It was once common in the delinquency literature to distinguish between homes broken by divorce and those broken by death. This distinction recognized the difficulty of separating the effects of the people involved in divorce from the effects of divorce itself. Indeed, it is common to find that involuntarily broken homes are less conducive to delinquency than homes in which the parent was a party to the decision to separate.

With the continued popularity of marriage, a possible complication enters the picture. The missing biological parent (in the overwhelming majority of cases, the father) is often replaced at some point by a stepparent. Is the child better or worse off as a result of the presence of an "unrelated" adult in the house?

The model we are using suggests that, *all else being equal*, one parent is sufficient. We could substitute "mother" or "father" for "parents" without any obvious loss in child-rearing ability. Husbands and wives tend to be sufficiently alike on such things as values, attitudes, and skills that for many purposes they may be treated as a unit. For that matter, our scheme does not even require that the adult involved in training the child be his or her guardian, let alone a biological parent. Proper training can be accomplished outside the confines of the two-parent home.

But all else is rarely equal. The single parent (usually a woman) must devote a good deal to support and maintenance activities that are at least to some extent shared in the two-parent family. Further, she must often do so in the absence of psychological or social support. As a result, she is less able to devote time to monitoring and punishment and is more likely to be involved in negative, abusive contacts with her children.

Remarriage is by no means a complete solution to these problems. As compared to natural parents, stepparents are likely to report that they have no "parental feelings" toward their stepchildren, and they are unusually likely to be involved in cases of child abuse (Burgess 1980). The other side of the coin is the affection of the child for the parent. Such affection is conducive to nondelinquency in its own right and clearly eases the task of child-rearing. Affection is, for obvious reasons, less likely to be felt toward the new parent in a reconstituted family than toward a biological parent in a continuously intact family

The Mother Who Works Outside the Home

The increase in the number of women in the labor force has several implications for the crime rate. To the extent this increase contributes to the instability of marriage, it will have the consequences for crime just discussed. Traditionally, however, the major concern was that the mother working outside the home would be unable to supervise or effectively rear her children. Sheldon and Eleanor Glueck (1950) found that the children of women who work, especially the children of those who work "occasionally" or "sporadically," were more likely to be delinquent. They also showed that the effect on delinquency of the mother's working was *completely* accounted for by the quality of supervision provided by the mother. (Such complete explanations of one factor by another are extremely rare in social science.) When the mother was able to arrange supervision for the child, her employment had no effect on the likelihood of delinquency. In fact, in this particular study, the children of regularly employed women were least likely to be delinquent when supervision was taken into account. This does not mean, however, that the employment of the mother had no effect. It did have an effect, at least among those in relatively deprived circumstances: the children of employed women were more likely to be delinquent.

More commonly, research reports a small effect of mother's employment that it is unable to explain. The advantage of the nonemployed mother over the employed mother in child-rearing remains when supervision and other characteristics of the mother, the family, and the child are taken into account. One possible implication of this explanatory failure is that the effects of employment influence children in ways not measurable except through their delinquency. One way of addressing this question would be to examine the effect of mother's employment on measures of inadequate self-control other than the commission of criminal acts—such as on accidents or school failure. If we are dealing with a social-control effect rather than a socialization effect, it should be possible to find a subset of deviant behaviors that are more affected than others by mother's employment. Although our scheme does not allow us *a priori* to separate the enduring effects of child "rearing" from the temporary effects of child "control," it alerts us to the fact that self-control and supervision can be the result of a single parental act.

Another consequence of female labor-force participation is that it leaves the house unguarded for large portions of the day. The unoccupied house is less attractive to adolescent members of the family and more attractive to other adolescents interested only in its contents. As we indicated earlier, research shows that the absence of guardians in the home is a good predictor of residential burglary.

Child Rearing and Self-Control: The School

Most people are sufficiently socialized by familial institutions to avoid involvement in criminal acts. Those not socialized sufficiently by the family may eventually learn self-control through the operation of other sanctioning systems or institutions. The institution given principal responsibility for this task in modern society is the school. As compared to the family, the school has several advantages as a socializing institution. First, it can more effectively monitor behavior than the family, with one teacher overseeing many children at a time. Second, as compared to most parents, teachers generally have no difficulty recognizing deviant or disruptive behavior. Third, as compared to the family, the school has such a clear interest in maintaining order and discipline that it can be expected to do what it can to control disruptive behavior. Finally, like the family, the school in theory has the authority and the means to punish lapses in self-control.

All else being equal, it would appear that the school could be an effective socializing agency. The evidence suggests, however, that in contemporary American society the school has a difficult time teaching self-control. A major reason for this limited success of the modern school appears to stem from the lack of cooperation and support it receives from families that have already failed in the socialization task. When the family does not see to it that the child is in school doing what he or she should be doing, the child's problems in school are often directly traceable to the parents. For example, according to Robins (1966), truancy begins in the first and second grades (and is not, as some assume, solely an adolescent problem). Truancy or absence in the first and second grades can hardly be attributed to the child alone. Whatever the source of such truancy, it is highly predictive of low self-control later in life.

The question, then, is whether inadequate socialization by the family could be corrected by the school if it were given the chance—that is, if the family were cooperative. Robins, whose analyses of the stability of the antisocial personality are not ordinarily optimistic, notes that the school could be used to locate preadolescents with low self-control and that it might be effective in doing what the family has failed to do: "Since truancy and poor school performance are nearly universally present in pre-sociopaths, it should be possible to identify children requiring treatment through their school records. . . . [T]he fact that a gross lack of discipline in the home predicted long-term difficulties suggests trying a program in which the schools attempt to substitute for the missing parental discipline in acting to prevent truancy and school failures" (1966: 306–7).[3]

Even without parental support, in our view, the net effect of the school must be positive. As a result of the school experience, some students learn better to appreciate the advantages and opportunities associated with self-control and are thus effectively socialized regardless of their familial experiences. One of the major school correlates of crime has always been the mundane homework. Those who do it are by definition thinking about tomorrow. Those who do not do it have a shorter time frame. One mark of socialization is considering the consequences of today's activities for tomorrow. Homework thus indexes and perhaps contributes to socialization.

Another major predictor of crime is not liking school. This connec-

---

[3] In subsequent chapters we emphasize the limited power of institutions to create self-control later in life when it has been theretofore lacking. Our theory clearly argues, however, that it is easier to develop self-control among people lacking it than to undermine or destroy self-control among those possessing it. Consistent with this position, the data routinely show that preadolescents without behavior problems rarely end up with significant problems as adults (see, e.g., Robins 1966; Glueck and Glueck 1968).

tion is so strong that the statement "delinquents do not like school" does not require much in the way of qualification (Glueck and Glueck 1950: 144). The connection speaks well for the school as a socializing institution. Socializing institutions impose restraints; they do not allow unfettered pursuit of self-interest; they require accomplishment. Lack of self-control activates external controls, controls that are not applied to or felt by everyone, thus resulting in differences in attitude toward the school.

School performance also strongly predicts involvement in delinquent and criminal activities. Those who do well in school are unlikely to get into trouble with the law. This, too, supports the view of the school as a potentially successful training ground for the development of self-control. Students who like school and do well in it are likely to perceive a successful future and are thus susceptible to school sanctions (Stinchcombe 1964).

The crime and low self-control perspective organizes and explains most facts about the relation between schooling and crime, one of the staples of delinquency research. We will have more to say about the school and crime in later chapters, especially Chapter 6. For now, suffice it to say that self-control differences seem primarily attributable to family socialization practices. It is difficult for subsequent institutions to make up for deficiencies, but socialization is a task that, once successfully accomplished, appears to be largely irreversible.

The Stability Problem

Competent research regularly shows that the best predictor of crime is prior criminal behavior. In other words, research shows that differences between people in the likelihood that they will commit criminal acts persist over time.[4] This fact is central to our conception of criminality. In the next chapter we show how it calls into question the many theories of crime that depend on social institutions to create criminals from previously law-abiding citizens. For now, we briefly reconcile the fact of stability with the idea that desocialization is rare.

Combining little or no movement from high self-control to low self-control with the fact that socialization continues to occur throughout life produces the conclusion that the proportion of the population in the potential offender pool should tend to decline as cohorts age. This conclusion is consistent with research. Even the most active offenders burn out with time, and the documented number of "late-

[4] We described the research documenting the stability of "aggression" in Chapter 3, and the research documenting the stability of "criminality" is discussed at length in Chapter 11 in reference to methodologies for studying crime and criminality.

comers" to crime, or "good boys gone bad," is sufficiently small to suggest that they may be accounted for in large part by misidentification or measurement error. (This result is also consistent with Bentham's theory in that all sanction systems work against the possibility of lengthy careers in crime.) Put another way, the low self-control group continues over time to exhibit low self-control. Its size, however, declines.

Such stability of criminality is a staple of pragmatic criminology. The criminal justice system uses this fact in much the same way that educational institutions use prior academic performance to sort students and select personnel—that is, without much concern for the meaning of the variable. (A variant of the pragmatic response seeks to identify career criminals or high-rate offenders and thereby refine selection decisions, but here too nothing is usually said about what it is that produces long-standing differences in the level of involvement in crime [Blumstein et al. 1986].)

The traditional theoretical response denies stability and constructs theories that do not deal with "individual-level" variables. These theories automatically suggest that the causes of the "onset" of crime are not the same as the causes of "persistence" in crime. They also suggest that "desistance" from crime has unique causes. On analysis, however, most criminological theories appear to deal with onset and remain agnostic or silent on the persistence and desistence issues.

Thus no currently popular criminological theory attends to the stability of differences in offending over the life course. We are left with a paradoxical situation: a major finding of criminological research is routinely ignored or denied by criminological theory. After a century of research, crime theories remain inattentive to the fact that people differ in the likelihood that they will commit crimes and that these differences appear early and remain stable over much of the life course. Perhaps a major reason for ignoring the stability of low self-control is the assumption that other individual traits are stable and thereby account for apparently stable differences in criminal behavior. These are the so-called personality explanations of crime.

Personality and Criminality

Sociological criminology takes the position that no trait of personality has been shown to characterize criminals more than noncriminals (Sutherland and Cressey 1978: ch. 8). Psychological criminology takes the position that many personality traits have been shown to characterize criminals more than noncriminals (Wilson and Herrnstein 1985: ch. 7). We take the position that both views are wrong. The level of self-control, or criminality, distinguishes offenders from nonoffenders, and the degree of its presence or absence can be established before (and after) criminal acts have been committed. This enduring tendency is well within the meaning of "personality trait" and is thus contrary to the sociological view. Contrary to the psychological view, the evidence for personality differences between offenders and nonoffenders beyond self-control is, at best, unimpressive. Most of this evidence is produced by attaching personality labels to differences in rates of offending between offenders and nonoffenders—that is, by turning one difference into many.

For example, Wilson and Herrnstein (1985: ch. 7) report that delinquents score higher than nondelinquents on the following dimensions of personality (see also Herrnstein 1983):

1. "Q" scores on the Porteus Maze Tests.
2. Assertiveness.
3. Fearlessness.
4. Aggressiveness.
5. Unconventionality.
6. Extroversion.
7. Poor socialization.
8. Psychopathy.
9. Schizophrenia.
10. Hypomania.
11. Hyperactivity.
12. Poor conditionability.
13. Impulsiveness.
14. Lefthandedness.

All of these "personality" traits can be explained without abandoning the conclusion that offenders differ from nonoffenders only in their tendency to offend. One problem that has historically plagued personality research is the failure of its practitioners to report the content of their measuring instruments. This failure may be justified by the fact that the tests have commercial value, but the scientific result is the reporting of what are rightly considered "empirical tautologies," the discovery that two measures of the same thing are correlated with each other. In the present case, it seems fair to say that no one has found an independently measured personality trait substantially correlated with criminality. For example, the Minnesota Multiphasic Personality Inventory has three subscales said to distinguish between delinquents and nondelinquents. The major discriminator is the Psychopathic Deviate subscale. As Wilson and Herrnstein note, this subscale includes "questions about a respondent's past criminal behavior" (1985: 187). But if this is so, then scale scores obviously cannot be used to establish the existence of a trait of personality independent of the tendency to commit criminal acts.

The situation is the same with the socialization subscale of the

California Personality Inventory. This subscale contains items indistinguishable from standard self-report delinquency items. That it is correlated with other measures of delinquency supports the unremarkable conclusion that measures of delinquency tend to correlate with one another. By the same token, a high score on the Q scale of the Porteus Maze Tests indicates subjects who frequently "break the rules by lifting his or her pencil from the paper, by cutting corners, or by allowing the pencil to drift out of the maze channels" (Wilson and Herrnstein 1985: 174). This measure is reminiscent of the measure of cheating developed by Hugh Hartshorne and Mark May (1928). That people who lie, cheat, and steal are more likely to cheat is not particularly instructive.

Earlier we examined the misleading suggestion that offenders can be usefully characterized as highly aggressive. Because measures of aggressiveness include many criminal acts, it is impossible to distinguish aggressiveness from criminality (see Chapter 3). And so on through the list above. The measures of personality are either direct indicators of crime or conceptually indistinguishable from low self-control. Some, of course, are simply not supported by credible research (such as lefthandedness), and their continual reappearance should by now begin to undermine the credibility of psychological positivism.

The limited life of personality-based theories of crime is illustrated by the work of Hans Eysenck. He concluded that "persons with strong antisocial inclinations [should] have high P, high E, and high N scores," where P is psychoticism, E is extraversion, and N is neuroticism (1964: 58). Eysenck provided detailed descriptions of persons scoring high on extraversion and psychoticism. For example, the extravert is "sociable, likes parties, has many friends, needs to have people to talk to, and does not like reading and studying by himself. . . . He prefers to keep moving and doing things, tends to be aggressive and loses his temper quickly; his feelings are not kept under tight control and he is not always a reliable person" (pp. 50–51). In contrast, the person scoring high on the P factor is "(1) solitary, not caring for other people; (2) troublesome, not fitting in; (3) cruel, inhumane; (4) lack of feeling, insensitive; (5) lacking in empathy; (6) sensation-seeking, avid for strong sensory stimuli; (7) hostile to others, aggressive; (8) [has a] liking for odd and unusual things; (9) disregard for dangers, foolhardy; (10) likes to make fools of other people and to upset them" (p. 58).

Although Eysenck is satisfied that research supports the existence of these dimensions and the tendency of offenders to score high on them (Eysenck 1989), many scholars (e.g., Rutter and Giller 1984) have not been convinced of the utility of Eysenck's personality scheme. (Wilson and Herrnstein do not include Eysenck's dimensions among the many personality traits they list.) In the current context, this scheme epitomizes the difficulties of the personality perspective (whatever the assumed source of personality differences) when applied to criminal behavior. In Eysenck's case, these difficulties are manifest in the obvious conceptual overlap of the personality dimensions and in the inability to measure them independently of the acts they are meant to produce.

The search for personality characteristics common to offenders has thus produced nothing contrary to the use of low self-control as the primary individual characteristic causing criminal behavior. People who develop strong self-control are unlikely to commit criminal acts throughout their lives, regardless of their other personality characteristics. In this sense, self-control is the only enduring personal characteristic predictive of criminal (and related) behavior. People who do not develop strong self-control are more likely to commit criminal acts, whatever the other dimensions of their personality. As people with low self-control age, they tend less and less to commit crimes; this decline is probably not entirely due to increasing self-control, but to age as well (see Chapter 6).

Although the facts about individual differences in crime are consistent with our theory, they are also consistent with theories designed explicitly to account for them. Differences between these theories and our own should therefore be specifically discussed.

Alternative Theories of Criminality

It is common to say that there are multitudes of theories of criminality. In fact, however, the number of truly distinct explanations is small. One reason the number is limited is that the assumptions underlying theories are themselves limited and tend to cluster logically. Some theories assume that humans are naturally inclined to law-abiding or social behavior; others assume that humans are naturally inclined to criminal or antisocial behavior; still others try to make neither of these assumptions. Some assume that the motivation to commit crime is different from the motivation for lawful activities; others make no such assumption. Some assume that human behavior is governed by forces in the immediate situation or environment; others assume that stable personality characteristics govern conduct. Some assume that each item of behavior has unique determinants;

others assume that many items of behavior may have causes in common. In subsequent chapters, our theory will be frequently distinguished from other theories by the position it produces on various empirical and policy issues. Here we want to locate the theory along methodological dimensions as a means of exposing in some systematic way opportunities for further development.

One way to look at theories of crime is in terms of their assumptions about human nature and society. Another is to examine their intended scope, the range of deviant acts they encompass. Still another is to contrast the empirical tests that may be derived from them. Finally, one may ask where the theories are located in the temporal sequence leading to a particular criminal act. Taking the last first, it is relatively easy to describe current theories in terms of the proximity of their causal forces to the actual behavior they attempt to explain.

The Temporal Position of Criminality vis-à-vis Crime

Some theories (e.g., Becker 1974; Wilson and Herrnstein 1985; Cornish and Clark 1986) focus on decisionmaking in the immediate situation in which the offense is or is not committed. At an intermediate remove, other theories (e.g., Merton 1938; Cloward and Ohlin 1960) focus on the forces in adolescence that produce offenders—that is, people embarked on a course of life that ultimately leads to the commission of criminal acts. Still other theories (e.g., Mednick 1977; Colvin and Pauly 1983) focus on hereditary or class factors present at or before birth, factors that operate at great distance from the events they cause.

Traditionally, the more distant the causes from the criminal act, the harder it is to construct a plausible theory using them. As a result, "distant" theories tend to exaggerate differences between offenders and nonoffenders, or to suggest causes that eventually *require* criminal acts. The model for such explanations is Lombroso's born criminal, a person destined to commit criminal acts from the point of conception. Only slightly less deterministic is the predispositional theory of the biologist or psychologist. These theories, too, suggest that once people have developed their respective dispositions the criminal behavior of some of them is a foregone conclusion.

Even temporally intermediate theories tend to divide the population into sharply distinct categories and to suggest that those in the potential offender category must go on to commit their quota of criminal acts. For example, once the lower-class boy has adapted to strain by giving up allegiance to the legitimate means to wealth, criminal acts ineluctably follow; once the person has learned an excess of definitions favorable to the violation of law, the outcome in criminal behavior is fixed. (The labeling theory saves itself from this problem by retaining the proviso that labels do not always "stick." Fair enough. But if they do stick, delinquency is inevitable.)

Theories that focus on the immediate decisionmaking situation are accordingly least concerned about differences between offenders and nonoffenders. In fact, since they do not require differential tendencies to commit crime, these theories are inclined to suggest that such differences are trivial or nonexistent. Theories that combine distant *and* proximate causes, such as our own, thus combine opposing tendencies, and risk inconsistency.

In principle, distant and proximate theories should be consistent. On inspection, however, they are usually inconsistent. The marked differences that in distant theories require crime do not permit unrestricted decisionmaking from moment to moment depending on the situation. For example, Wilson and Herrnstein advance a theory in which the offender chooses between crime and noncrime on the basis of the costs and benefits accruing to both lines of action:

The larger the ratio of the rewards (material and nonmaterial) of noncrime to the rewards (material and nonmaterial) of crime, the weaker the tendency to commit crimes. The bite of conscience, the approval of peers, and any sense of inequity will increase or decrease the total value of crime; the opinions of family, friends, and employers are important benefits of noncrime, as is the desire to avoid the penalties that can be imposed by the criminal justice system. The strength of any reward declines with time, but people differ in the rate at which they discount the future. The strength of a given reward is also affected by the total supply of reinforcers. [1985: 61]

The criminal described by Wilson and Herrnstein is a person without a conscience who cares about the approval of his friends and has a strong sense that he has not been treated fairly. Those knowledgeable about basic criminological theories will see the resemblance between these characteristics of the offender and those described by control theory, cultural deviance theory, and strain theory—in that order—and will be troubled by the contradictory images these theories have always projected (Kornhauser 1978). For present purposes, the problem is that cultural deviance theory and strain theory do not take approval of one's friends or a sense of inequity as momentary decisionmaking criteria. On the contrary, these theories suggest that such considerations override concerns for legitimate employment, the opinion of family and friends, and the desire to avoid the penalties of the criminal law. If so, the decision to commit a criminal act is no decision at all.

Wilson and Herrnstein argue that delinquents discount future consequences more than nondelinquents do. This is inconsistent with strain theory. In the Merton and the Cloward and Ohlin versions of this theory, the potential delinquent looks into the future and sees dismal prospects. As a consequence, he turns to a life of crime designed to brighten these prospects. In other words, in strain theory the delinquent is especially future-oriented as compared to the nondelinquent. (We believe Wilson and Herrnstein may be correct about the decisionmaking [crime] portion of their theory. The point is that the crime portion of their theory cannot be squared with its criminal portion.) The idea that offenders are likely to be concerned with equity is also contrary to the notion that they more heavily discount time: equity concerns, as described by Wilson and Herrnstein, require that the person compare his effort/reward ratio with the effort/reward ratios of others. Such calculations obviously require rather broad perspectives on the social order, but for present purposes the important point is that people who feel inequitably treated must have put forth the effort that justifies their feelings (otherwise we would be talking about envy). But people who discount the future do not exert themselves for uncertain future benefits, and the notion of inequity at the point of crime is therefore incompatible with the image of the offender at the point of criminality.

The problems encountered by Wilson and Herrnstein are endemic to social learning theories, theories that also attempt to consider crime and criminality simultaneously. Social learning theories suggest that people learn to commit criminal acts because they provide benefits from valued groups in excess of their costs from neutral or disvalued groups (and apart from any benefits obtained from the criminal act itself). To the extent this is so, the idea that criminals differ from noncriminals in such things as time-discounting, aggressiveness, or impulsiveness is hard to sustain. On the contrary, such theories suggest that if there are differences between criminals and noncriminals, they are opposite to those usually suggested by theories of criminality. Such inconsistencies between the demands of theories of choice and theories of criminality are hard to ignore. Since data bearing on both theories are abundantly available, they are even harder to ignore. In our view, they survive only because of the disciplinary interests they appear to serve.

Our theory was in part devised by working back and forth between an image of crime and an image of criminality. Because crimes tend to combine immediate benefit and long-term cost, we are careful to avoid the image of an offender pursuing distant goals. Because crimes tend to be quick and easy to accomplish, we are careful to avoid the image of an offender driven by deep resentment or long-term social purposes. Because crimes tend to involve as victim and offender people with similar characteristics, we are careful to avoid the image of an offender striking *out* against class or race enemies.

Because lack of self-control is not conducive to hard work, delayed gratification, or persistence in a course of action, we are careful to avoid an image of crime as a long-term, difficult, or drawn-out endeavor. Because lack of self-control is conducive to unpredictability or unreliability in behavior, we are careful to avoid an image of crime as an organized activity. And, because lack of self-control shows itself in many noncriminal as well as in criminal acts, we are careful to avoid an image of deviance as exclusively illegal behavior.

Our theory applies across the life course, and it applies from the point of decisionmaking back to the origins of differences in degree of self-control. In infancy and preadolescence it is a theory of socialization and social control, accounting for a variety of deviant acts— defiance, truancy, school failure—and constructing people unlikely in future years to commit criminal acts. In adolescence and the early adult years, the socialization component declines and the theory focuses largely on social control, accounting for an even greater variety of deviant and criminal acts: truancy, dropout, drug use, theft, assault, accidents, pregnancy. As adulthood approaches, natural (i.e., biological and physical) controls play an increasingly larger part, and there is a tendency for the rate of deviant behavior to decline. As a result of declining rates, the diversity of offenses committed by individual offenders tends to decline, but differences established earlier continue to explain the whole set of offenses, along with other manifestations of low social control.

The Scope of Theory

In principle, theorists must choose between broad theories roughly applicable to a wide variety of vaguely defined conduct and narrow theories directly applicable to specific, precisely defined acts. This choice is often seen as being broad, important, and wrong versus being narrow, trivial, and correct. Positivists have historically chosen the latter position. Unfortunately, the positivist assumption that the correctness of their theories compensates for their limitations is called into question by the frequency with which positivistic research disputes the correctness of positivistic explanations.

Theories that focus on decisionmaking have traditionally sought to explain all behavior with a single principle. This principle tends to be complicated beyond recognition the moment it confronts individual differences that transcend properties of the immediate environment.

Previous efforts at compromise have not been particularly successful. Wilson and Herrnstein take the novel approach of using their general theory to explain a *narrowly* described set of acts:

> The word "crime" can be applied to such varied behavior that it is not clear that it is a meaningful category of analysis. Stealing a comic book, punching a friend, cheating on a tax return, murdering a wife, robbing a bank, bribing a politician, hijacking an airplane—these and countless other acts are all crimes. Crime is as broad a category as disease, and perhaps as useless. [1985: 21]

These considerations lead Wilson and Herrnstein to concentrate on those persons who "commit serious crimes at a high rate." By doing so, they argue, they "escape the problem of comparing persons who park by a fire hydrant to persons who rob banks" (1985: 21). By "serious crimes," Wilson and Herrnstein mean "predatory street crimes," those acts "regarded as wrong by every society, preliterate as well as literate; . . . among these 'universal crimes' are murder, theft, robbery, and incest" (ibid., p. 22).

One question that arises is why Wilson and Herrnstein would wish to restrict the range of their dependent variable without clear evidence that such restriction is necessary. What evidence do they use to justify dividing the domain of crime into serious street crime and other crime? For one thing, they are skeptical of the view that a general theory can explain crime across cultures or that it can explain all of the myriad crimes within a given culture. Clearly, the *a priori* conclusion that a theory should set its boundaries narrowly need not be taken to mean that the boundaries have been accurately described. The boundaries of a theory require theoretical justification. In its absence, concern for boundaries rightly suggests the operation of nontheoretical criteria.

The seriousness of crime is, in our view, a nontheoretical criterion. It is of course no accident that theorists prefer to limit their interests to "serious" matters—in the mistaken belief that the importance of the phenomenon has something to say about the importance of the theory. The fact of the matter is that the importance or seriousness of a phenomenon is often hard to assess anyway. Individually, serious crimes may tend to produce more injury or loss, but collectively they may produce much less injury or loss than less serious crimes. By the same token, hard drugs such as heroin may produce less harm in the aggregate than drugs such as tobacco or alcohol. Arguably, reducing the rate of cigarette smoking would be a greater contribution to the resolution of a serious problem than would reducing the rate of drug addiction.

In any event, we do not share Wilson and Herrnstein's skepticism about the possibility of a general theory of crime, and we note that limits on the range of a theory should not be taken too seriously unless those stating the limits provide evidence that it will not work outside the narrow domain they specify. (Put another way, modesty per se is not a virtue of a theory.)

Tests of generality or scope are, in our view, easy to devise. In criminology it is often argued that special theories are required to explain female and male crime, crime in one culture rather than another, crime committed in the course of an occupation as distinct from street crime, or crime committed by children as distinct from crime committed by adults. As subsequent chapters will show, we intend our theory to apply to all of these cases, and more. It is meant to explain all crime, at all times, and, for that matter, many forms of behavior that are not sanctioned by the state.

Human Nature and Society

Useful theories of crime make assumptions about human nature. The range of possible assumptions is limited. A theory can assume, as ours does, that people naturally pursue their own interests and unless socialized to the contrary will use whatever means are available to them for such purposes. In this view, people are neither naturally "good" nor naturally "evil." They are, however, expected to behave in predictable ways. The standard social-contract assumption thus has useful properties, properties described throughout this book.

In contrast, a theory can assume, as nearly all sociological theories do, that people naturally tend to pursue group interests and will continue to do so unless forced to do otherwise—that is, that people are naturally good or social. Such theories also have useful properties. They make possible specific predictions about the causes or correlates of crime, predictions that tend to conflict with the predictions derived from theories that do not share their assumptions about human nature. Throughout the book we take advantage of this fact by comparing the adequacy of the hypotheses derived from these distinct perspectives.

Some theorists argue either explicitly (Elliott, Huizinga, and Ageton 1985) or implicitly (Wilson and Herrnstein 1985) that these various perspectives can be usefully combined without fear of contradiction or ambiguity. In fact, however, as is easily shown, theorists arguing for "integration" of these divergent views usually simply adopt one set of assumptions at the expense of the other or refuse to make assumptions and thus weaken what claims to theory they may have had. In the first case, most sociological integrationists simply adopt "social behavior" assumptions about crime and reject "individual interest" assumptions on the grounds that the assumptions favored by their discipline are correct (Johnson 1979; Elliott, Huizinga, and Ageton 1985; see also Hirschi 1979). In the second case, some psychologists think the assumption issue can be finessed by adopting an assumption-free psychological learning theory. Unfortunately, the idea that all views (strain, cultural deviance, social control, and rational choice) can be subsumed under a single learning theory abrogates the responsibility of the theorist to theorize about the sources of crime. For example, Wilson and Herrnstein advance the proposition that, in a situation of choice, people select the outcome they prefer (1985: 43). It is possible to make a theory from this statement by introducing bias into preference, by asserting or believing that some tendency acts on choice in the first instance; for example, one could say that, other things being equal, people will prefer outcomes that reduce their wealth and happiness (hard to believe, but at least testable). In the absence of such a bias, all preferences are possible and the theory asserts nothing. Evidence that it asserts nothing comes from the fact that it is said to *subsume* strain, cultural deviance, and social control theories, theories often used to illustrate conflicting assumptions and predictions. (In Chapter 4, we demonstrated the incompatibility of the strain and cultural deviance components in the Wilson-Herrnstein theory; see also Kornhauser 1978.)

Empirical Tests of the Crime and Criminality Perspective

Our stability postulate asserts that people with high self-control are less likely under all circumstances throughout life to commit crime. Our stability notion denies the ability of institutions to undo previously successful efforts at socialization, an ability other theories take as central to their position.

Similarly, our versatility construct suggests that one avenue available for the identification of persons with low self-control is via its noncriminal outlets. Other theories predict no correlation or even negative correlation between the various forms of deviance. Our conception of versatility also predicts that one can study crime by studying other noncriminal manifestations of low self-control without being misled by the results.

Our idea of crime asserts that complex, difficult crimes are so rare that they are an inadequate basis for theory and policy. Other perspectives suggest that exotic crimes are as theoretically useful as mundane crimes and just as likely to occur. Our idea of crime predicts that the vast majority of crimes will be characterized by simplicity, proximity of offender and target, and failure to gain the desired objective. Other theories make no room for failure, assuming that crime satisfies strong forces and desires and thus reinforces itself. Our perspective asserts that crime can be predicted from evidence of low self-control at any earlier stage of life. No sociological or economic theory allows such predictions. Our perspective also asserts that low self-control can be predicted from crime at any earlier stage of life; most sociological theories do not allow such a prediction.

Our perspective asserts that many of the traditional causes of crime are in fact consequences of low self-control—that is, people with low self-control sort themselves and are sorted into a variety of circumstances that are *as a result* correlated with crime. Our theory predicts that prevention of one form of deviant behavior will not lead to compensating forms of behavior, but will reduce the total amount of deviant behavior engaged in by the population in question. Other theories predict displacement and suggest constant levels of deviance in a constantly "predisposed" population. We address these and other differences between our theory and rival perspectives in the pages that follow.

Conclusions

Theories that cannot incorporate or account for the stability of differences in offending over time are seriously at variance with good evidence. Theories that assume specialization in particular forms of crime or deviant behavior are seriously at odds with good evidence. Theories that propose to examine the parameters of criminal careers (such as onset, persistence, and desistence) or the characteristics of career criminals are at odds with the nature of crime. Theories that assume that criminal acts are means to long-term or altruistic goals are at odds with the facts.

Our theory explicitly addresses the stability and versatility findings. It accounts for them with the concept of self-control: with deferred gratification at one extreme and immediate gratification at the other, with caution at one extreme and risk-taking at the other. The mechanism producing these differences has been described as differences in child-rearing practices, with close attention to the behavior of the child at one extreme and neglect of the behavior of the child at the other.

The theory incorporates individual properties insofar as they have an impact on crime or on self-control. These properties are elucidated in subsequent chapters, where we apply our model to the facts about crime and deviant behavior. For now, we note that the theory is a direct response to analysis of the concept of crime and to our analysis of the failings of the theories of the positivistic disciplines. It incorporates a classical view of the role of choice and a positivistic view of the role of causation in the explanation of behavior. It produces a general explanatory concept that can be measured independently of the phenomenon it is alleged to cause, and it is thus directly testable.

We turn now to application of the theory to various topics in crime causation, research methods, and public policy.

III

APPLICATIONS OF
THE THEORY

6

Criminal Events and
Individual Propensities: Age,
Gender, and Race

After sociological positivism replaced biological positivism as the dominant force in criminology, individual correlates of crime were generally ignored in favor of social variables such as urbanization, class, and culture. Theorists set out to explain the delinquency of the urban, lower-class, gang boy, a boy explicitly lacking such individual attributes as race or IQ. Thus sociology handled sex, race, age, IQ, and physique by holding them constant, by ignoring variation in crime rates across their categories.

Once these biology- and psychology-free theories had been developed, sociologists simply applied them to the differences they had initially ignored. For example, the theory of differential association was applied to the crime differences between blacks and whites via the simple (and erroneous) assertion that black culture values violence more than white culture (Wolfgang and Ferracuti 1967; Curtis 1974). Perhaps more commonly, ethnic differences were explained by making nonwhite racial status equivalent to membership in the lower class identified by social theories. This device was applied to age differences as well, with adolescence interpreted as equivalent to a lower class or deprived status (Greenberg 1979). Gender differences were explained by application of a form of labeling theory, according to which the female "script" differs from that offered males (Harris 1977). Such traditional, individual-level variables as intelligence and physique were ignored, denied, or explained by strain or, more frequently, labeling concepts.

With the failure of sociological theories to explain the variables they were initially designed to explain (Kornhauser 1978), their utility as explanations of the large correlates of crime—age, gender, and race—were no longer plausible. In fact, the evidence suggests that no current theory of crime can accommodate what are perhaps the largest correlates of crime.

In this chapter we review the evidence about age, gender, and race, and we show how the crime and self-control perspective is useful in interpreting these differences in crime rates. Our first awareness of the inadequacy of contemporary theories and of the need for a new perspective was generated by examining the research literature on the relation between age and crime. This examination led us to the tentative conclusion that the age effect is everywhere and at all times the same. This invariance thesis has far-reaching implications and therefore deserves detailed discussion.

Invariance of the Age Effect

Theoretical and textbook discussions of the age effect usually assume variation in this effect over time, place, demographic group, and type of crime (Empey 1982; Glaser 1978; Wilson and Herrnstein 1985: 126–47; Farrington 1986a). Typically, the current age distribution of crime in the United States as revealed by the *Uniform Crime Reports* (e.g., U.S. Department of Justice 1985) is shown and the reader is left with the impression that this distribution is only one of many such distributions revealed by research.

Figures 2, 3, and 4 show three age distributions of crime: one from England and Wales in 1842–44 (Neison 1857), another from England in 1908 (Goring 1913), and another from contemporary U.S. data (U.S. Department of Justice 1979). Goring concluded that the age distribution of crime conformed to a "law of nature." The similarity between the three distributions is sufficient to suggest that little or nothing has happened to Goring's law of nature since he discovered it—in fact, the shape or form of the distribution has remained virtually unchanged for about 150 years. Recent data, the basis for many assertions of variability in the age distribution, force the same conclusion: "While population arrest rates have changed in absolute magnitude over time (almost doubling between 1965 and 1976), the same pattern has persisted for the relative magnitudes of the different age groups, with fifteen- to seventeen-year-olds having the highest arrest rates per population of any age group" (Blumstein and Cohen 1979: 562).

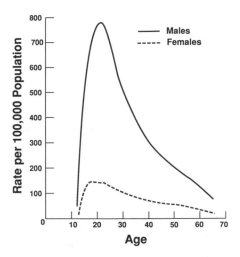

Fig. 2. Age and Sex Distribution of Criminal Offenders in England and Wales, 1842–44. Adapted from Neison 1857: 303–4.

Fig. 3. Age Distribution of Male Criminals at First Conviction as a Percentage of the Age Distribution in the General Population, England, 1908. Adapted from Goring 1913: 201–2.

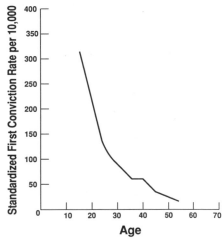

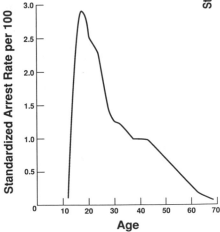

Fig. 4. Age Distribution of People Arrested for All Offenses, Standardized for Their Representation in the General Population, United States, 1977. Adapted from U.S. Department of Justice 1979: 171. Note That Data Are Approximate.

We do not know all of the ways that England and Wales in the 1840's differed from the United States in the 1970's. Presumably the differences are large across a variety of relevant dimensions. We do know, however, that in the 1960's the age distribution of delinquency in Argentina (DeFleur 1970: 131) was indistinguishable from the age distribution in the United States, which was in turn indistinguishable from the age distribution of delinquency in England and Wales at the same time (McClintock and Avison 1968).

Demographic Groups

Most discussions of the age distribution in a theoretical context assume important differences for demographic subgroups. Textbooks often compare rates of increase in crime for boys and girls for particular offenses, thus suggesting considerable flexibility in the age distribution by sex. "Age-of-onset" studies note that, for example, black offenders appear to "start earlier" than white offenders; such a suggestion gives the impression that the age distribution of crime varies across ethnic or racial groups (see, e.g., Wolfgang, Figlio, and Sellin 1972: 131). Figures 5 and 6 (delinquency rates by sex and race, respectively) show that such suggestions tend to obscure a basic and persistent fact: available data suggest that the age-crime relation is *invariant* across sex and race.

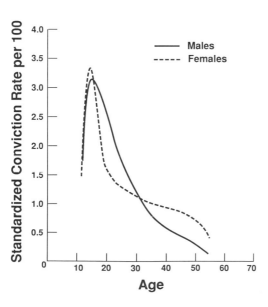

Fig. 5. Age Distribution of Males and Females Found Guilty of Indictable Offenses, Standardized for Their Representation in the General Population, England and Wales, 1965. Adapted from McClintock and Avison 1968: 170.

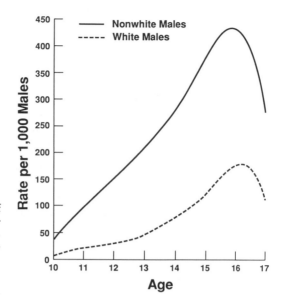

Fig. 6. Delinquency Rates of Males Born in 1945 in Philadelphia, by Race and Age. Adapted from Wolfgang, Figlio, and Sellin 1972: 109.

Types of Crime

As we have noted, positivistic research routinely assumes causal differences across types of crime. In fact, the principal data for criminology, the "official" statistics provided by the *Uniform Crime Reports*, distinguishes dozens of offenses, categorizes acts into "Part I" and "Part II" crimes depending on their "seriousness," and reports "variability" in these categories by such things as age, gender, and race. When positivistic criminologists encounter this variability, they automatically see it as requiring a substantive explanation. As we have indicated, specific crimes have causes distinct from properties of offenders; they require victims, opportunity, substances, and the like. These crime properties may obviously account for variation in specific offenses from time to time and place to place. Yet it is hard to disentangle the properties of offenses from the properties of offenders, many of which may be more readily available and easily measured (such as age). As a result, it is not surprising that data reflecting variation in age distributions for various crimes have been available for quite some time. For example, a consistent difference in the age distributions for person and property offenses appears to be well established, at least for official data. In such data, person crimes peak later than property crimes, and the rate declines more slowly with age. The significance of this fact for theories of criminality is, however, problematic. We cannot assume that such variability is attributable to the properties of offenders, something that virtually all positivists have assumed. In fact, since offenders commit all types of crimes at all ages, and since the "seriousness" of offending does not increase with age, there is strong reason to doubt that differences in the age distributions for crimes are attributable to variations in the criminality of the offenders by age. In addition, self-report data do not support the age difference between person and property offenses; they show instead that both types of offenses peak at the same time (see, e.g., Elliott, Ageton, and Huizinga 1978) and decline at the same rate with age (Tittle 1980). Consistent with this position, the slower decline of person offenses in official data may simply reflect the fact that a greater portion of such offenses involve primary-group (i.e., immediate-family) conflicts. Primary-group conflicts may be assumed to be relatively constant over the age span and to produce a relatively stable number of assaultive offenses during the period of capability (i.e., among those neither very young nor very old). If these offenses were subtracted from the total number of person offenses, the form of the curve for person offenses would approximate more closely that for property offenses. Such speculations are consistent with the self-report finding of no difference between person and property crimes with respect to the long-term effects of an offender's age (Tittle 1980: 92).

Since our thesis is that the age effect is invariant across social and cultural conditions, it may appear that our explanation of the apparent difference in person and property crimes requires modification of our thesis. Actually, in some conditions, the effects of age may be muted. For example, as people retreat into the primary-group context with increasing age, the relatively rare criminal events that occur in this context may continue to occur. Outside of the primary-group context, the effects of age on person offenses show themselves even more clearly. So, although we may find conditions in which age does not have as strong an effect as usual, the isolation of such conditions does not lead to the conclusion that age effects may be accounted for by such conditions. On the contrary, it leads to the conclusion that in particular cases the age effect may be to some extent obscured by countervailing crime factors.

Artificial Conditions and Behavior Analogous to Crime

As indicated in Chapter 5, our theory can be tested by using non-criminal events defined by it as equivalent to crime. We can, if nec

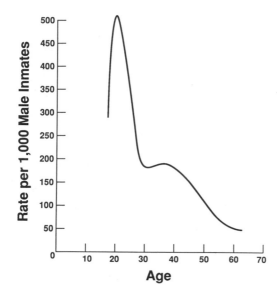

Fig. 7. Prison Infractions per 1,000 Male Inmates, New York State, 1975. Analysis of Raw Data from Flanagan 1979 and New York State 1976.

essary, study criminality among children too young to attract the attention of officials, and, if necessary, we can study criminality among those incapable of committing offense because of their incapacitation by the state. We can even study criminality by examining behavior that is nowhere considered criminal (such as accidents). This allows us to examine the effects of age (or any other variable) under conditions that eliminate competing explanations of the effect.

Explanations of age effects typically focus on the social position of youth vis-à-vis adults, suggesting that if their situations were identical, the differences in their crime rates would disappear. One way to test such theories would be to construct an environment in which age varies and the forces said to create the age relation are held constant. For example, if differential labor-force participation is said to account for the age effect, we could test this thesis by creating an environment in which no one participates in the labor force. Such an environment is approximated in prisons. Prison populations have the advantage of being relatively homogeneous on many crime causal variables, since they are relatively homogeneous on crime. As shown in Figure 7, which presents prison infraction rates by age, when "practically everything" is held relatively constant, the age effect is much like the age effect in the free world (see also Zink 1958; Wolfgang 1961; Ellis, Grasmick, and Gilman 1974; Flanagan 1979, 1981; Mabli et al. 1979).

Another way to approach the problem of the confounding of age

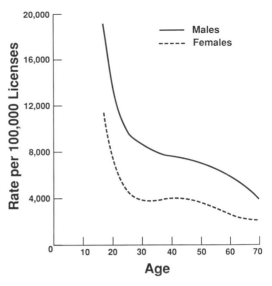

Fig. 8. Motor Vehicle Accidents by Age and Sex, New
York State, 1977. Adapted
from New York State 1979.

with other causal variables is to isolate an item of behavior analogous to crime, such as automobile accidents. Figure 8 shows the motor vehicle accident rate in New York state among those eligible to drive, by age. As is evident, these data closely parallel those for crime. Obviously, standard theories of crime cannot explain this similarity. Indeed, most of them are falsified by it (a subculture of accidents?)

The Age Critique of Theories of Criminality

Most current theories of crime concentrate on the adolescent and late teen years, when the rate of crime is at or approaching its maximum level. The general strategy is to identify or construct high- and low-rate groups, to differentiate between delinquents and nondelinquents. However differentiation is accomplished—whether by labeling, exposure to definitions favorable to delinquency, lack of legitimate opportunity, reinforcement of incipient delinquent conduct, or lack of social restraint—the result is identification of groups unusually likely to commit criminal acts.

Standard research procedure in testing such theories is to compare the actual crime rates of the groups they identify. Although in practice the theories may be difficult to test because of ambiguity or inconsistency, there is in principle little disagreement about how they should be tested. If differential opportunity is said to be the key to delinquency, one defines opportunity operationally and compares the rate of those having more with those having less. Up to the actual initiation of tests, there appears to be no necessary empirical defect in such theories. And since they are, at least in principle, testable, there would appear to be no necessary logical defect in them either.

Enter the brute fact, the age distribution of those who commit crime. Just at the point where the criminal group has been created, it begins to decline in size. "Maturational reform" or some equivalent, unexplained process takes over. The theory is then said to be able to explain the onset of crime but unable to explain desistance from crime. Since "desistance" is equal in theoretical significance to "onset," this failing of the theory is considered to be a failing sufficiently serious to bring its explanation of the onset of crime under a cloud of suspicion: "Since most delinquents do not become adult criminals, can we assume that somehow their social bonds eventually are strengthened? How is this possible? Control theory does not adequately answer these and similar questions" (Siegel and Senna 1981: 139). And: "Social process theories do not account for the 'aging out' factor in delinquency. This is a fault of the . . . social structure approach as well" (ibid., p. 147).

This traditional criticism should be understood for what it is: a theoretical argument dressed as a logical and empirical argument. The empirical fact of a decline in the crime rate with age is beyond dispute. The requirement that theories account for facts is also beyond controversy. But it does not follow that a theory that adequately differentiates criminals from noncriminals will also account for the effects of age. What makes the argument theoretical is that it *requires* that the age distribution of crime be accounted for by the variables explaining crime-rate differences at a given time. This amounts to an assertion that the age effect on crime cannot be independent of the variables employed by an accurate theory of crime. Yet it could be that a given theory, in which the rate for the low-rate group is simply a constant proportion of that for the high-rate group, holds true at all age levels. Figure 9 illustrates this possibility. It shows a true theory unaffected by "maturational reform." This theory differentiates offenders from nonoffenders throughout the life cycle. Its failure to account for the "aging-out" factor in crime cannot therefore be taken as a "fault" of the theory, since the aging-out effect occurs constantly in each group. Clearly, until evidence against this plausible hypothesis has been located, there is no justification for using age as a critical weapon against any current theory of crime.

This point may be illustrated by applying the logic of age-based

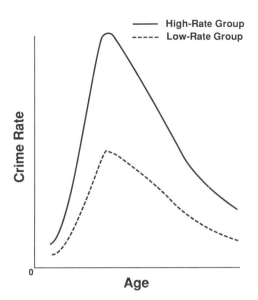

Fig. 9. True Theory Unaffected by Age.

critiques of social theories of crime to the motor vehicle accident data displayed in Figure 8. No one would argue that the impact of driver training on accidents is inadequate as an explanation of variation among drivers because it fails to account for the age effect. Indeed, insurance companies that routinely give premium discounts for persons with driver training do not neglect the age variable. More generally, it is beyond question that age affects the likelihood of motor vehicle accidents regardless of the social characteristics of drivers. It should be mentioned also that the physical costs of accidents are usually far greater than the social costs and/or legal penalties. There is, therefore, no reason to believe that social control can account for the shape of the age distribution of accidents.

Thus, if the possibility depicted in Figure 9 describes the actual situation, efforts to bring theories into line with the age distribution, to encompass the effects of age, may lead the theorist into assertions contrary to fact. For example, Edwin Sutherland and Donald Cressey (1978: 130) argue that the theory of differential association can account for the apparent effects of age. Presumably this means that age is correlated with exposure to particular constellations of definitions favorable to the violation of law and that, in groups where there is no change in definition, there will be no change in the likelihood of crime over the life course. Yet research shows that, in accord with our thesis, "even with equal exposure to criminal influences, propensity toward crime tends to diminish as one grows older" (Rowe and Tittle 1977: 229).

Again, this fact does not invalidate the theory of differential association. On the contrary, it is exactly what we would expect were the theory true *and* independent of age. The reader will note that Figure 9, though hypothetical, closely approximates actual subgroup differences reported earlier. It therefore seems safe to say that (1) the argument that theories of crime must take age into account is itself a theory of crime, and (2) the theory underlying this argument is contrary to fact.

These hypotheses about age have proven to be controversial (Greenberg 1985; Farrington 1986a; Blumstein, Cohen, and Farrington 1988a, 1988b; Tittle 1988). The empirical challenge to our invariance thesis has boiled down to a search for statistical variation in the age distribution of crime with respect to such things as mode, level, or skew (Steffensmeier et al. 1989). Often (e.g., Farrington 1986a) this search is unguided by theoretical purpose. As a result, it tends to lead to the improper conclusion that nonsubstantive and unexplained variations in the age distribution of crime bear on the invariance thesis. As indicated above, it is a caricature of our position to suggest that it denies the possibility of change in the level of crime over time (such as between 1965 and 1980) or the possibility of trivial shifts in the modal age for a particular "crime type."

Still, it is clear that many researchers do not share our perceptions of similarity and difference. Positivists tend to see difference where we see similarity. We believe our bias can be justified by its consequences. For example, the conclusion that the age distribution of crime is substantially invariant leads directly to several propositions about crime that can themselves be validated (see Hirschi and Gottfredson 1983, 1986, 1987), as indicated by the discussion below. The contrary and standard conclusion is that the age distribution of crime varies from year to year, place to place, crime type to crime type, and group to group (see Sutherland and Cressey 1978: ch. 6; Wilson and Herrnstein 1985: ch. 5). As we have seen, such observation of statistical variation absent theoretical interest is a fundamental liability of positivism, leading as it does to further observation of ever more detailed and meaningless variation. Certainly science does not require the conclusion that trivial variation is more meaningful than the fundamental similarity in the distributions at issue.

Three-quarters of a century ago, Goring (1913) found statistically significant differences in age distributions and concluded that such differences were scientifically trivial. Farrington (1986a) replicated

Goring's results but reached the opposite conclusion. We agree with Goring and with Louis Guttman, who notes that "a test of statistical significance is not a test of scientific importance. . . . No one has yet published a scientific law in the social sciences which was developed, sharpened, or effectively substantiated on the basis of tests of significance. The basic laws of physics were not facilitated this way. Estimation and approximation may be more fruitful than significance in developing science, never forgetting replication" (1977: 92).

In our view, the question for criminology is whether the glass is 97 percent full or 3 percent empty—that is, whether to pursue the important implications of a remarkably robust age effect or to continue to revel in the statistical noise generated by atheoretical research. Given the clear inconsistency between traditional criminology theories and the age-crime relation, let us invoke the distinction between crime and criminality as a mechanism for resolving this theoretical impasse.

Age and the Distinction between Crime and Criminality

In *Delinquency and Drift* (1964), David Matza argued that a basic defect in positivistic explanations of crime is that they are incapable of explaining maturational reform, the tendency for delinquency to decline from its peak level in the middle teens. According to Matza, positivistic theories create a criminal required by the laws of determinism to do as he does (that is, commit criminal acts). Alas for such theories, at the moment the offender is fully created, at the moment he is complete, he begins to do what he does less and less frequently, and the theory that created him cannot explain why he no longer does what he was designed to do. Matza's solution to this problem was to resurrect the notion of "will," to make a delinquent, if not totally free of deterministic constraints, at least freer than he is normally pictured in positivistic accounts of his behavior. Matza's specific solution is not often encountered today, but the idea that theory must be able to deal with change in the offender's behavior over time has become part of the common sense of criminology, and those solutions now offered to Matza's problem retain much of the flavor of the original.

In one of the more remarkable statements in the delinquency literature, Matza tells us that "biological theories are hardest hit by the frequency of maturational reform if only because the compulsion of biological constraint has a more literal meaning than psychic or social constraint and has been so taken" (1964: 22). Maturational reform is of course another word for change in behavior over time, for change in behavior with advancing age. Change in behavior with age would normally lead one to suspect that age might be in some way responsible for the change in behavior (since change in behavior cannot be responsible for advancing age). But age suggests biology, and in criminology biology connotes fixation, immutability, or even destiny, and Matza is thus able to say that an obviously biological correlate of crime poses a direct threat to the ability of the biological perspective to explain criminality.

Matza is not alone in this logic. In a thoughtful piece written some years later, Gordon Trasler addresses the issues posed by "spontaneous desistance" for conscience theories of crime:

The significance of [spontaneous desistance] escaped us, or rather we misinterpreted it, because we still clung to the belief that criminality was primarily a characteristic of persons, a disposition to dishonesty or violence which was rooted in some abnormality or developmental deficit, and which, therefore, would persist unless it was modified or restrained by treatment or deterrence. . . . [Spontaneous desistance] poses problems for those (such as Eysenck, Mednick, and myself) who have regarded conscience as the key mechanism in restraining people from behavior which is contrary to laws . . . and have explained criminality mainly in terms of inadequacies in the functioning of conscience. For the essential characteristic of conscience is that it is largely or entirely situation independent. [1980: 10, 12; see also Trasler 1987]

Trasler's problem is identical to Matza's: how can change in behavior be explained by a person's characteristics—characteristics that, once attained, are relatively fixed? Trasler's solution to his problem comes very close to Matza's:

The simplest and (in my view) the most satisfactory explanation of spontaneous desistance from adolescent crime is one which concentrates upon the satisfactions of delinquent conduct—as Skinner would put it, the reinforcers which maintain such behavior during adolescence, but cease to do so when the individual becomes an adult. I suggested earlier that much teenage crime is fun. . . . But as they grow older most young men gain access to other sources of achievement and social satisfaction—a job, a girlfriend, a wife, a home, and eventually children—and in doing so become gradually less dependent upon peer-group support. What is more to the point, these new life-patterns are inconsistent with delinquent activities. [Trasler 1980: 11–12]

Trasler concludes that so-called spontaneous desistance is produced by change in the situation of youth—in other words, that desistance is situation-dependent. He then draws the same moral drawn by Matza: If change in crime is situation-dependent, then criminality too is situation-dependent. If this is so, then a situation-independent construct like conscience (which is, after all, "an internalized system of values and proscriptions") must be reconsidered as an explanation of criminality. Matza and Trasler come to the problem of maturational reform or spontaneous desistance from markedly different backgrounds and perspectives. Yet both follow the same path to essentially the same conclusion. Crime declines with age; this decline may be explained by change in a person's social situation; if the social situation of the person can explain the decline in crime with age, it can also explain differences at any given age; therefore, explanations of crime that focus on a person's characteristics, whether these characteristics be biological, psychological, or, for that matter, sociological are (at best) suspect and (at worst) wrong.

An alternative interpretation of maturational reform or spontaneous desistance is that crime declines with age (Hirschi and Gottfredson 1983). This explanation suggests that maturational reform is just that, change in behavior that comes with maturation; it suggests that spontaneous desistance is just that, change in behavior that cannot be explained and change that occurs regardless of what else happens. We believe this interpretation is consistent with the evidence. We also believe it requires more careful specification of such terms as delinquency and crime.

The literature on maturational reform typically focuses on the decline in crime among those with high rates ("delinquents") and ignores a possibly similar decline in crime among those with low rates ("nondelinquents"). This oversight leads to the suggestion that delinquents tend over time to become nondelinquents—that the two groups, if they do not actually trade places, are at least eventually intermingled. This leads, as we have seen, to the conclusion that delinquency is unstable over time and that it therefore cannot be explained by characteristics that are stable over time. In fact, however, as we have shown, delinquency is relatively stable over time, and it is reasonably stable during the years of decline in the crime rate. For example, Lyle Shannon reports a correlation of .52 between the number of police contacts through age eighteen and the number of police contacts after age eighteen (1978: table 4). More concretely, Shannon's data show that 5 percent of people with no police contacts through age eighteen have five or more police contacts by the time they are 32, whereas 64 percent of people with five or more police contacts through age eighteen have five or more police contacts by the time they are 32 (1978: table 2).

Obviously, if crime declines and delinquency remains stable, we need more than one concept to account for this result. The theory we have described was in fact built in part on this necessity. It provides the two concepts necessary for reconciliation of these seemingly contradictory results, "crime" and "criminality" (self-control). As we have defined these terms, crimes are short-term, circumscribed events that presuppose a peculiar set of necessary conditions (e.g., activity, opportunity, adversaries, victims, goods). Self-control, in contrast, refers to relatively stable differences across individuals in the propensity to commit criminal (or equivalent) acts. Accordingly, self-control is only one element in the causal configuration leading to a criminal act, and criminal acts are, at best, imperfect measures of self-control. It follows that the frequency with which individuals participate in criminal events may vary over time and place without implying change in their self-control. It follows further that differences in propensity within groups may remain in the face of change in the group's overall rate of crime. Finally, it follows that low self-control can exist without crime (both before it begins and after it ends). Seen in the light of this distinction, those concerned with maturational reform appear to confuse change in crime (which declines) with change in tendency to commit crime (which may not change at all). Part of the reason for this confusion is that we tend to use the same indicator for both concepts. We allow a count of criminal acts to serve as a measure of crime and as a measure of criminality. It appears that this count is factorially complex in ways that we do not normally acknowledge, that criminality is only one of several factors accounting for its variation. With this problem in mind, it may be useful to apply the substantive distinction between crime and criminality to the facts about the age distribution of crime.

With the concept of crime and the concept of low self-control, we can distinguish between traditional "desistance" theory and an "age" theory of the same phenomenon. The desistance theory asserts that crime declines with age because of factors associated with age that reduce or change the criminality of the actor. The age theory asserts that crime, independent of criminality, declines with age. The evidence, in our view, clearly favors the age explanation. Let us briefly explore some of this evidence.

Situational and Age Explanations of Maturational Reform

Trasler argues that the decline in crime that begins in the late teens is accounted for by change in the social situation of youth. Trasler's theory is unusually explicit: he lists "sources of achievement and social satisfaction" that lead to decline. This list includes "a job, a girl friend, a wife, a home, and eventually children" (1980: 11–12). As stated by Trasler, situational theory has no characteristic of persons it may use to predict institutional involvement or to condition its predictions of the impact of such involvement. As a result, it must assume that everyone, delinquent and nondelinquent, is equally likely to end up in and be influenced by the conventional institutions of society. Our theory, in contrast, assumes that a stable personal characteristic—self-control—is obviously relevant to institutional involvement and impact. In fact, it assumes that since conventional institutions almost by definition constrain behavior, those with little self-control are unlikely to be attracted to or influenced by them. Consequently, our theory is suspicious of the idea that such institutions change people in the ways suggested by situational explanations. Let us look at the evidence on jobs, girlfriends, wives, and children.

Employment. If rates of crime decline with age, one reason almost invariably mentioned is that at the peak age of committing crime, young people begin to enter the labor force. The job, with its regular hours, its restrictions, and its compensation, settles the adolescent down and satisfies his previously unsatisfied wants. If work is the curse of the drinking man, it is also the curse of all who would engage in other unconventional or illegitimate pleasures. Or, so the story goes, as it is endlessly repeated in the crime literature. Job theories are easy to state, but they are hard to test. They appear to imply, at least in the context of arguments against person-oriented explanations of crime, that jobs somehow attach themselves to persons and proceed to modify their behavior. If this were so, we could merely compare persons with jobs to persons without them and expect to find that those without jobs are more likely to be delinquent. When we try such passive observation under natural conditions, at least in the late teens when employment is increasing and delinquency declining, we find that persons with jobs attached to them are *more* rather than less likely to be delinquent (Hirschi 1969: 188; West and Farrington 1977).

This finding requires that we modify job theory in fundamental ways. We do so by qualifying the idea of a job, or by restating the connection between jobs and people, or some combination of the two. Once we do begin to talk about "meaningful" work or about personal characteristics that lead people to seek or maintain jobs, we create a complex model whose significance for the age question is no longer clear. One thing *is* clear: once a situational variable has been contaminated by the characteristics of persons, it is no longer legitimate to use its effects as an argument against person-oriented explanations of crime. The modified job theory, recognizing that jobs do not exist in a vacuum, would probably state that, other things being equal, those with jobs are less likely to be delinquent than those without them. To test this theory, we assign some people jobs and withhold jobs from others. When this is done, it seems fair to say that the results are not those "job theory" has led us to expect. Differences in rates of crime are small, nonexistent, or even in the wrong direction (Berk, Lenihan, and Rossi 1980). When, in contrast, everyone is assigned the same job regardless of past history of delinquency, as happened in World War II, differences in delinquency persist and the gradual decline in crime with age continues (Glueck and Glueck 1968). We therefore conclude that employment does not explain, or help to explain, the reduction in crime with age, and that it is not relevant to theories that differentiate between offenders and non-offenders.

A girlfriend. The plausibility of the girlfriend or wife as a reason for the decline in crime with age stems from several sources. As Franklin Zimring notes, "adolescents commit crimes, as they live their lives, in groups" (1981: 867). The evidence Zimring presents in favor of this statement is overwhelming. If we add one qualification to his statement, its implications for the age question are apparent: "adolescents commit crimes, as they live their lives, in groups homogeneous on sex." If this is so, breaking up the single-sex group should lead to a reduction in crime, whether the reduction is real or apparent. In this view, one shared by Trasler and by Wilson and Herrnstein (1985: 147), the girlfriend functions to keep the boyfriend away from his peers, to shield him from the temptations of gang life. Since girlfriends, like jobs, appear more frequently as boys grow into men, they could account for the decline in crime that occurs as boys grow into men. Do they? Once again, the evidence is distressingly in the wrong direction: boys with girlfriends appear more likely to commit delinquent acts than boys without them. In fact, this tendency is so strong that dating can be equated with smoking and drinking in terms of its connection with delinquency. This equation, by the way, is commonly encountered in the delinquency literature (Hirschi 1969: 163–70; Wiatrowski, Griswold, and Roberts 1981). Apparently, girlfriends, like jobs, do not simply attach themselves to boys. Instead, there is some sort of self-selection to the treatment condition. If this "treatment" is conducive to nondelinquency, we are forced once again to the strange conclusion that delinquents are peculiarly attracted to situations inconsistent with their delinquent behavior. It seems more reasonable, and certainly more consistent with what we know about self-selection, to assume that delinquents will be attracted to situations or activities consistent with their delinquent behavior.

Since we have introduced such activities, it may be worthwhile to explore their implications for the question at hand. The use of alcohol, tobacco, and drugs increases through the adolescent years. In other words, its tendency is in the direction opposite to other forms of delinquent behavior. Given this familiar pattern, we could suggest the possibility that alcohol acts as a substitute for other forms of delinquency, that its pleasures make at least some other pleasures unnecessary. Given this logic (which is of course identical to situational explanations of the decline in crime with age), we would predict that those who use alcohol will be less likely to commit criminal acts. But we know that this is not true; on the contrary, alcohol and delinquency tend to go together. The reason they go together is that they both reflect a characteristic of the person: low self-control, the tendency to pursue short-term, immediate pleasures. Apparently, such pleasures do not preclude one another. Apparently, too, change in the frequency with which one of them is pursued does not necessarily imply change in the frequency with which others are pursued; nor does change in the frequency with which one of these pleasures is pursued necessarily imply change in the general propensity of the person to pursue such pleasures as a whole. In this regard, the Gluecks' longitudinal studies of delinquents consistently show that increases in arrests for drunkenness almost make up for decreases in arrests in other crime categories. The McCords' follow-up data show strong trends in the same direction (see Cline 1980: 658–61). Pursuit of this line of thought leads to the conclusion that a girlfriend, at least in the teen years, does not so much restrain the delinquent as she reflects and even encourages his short-term orientation to life. This conclusion has the virtue that it is consistent with the data as well as with a general conception of delinquency, a conception consistent with the decline in some kinds of pleasure-seeking with age.

Wives, home, and children. Wives and homes raise the same problems as jobs and girlfriends. They sound nice, and they are almost by definition inconsistent with crime, but they too may be abandoned if they prove inconvenient or overly restrictive. As a consequence, they do not seem to have an impact on the likelihood of crime. More to the point, they do not account for the decline in crime with age (Farrington 1979; Tittle 1980). Children are an even more interesting case. It is generally reported that people with criminal records do not want their children to be delinquent. It seems to follow that children would therefore have an inhibiting effect on a parent's behavior: the parent interested in his or her children will try to provide a proper model for them and be willing to devote the immense amount of time and energy necessary to train them. But as we noted in Chapter 5, many parents do not behave as expected. The training of children requires self-denial and a willingness to sacrifice immediate pleasure for long-term, uncertain benefit, characteristics offenders are likely to lack in the first place. The fact that their children are unusually likely to become offenders is consistent with the conclusion that offenders do not change their own behavior in the way the children hypothesis would suggest; instead, as parents, they maintain the short-term orientation of their youth.

In summary, the life-course or situational explanation of the decline in crime with age says that a person gains sources of satisfaction inconsistent with crime as he or she grows older. If one set of satisfactions is inconsistent with another, there is good reason to conclude that the person switching from one set to another has changed: he or she has given up something and accepted something rather different in its place. Put in bald form, the irresponsible, thoughtless offender has become the responsible, thoughtful law-abiding citizen. The data, however, do not conform to this picture. The institutions thought to restrain the offender do not produce the expected results. On the contrary, the offender tends to convert these institutions into sources of satisfaction consistent with his previous criminal behavior. As a result, individual differences in the likelihood of crime tend to persist across the life course; there is no drastic reshuffling of the criminal and noncriminal populations based on unpredictable, situational events.

There is, however, a decline in crime with age. Since this decline cannot be explained by change in the person or by his exposure to anticriminal institutions, we are left with the conclusion that it is due to the inexorable aging of the organism. We are also left with the conclusion that change in crime with age is not the problem for individual-level explanations it is usually taken to be; on the contrary, the theories that appear to be jeopardized by change are those theories used unsuccessfully to explain it, theories that focus on the controlling influence or deterrent effects of participation in conventional institutions.

Social Theories of Crime and the Age Effect

To this point, we have focused on the decline in crime with age, taking "remission" as the problem of interest. In this respect, we have merely followed tradition. The other side of the age curve is of at least equal theoretical interest. Why is it generally ignored? One reason seems to be that we think it is not ignored, that theory deals with the increase in crime with age up to the middle teens, and that it therefore has no difficulty with *change* in criminal behavior until decline begins. Inspection of the major theories of delinquency reveals, however, that they do not really attend to either side of the age distribution, or, if they focus on one side, they ignore the other. Matza's discussion, focusing on remission, makes no mention of age of onset or analogous concepts. In fact, Matza's theory begins where delinquency is at its peak. Matza, then, takes delinquency as given: he begins and ends with the idea that the behavior of the delinquent must be explained, telling us nothing about how or when the delinquent came to be delinquent in the first place.

Cloward and Ohlin (1960) devote several brief sections of their book to the integration of age levels in the delinquent subculture, but it is not clear how the system of recruitment and training they describe squares with the age distribution of crime, since, as far as we can determine, they do not mention the specific ages of any of the people they describe. It seems fair to say, however, that Cloward and Ohlin describe a process through which people formerly nondelinquent are transformed into delinquents, and that this process involves participation in the conventional institutions of society—in particular, of course, the school. There is good reason to believe, then, that the Cloward and Ohlin theory stems ultimately from an image of the age distribution of crime, the image in which it starts from nowhere and rises to its peak in the middle teens. There is good reason, too, to believe that this theory is unlikely to be correct, since it mistakes the age distribution of crime for the age distribution of criminality, asking us to believe that criminality also comes from nowhere or, worse, to believe that good boys are transformed into bad boys by good institutions, a sequence we have learned to doubt from our experience with desistance theory.

Albert Cohen (1955) also does not mention specific age periods when the events he describes are supposed to occur, but these events can be located with reasonable precision in the life course. For example, Cohen spends a good deal of time describing what boys are like when they are turned over to the school by the family. We may not know exactly when this happens, but we do know it happens before officially noticed delinquency begins. Cohen describes in some detail two polar types of boys received by the school: boys who accept and boys who reject the following set of standards or values:

1. Ambition is a virtue: its absence is a defect. . . . Ambition means a high level of aspiration, aspiration for goals difficult of achievement. It means also

an orientation to long-run goals and long-deferred rewards. 2. Individual responsibility [is applauded]. . . . 3. [T]here is special emphasis on academic achievement and the acquisition of skills of *potential* economic and occupational value. 4. [G]reat value [is placed] on . . . a readiness and an ability to postpone and to subordinate the temptations of immediate satisfactions and self-indulgence in the interest of the achievement of long-run goals. . . . 5. Rationality is highly valued, in the sense of the exercise of fore-thought, conscious planning, and budgeting of time. . . . 6. [M]anners, courtesy, and personability [are valued]. . . . 7. The . . . ethic emphasizes the control of physical aggression and violence. . . . 8. [R]ecreation should be wholesome. . . . 9. Lastly, [these] values emphasize "respect for property" . . . [which] includes . . . the *right* of the owner to do as he wishes with his belongings. [1955: 88–91; first emphasis added]

Cohen's description of middle-class values is quoted at length because it is a detailed conceptualization of what we mean by self-control. In fact, just as we suggest that crime is a by-product of a tendency to seek immediate pleasure, Cohen suggests that those untrained to postpone pleasure are also untrained to avoid theft and violence. If so, it seems fair to say that in Cohen's theory marked differences in criminality have been produced by the time the family turns the child over to the school.

If differences in *criminality* appear early in life, there are two ways to handle the fact that crime does not appear until adolescence. One is to let age fill the gap, to assume that differences in crime potential, at whatever age they are established, will show themselves when the passage of time makes crime possible. The way adopted by Cohen is to fill the intervening period with theory; he gives boys who are untrained to postpone pleasure, to avoid violence, or to respect property one antidelinquent trait: concern for the opinion of middle-class people. Cohen then needs time, and an institutional experience, to get rid of this trait. Once again, then, an institution is required to transform the individual, in this case to turn a hypersensitive kid into a malicious offender. The theoretical effort required to produce this transformation is prodigious. Even though Cohen begins with a child who, if left alone, would almost certainly get into trouble eventually, that part of his theory most often cited and tested deals with the transformation question. We are forced to conclude that Cohen's theory, too, has been influenced by disciplinary preconceptions and an image of the age distribution of crime, the same image held by Cloward and Ohlin, according to which delinquency appears suddenly in early adolescence. These explanations of delinquency are thus mirror images of explanations of nondelinquency one finds on the down side of the age distribution: on the down side, a delinquent enters conventional institutions and is transformed into a nondelinquent; on the up side, a nondelinquent enters a conventional institution and is transformed into a delinquent. In both sets of theory, the outcome is inconsistent with at least some of the initial properties of the person. In the up-side theory, the outcome is inconsistent with initial properties of the person and with the thrust of the institution he enters. If age is allowed to account for change in crime over time, many of the complications of transformation theory are avoided.

The distinction between crime and self-control thus provides a device for solving one of the major empirical dilemmas of criminology: the fact that crime everywhere declines with age while differences in "crime" tendency across individuals remain relatively stable over the life course. Once this distinction between propensities and events has been made, it is hard to return to crime theories that operate without it. Theories that fail to make this distinction were identified in Chapters 3 and 4 as representing the various brands of disciplinary positivism. Because the positive disciplines do not have a concept of crime, their theories focus on the criminal. At the same time, they are reluctant to acknowledge the idea of a stable characteristic of the individual bearing on his criminal behavior—that is, criminality. As a consequence, positive criminology has no clear conception of its primary dependent variable; it has no way to integrate findings about characteristics of people with those about characteristics of situations; and it has no way of permitting choice and causation to coexist in a single act.

Let us take these notions to two additional correlates of crime that have been extremely difficult for other schemes to deal with: gender and race.

Gender and Crime

Most scholars agree that gender is a major, persistent correlate to crime:

None of these studies quarrels with the invariant findings that males commit more offenses than females, and that male offenses are in general more serious than those of females. [Warren 1981: 8]

Such differences are striking indeed: sex appears to explain more variance in crime across cultures than any other variable. This appears so *regardless* of whether officially known or hidden ("true") rates of crime are indexed. [Harris 1977: 4]

Given's 1977 careful analysis of historical documents notes that homicide in 13th-century England "was an overwhelmingly male phenomenon" . . . and surveys of research worldwide confirm this kind of finding. [Nettler 1982: 16; Nettler's citations omitted]

The relation between gender and criminality is strong and is likely to remain so. Women have traditionally been much less likely than men to commit violent crimes and that pattern persists today. . . . While the relative increase in women's property crime involvements is significant, female participation even in these crimes remains far less than that of men. [Nagel and Hagan 1983: 91]

Our review of the data on gender and crime can be brief because of these recent extended treatments of the subject in the literature. For crimes involving force and fraud, male arrests account for 60–99 percent of those arrested. This disproportionality characterizes all official data since the FBI began collecting statistics in the 1930's in the United States. Similar differences have been documented for England (Douglas et al. 1966; Wadsworth 1979; Farrington 1986a), Sweden (Jonsson 1967), and Denmark (Christiansen and Jensen 1972), as well as for many other countries (see Adler 1981).

Unofficial statistics, it is now agreed, confirm the official portrait. Large differences between boys and girls are a persistent feature of self-report data. For example, Table 5 shows that male-female self-report differences from many studies consistently reveal a substantial disproportionality for serious offenses, and these differences are in all cases consistent with official data. According to the National Academy of Sciences: "The most consistent pattern with respect to gender is the extent to which male criminal participation in serious crimes at any age greatly exceeds that of females, regardless of source of data, crime type, level of involvement, or measure of participation" (Blumstein et al. 1986).

The Stability of the Gender Effect

As was true of age, gender differences appear to be invariant over time and space. Men are always and everywhere more likely than women to commit criminal acts. As was also true of age, this fact is often obscured by the tendency to emphasize "recent" trends toward similarity, or theories that predict eventual similarity. Thus, for example, it was for a long time routinely assumed that with greater equality of status between men and women there would be greater equality in their crime rates (Simon 1975; Nettler 1984). However, the persistence of large differences within class and ethnic groups during a period of increase in the labor-force participation of women in the

TABLE 5

*Male-to-Female Sex Ratios for Commonly Used Self-Report Items,
Ranked by Magnitude of Median Sex Ratio*

Item	Range of sex ratios	Median sex ratio	Number of samples
Run away	.35–2.31	1.00	13
Hit parents	.79–1.09	1.00	4
Defy parents	.67–1.20	1.02	5
Smoke marijuana	.68–4.40	1.08	9
Drink alcohol	.85–1.75	1.28	20
Be truant	1.06–1.91	1.28	12
Drive without license	1.08–3.32	1.50	8
Steal less than $2	1.16–2.02	1.75	12
Steal $2–$50	1.48–5.03	2.70	12
Have sexual relations	1.51–83.86	2.86	8
Commit robbery	1.00–8.00	2.87	10
Damage/destroy property	1.17–5.15	2.92	14
Participate in gang fight	2.50–4.60	3.28	11
Take car	1.48 13.26	3.37	15
Beat up/assault	1.17–6.50	3.61	10
Steal more than $50	1.75–6.60	3.68	11

SOURCE: Adapted from Hindelang, Hirschi, and Weis (1981: 140). The data are derived from samples constructed from thirteen studies.

United States suggests that the equality thesis or role theory is incorrect.

But the major device for questioning the universality of the gender effect is to cite variation in the magnitude of the difference across conditions. This suggests that there *could be* conditions under which no difference would be found. In fact, however, these conditions have not been empirically discovered (Jensen and Eve 1976). In the United States, for example, the convergence of arrests for white-collar crimes does not falsify the idea that men are more likely than women to commit such crimes. It reflects, instead, the fact that women are greatly overpresented in occupations where such offenses are possible (e.g., women outnumber men in many white-collar occupations, such as bank tellers and clerical workers). When opportunity is controlled, the traditionally higher rate of fraud among males is again revealed (Hirschi and Gottfredson 1987).

Even if role or opportunity-based explanations of gender differences in crime could account for property-crime differences and their purported convergence, such explanations lack credibility when applied to violent conduct. The opportunities for women to commit assault or homicide are equivalent to those available to men. In fact, women spend much more time in unsupervised interaction with children, and the amount of time they spend in contact with other people is as large or larger than that of men.

Another common explanation of gender differences in sociology is labeling theory, according to which women are less likely to be defined as deviant and therefore less likely to behave in a deviant way. However, as Rutter and Giller (1984: 121) point out, the evidence overwhelmingly demonstrates that girls have been more harshly treated than boys by the criminal justice system. They are more likely to be taken into custody for offenses that would not involve custody for adults. Indeed, several recent reviews suggest insufficient bias in processing to produce the large gender differences in crime—a research outcome that is consistent with the official/self-report comparisons mentioned earlier (Hindelang 1981; Warren 1981; Empey 1982; Nagel and Hagan 1983).

Gender differences in behavior analogous to crime are similar to those found for crime, further serving to question the idea that role differences account for behavioral differences. For example, Figure 8 (p. 130) revealed consistent and large differences in motor vehicle accident rates for males and females regardless of age. Differences of the same magnitude are reported for most accidents, including drowning, burning, and falling. Alcohol and drug abuse are also more common among men than women (Miller 1982).

What does the crime and criminality distinction say about gender differences in crime? Note first that gender differences for all types of crime are established early in life and that they persist throughout life. This fact implies a substantial self-control difference between the sexes. Note second that there are obvious crime differences between men and women, such as rape and prostitution, and equally obvious differences between them in the sanctioning of deviant behaviors, such as the differential consequences for boys and girls of premarital pregnancy. This fact suggests that gender differences may be due to differences in crime rather than criminality, and that differences in opportunity may account for much of the male-female difference in crime rates. The latter hypothesis is the more prevalent in the literature. The theory we offer provides the means for beginning to resolve the question of the extent to which gender differences are crime or criminality related. Let us briefly illustrate how the perspective can be applied to this dispute.

At first glance, the gender difference in crime appears to be largely a result of opportunity variables or supervision. Historically, girls and women have been more closely supervised than boys and men. Parents tended to watch their daughters more closely than their sons, a tendency that persists at the present time, albeit at a somewhat diminished level (Felson and Gottfredson 1984). Schools and other community institutions followed parental practice in exercising tighter control over their female charges, a tendency that presumably also persists to the present day. The reason for greater control was not the presumption that girls are more criminally inclined than boys; it was the fact that most forms of delinquency are more costly to females than to males. In the extreme case, sexual misbehavior could result in pregnancy and reduced opportunities for a successful marriage. In general, the connection between good behavior and life chances was so much stronger for females than for males that their life chances could be damaged by all sorts of misbehavior that would have little impact on the life chances of males. Because most delinquency takes place in the absence of direct parental supervision, the tighter control on girls in and of itself could translate into lower rates of delinquency.

As a complete explanation, the direct-supervision thesis runs into trouble with the facts almost from the beginning. The male-female difference remains among adolescents who are equally supervised by their parents (Table 6). Boys have greater misconduct rates in school, where the sexes are comparably supervised. As a matter of fact, male-female differences in the use of force and fraud emerge early in life, well before differences in opportunity are possible, and persist into adulthood, where differences in supervision by agents of social control are minimal.

All of this suggests that social control and self-control have independent effects on the likelihood of criminal acts—that supervision and socialization are not synonymous. Indeed, parents do not appear to assume that supervision of their children is a necessary or sufficient means of socialization. Instead, they act as though their children are not sufficiently socialized to resist temptation in the absence of direct control. They therefore seek to minimize opportunities for crime, especially for daughters. But because supervision is not socialization, parents who supervise their sons and daughters differently may in fact socialize them similarly. Support for this idea is provided by the consistent finding that variables related to differences in criminality among boys are the same as those for girls (Glueck and Glueck 1934, 1950; Hindelang 1973; Jensen and Eve 1976; Warren 1981). Thus, for example, lack of attachment to parents is related to delinquency

TABLE 6

Self-Reported Delinquency by Parental Supervision and Gender (in percent)

Number of self-reported acts	Supervision, females			Supervision, males		
	Low	Medium	High	Low	Medium	High
0	31	51	65	16	27	38
1	28	33	25	20	32	29
2	23	10	8	23	21	17
3+	18	6	2	41	21	16
TOTALS	100	100	100	100	101	100
(N)	(65)	(134)	(394)	(334)	(337)	(663)

SOURCE: Richmond Youth Project data (Hirschi 1969).
NOTE: Supervision is measured by the items "Does your mother (father) know where you are when you are away from home?" and "Does your mother (father) know who you are with when you are away from home?" In the table, those scoring high on supervision answered "usually" to all four questions.

among both boys and girls. Likewise, academic ambition, good scholarly performance, and the belief that crime is wrong inhibit delinquency for both sexes. Clearly, parents may foster the same antidelinquent attitudes and behaviors in their children even as they supervise them differentially.

It seems to us to follow that the impact of gender on crime is largely a result of crime differences *and* differences in self-control that are not produced by direct external control. Given our discussion of the causes of self-control, this is not an altogether surprising conclusion. Direct supervision is only one of the elements necessary for the production of self-control. Other elements include the recognition of deviant behavior and the willingness to expend the effort necessary to correct it. Beyond these elements is the socializability of the individual. It is beyond the scope of this work (and beyond the reach of any available set of empirical data) to attempt to identify all of the elements responsible for gender differences in crime. However, by conceptualizing the problem as crime and criminality, available data may be examined in a new light.

Race, Ethnicity, and Crime

As with gender differences, there is substantial agreement that there are large, relatively stable differences in crime and delinquency rates across race and ethnic groups. In fact, John Laub (1983) has shown that the race differences in offending account for most of the apparent effect of urbanization on U.S. crime rates. Such differences are not unique to American society:

In virtually every society, there are differences in crime rates among some racial and ethnic groups. Americans of Chinese and Japanese origin have significantly lower crime rates than other Americans. . . . Even allowing for the existence of discrimination in the criminal justice system, the higher rates of crime among black Americans cannot be denied. . . . Every study of crime using official data shows blacks to be overrepresented among persons arrested, convicted, and imprisoned for street crimes. Blacks are about one-eighth of the population but accounted in 1980 for about one-half of all those arrested for murder, rape, and robbery, and for between one-fourth and one-third of all those arrested for burglary, larceny, auto theft, and aggravated assault. [Wilson and Herrnstein 1985: 459–61]

According to the National Academy of Sciences, "combining data from several studies with criminal participation broadly defined as nontraffic offenses, the black/white ratio averages 1.8:1; for index offenses, the ratio averages 3.1:1" (Blumstein et al. 1986: 41).

As John Conklin summarizes the data on this question:

Crime rates for Jews, Japanese-Americans, and Chinese-Americans are lower than rates for the total population, and . . . crime rates for blacks and Mexican-Americans are higher than rates for the total population. . . . In 1983 blacks constituted 12 percent of the population of the United States, but they accounted for 35.7 percent of the arrests for index crimes. Blacks comprised 47.5 percent of arrests for crimes of violence, and 32.7 percent of arrests for property crimes. [1986: 123]

The picture in official data of clear race-ethnic differences in crime rates is often ascribed to system bias against racial minorities, but this explanation is disconfirmed by victimization data, where victims report on the characteristics of those victimizing them. These victim surveys show differences in offending nearly identical to those revealed by official data (Hindelang 1978, 1981; Wilbanks 1986). The self-report method does not reveal differences of the magnitude shown in official and victim data, but this appears to be due to the differential validity of the method by race (Hindelang, Hirschi, and Weis 1981).

In Great Britain, Rutter and Giller report that "the findings of these various studies are quite clear-cut. Firstly, the delinquency rate for Asians has been equal to or lower than that for the white population at all times when it has been studied. Secondly, in sharp contrast to the situation in the 1950's and 1960's, the arrest rate for blacks is now substantially above that for whites, especially for violent crimes" (1984: 160–61).

The most popular explanation of racial variation in crime focuses on the American black-white rate difference and invokes a "subculture of violence" to explain it. According to subculture-of-violence theory, the deprivation of blacks leads to the development of values that condone or justify the use of violence in interpersonal disputes. Once developed, these values are passed on from generation to generation, even in the absence of the deprivation that stimulated their development in the first place (Wolfgang and Ferracuti 1967; Curtis 1974).

Such cultural models of what we call criminality are fully general: given that cultures can be assigned to racial or ethnic groups, and given that cultures can differ in the extent to which they permit or inhibit the development of the tendency to commit crime, any and all observed differences in crime rates among racial or ethnic groups may be "explained" by differences in racial culture.

Unfortunately for the cultural view of criminality, the empirical evidence supports virtually none of its assumptions. Social scientists have searched in vain for group differences in attitudes and values about the use of violence. First, all groups, whatever their racial or ethnic composition, condemn the use of force or fraud in human interaction (see, generally, Short and Strodtbeck 1965; Suttles 1968; Rossi et al. 1974; Newman 1976; Kornhauser 1978; Nettler 1984). Second, all groups, whatever their racial or ethnic composition, endorse values contrary to crime, values such as long-range planning, selflessness, and fair play. Third, offenders themselves, whatever their racial group or ethnic affiliation, do not endorse criminal acts, even those they commit (Matza 1964). Fourth, the characteristics of offenders tend to be the antithesis of those characteristics necessary for the intimate group participation necessary to full socialization, whatever the culture. That is, the characteristics of offenders suggest that they are less rather than more reflective of the cultural values of their groups (see Chapter 5). Fifth, the structure of criminal "organizations" is inconsistent with the premises of the cultural argument. Rather than highly organized, stable units capable of transmitting culture, organizations composed of people who tend toward criminality are likely to be ephemeral and inefficient (Yablonsky 1962; Suttles 1968; Reuter 1983; see also Chapter 10). Sixth, and perhaps most important, the cultural view misconstrues the nature of the criminal act. There is nothing in crime that requires the transmission of values or the support of other people. There is nothing in crime that requires the transmission of skills, or techniques, or knowledge from other people. On the contrary, it is in the nature of crime that it can be invented instantly, on the spot, by almost anyone, and its own reward is its justification.

Another explanation of race and ethnic differences is provided by strain theory. This explanation may focus on deprivation or poverty, suggesting that members of some racial groups are objectively deprived. Such deprivation theories find little support in criminological research. As Jackson Toby points out, "in point of fact, one thief in a thousand in urban industrial societies steals because he is hungry or cold; color television sets and automobiles are stolen more often than food and blankets" (1979b: 516).

More often, strain theory focuses on relative rather than absolute deprivation (for a recent revival, see Blau and Blau 1982). For example, black-white differences in crime may be explained by income *inequality* between blacks and whites. As Reid Golden and Steven Messner summarize the Blau thesis: "The ascribed nature of racial inequality renders it illegitimate and makes it a source of pervasive conflict. Furthermore, because opportunities for effective political action are in large measure restricted for the disadvantaged, the 'pervasive conflict' engendered by racial inequality tends to be expressed in diffuse forms of aggression, such as criminal violence" (1987: 525).

No good evidence exists for the inequality thesis. In fact, apart from the ecological correlations between race, poverty, and violent-crime rates provided by Judith and Peter Blau (1982), correlations subject to widely varying interpretations, the results of research run contrary to the inequality thesis (Sampson 1985; Golden and Messner 1987; see also Kornhauser 1978: 253, where the author concludes that "strain models are disconfirmed").

Our crime and criminality distinction is also contrary to strain models and can be used to expose their logical deficiencies as explanations of race differences in criminal behavior. For one thing, strain theorists misconstrue the nature of the criminal act, supplying it with virtues it does not possess. Strain theorists suggest that compelling social or psychological purposes govern the commission of criminal acts; in fact, they are governed by the proximity, ease, and convenience of their rewards. Strain theorists suggest that offenders tend to strike out against their class enemies or people more fortunate than themselves; in fact, offenders tend to victimize people who share their unfortunate circumstances (whether individuals or commercial establishments). In short, crime is an ill-conceived mechanism for the redistribution of wealth or for the extraction of revenge on one's oppressors, and no racial or ethnic group believes otherwise. As Kornhauser (1978) remarks, it is implausible to argue or to believe that the pain of inequality may be alleviated by assaulting, robbing, or stealing from similarly situated people.

In the more general versions of strain theory, offenders "turn to crime" as a device for alleviating the frustrations generated by a disjunction between democratically induced aspirations and realistic expectations of their achievement (Merton 1938; Cloward and Ohlin 1960). These versions were developed using "social class" as the element of stratification relevant to crime, but they have always been a major explanation of race differences as well (Silberman 1978).

In these versions of strain theory, crime is seen as an alternative route to material success, as a substitute for legitimate work. To the extent these versions are accurate, black offenders (and, for that matter, all offenders) should treat crime as an important source of livelihood, as an occupation or career that is pursued with long-term advantage in mind. None of these features can be reconciled with the nature of crime, which provides only uncertain, short-term benefits, as we have repeatedly shown. Furthermore, this image is inconsistent with known patterns of offending, where behavior contrary to the requirements of an occupation or career is commonplace (e.g., excessive drug use) and there is no tendency to specialize in a particular criminal act or to improve one's skill in any of them.

Given the inability of existing sociological theories to account for race or ethnic differences in crime, how can the crime and criminality perspective be applied?

Partitioning race or ethnic differences into their crime and self-control components is not possible with currently available data. Nearly all theories explain these differences as due to differences in levels of self-control or criminality rather than differences in opportunity or crime. In our view, the emphasis on self-control is appropriate. There seems little reason to believe that opportunity factors alone can account for the relationship. There are differences among racial and ethnic groups (as there are between the sexes) in levels of direct supervision by family, and thus there is a "crime" component to racial differences in crime rates, but, as with gender, differences in self-control probably far outweigh differences in supervision in accounting for racial or ethnic variations. Given the potentially large differences among racial groups in the United States in the elements of child-rearing discussed in Chapter 5 (monitoring, recognizing, and correcting evidence of antisocial behavior), it seems to us that research on racial differences should focus on differential child-rearing practices and abandon the fruitless effort to ascribe such differences to culture or strain. We return to the problem of ethnic differences in Chapter 8.

7

The Social Consequences of
Low Self-Control

The first test of a theory should be its ability to organize and explain the facts about crime and deviant behavior. In criminology today there is widespread agreement about the direction and relative magnitude of a large number of correlates of crime. In the previous chapter, we discussed the individual-level correlates of crime. In this chapter we discuss the social-level correlates: peer group, school, job, and marriage and family. In Chapter 8, we will turn our attention to cultural variables.

The Peer Group

The correlation between the delinquency of the subject and the delinquency of his or her friends is one of the strongest in the field. In 1950 the Gluecks reported that more than 98 percent of their 500 delinquents had largely delinquent friends, while the same was true of less than 8 percent of their 500 nondelinquents (1950: 163–64). Nearly every study of self-report delinquency has asked respondents, "Have any of your friends been picked up by the police?" Responses to this item are strongly correlated with self-reports of delinquent activity (Hirschi 1969; Gold 1970; Hindelang 1971; Elliott and Voss 1974). Michael Hindelang, Travis Hirschi, and Joseph Weis (1981: 205–6) report that the variable "friends picked up" is moderately to strongly related to a variety of measures of self-reported delinquency among blacks and whites and among males and females.

A related fact is the long-established tendency of adolescent youth to engage in delinquent activities in groups. Beginning with Clifford Shaw and Henry McKay (1942) and their classic studies of delinquent areas in Chicago, and continuing through the work of James Short and Fred Strodtbeck (1965) and Maynard Erickson and Gary Jensen (1977), to recent reiteration in data produced by the National Survey of Youth (Elliott, Huizinga, and Ageton 1985), a major assertion of sociological criminology is that adolescent delinquency is a group phenomenon.

Many modern theories of delinquency ascribe causal and theoretical significance to these peer-group correlations (Cohen 1955; Akers 1973; Sutherland and Cressey 1978; Elliott, Huizinga, and Ageton 1985). In fact, it is easy to conclude that the major claim of the sociological perspective is that differences in adolescent crime rates are due to differences in group membership:

Youths are not pushed into delinquency by strain or are unable to resist a natural impulse toward delinquency because of weak social controls; rather, they observe and learn in group interactions that some delinquent behaviors are encouraged and rewarded by the group, and that the anticipated rewards outweigh the potential costs or punishments associated with these behaviors in particular situations or settings. Although most social groups have a conventional orientation and provide social reinforcements for conforming behavior, others have an orientation that reinforces delinquent behavior (hereinafter referred to as delinquent groups). . . . The primary deviant learning context is the adolescent peer group; the greatest variation in normative orientations, delinquent behavior patterns, and social reinforcements for delinquent behavior are found in this social context. [Elliott, Huizinga, and Ageton 1985: 34–35]

Obviously, this kind of thinking about crime causation could not be further from our own. Let us, then, review the evidence as it bears on a choice between the "social learning" and the self-control perspectives.

To begin with, of course, there is the question of stability of differences in deviant behavior over the life course—or, put another way, the predictability of differences in delinquent behavior during and following adolescence from differences in behavior observable prior to the adolescent years.

A social-setting explanation such as that advanced by Delbert Elliott, David Huizinga, and Suzanne Ageton (and many other cultural deviance theorists) can account for observed stability by assuming constancy in the relevant characteristics of the settings in which people find themselves. For example, they can assume that, by chance alone, "delinquents" come from prodelinquent families, enter prodelinquent gangs, find prodelinquent wives and jobs, and acquire prodelinquent educations and prodelinquent children and adult friends.

The only alternative to this absurd scenario available to the cultural deviance theorist is to abandon at some point the assumption that delinquency is always situationally determined in favor of the view that learning in one setting is transferred to other settings, that people made delinquent by reinforcements at one point in life are likely to remain relatively delinquent *regardless of social setting* throughout the rest of life. If this alternative is selected, it is not clear (1) why the delinquent gang, rather than the temporally prior (and presumably more powerful) family, is the paramount socializing influence, or (2) how it may be concluded that instant "social" reinforcement is more important than past reinforcement, whether social or nonsocial.

This alternative solution has other problems as well. For example, it creates a "criminal," a person trained to commit criminal acts. Such a person would be expected to continue to commit criminal acts and to avoid noncriminal acts that might interfere with his or her criminal pleasures. All "positive" learning theories of crime thus lead to the conclusion that the offender will tend to repeat specific forms of deviant behavior, that he or she will learn to do it better and more often, and that some acts will be outside the repertoire of some offenders (since no direct learning of those acts has been available). Given the versatility finding, positive learning theories are thus clearly false.

All of which leaves the cultural deviance theory where it began, with the belief that delinquency is situationally produced in delinquent groups. This would be easier to believe if delinquency did not carry with it such antigroup behavior as unreliability, accidents, and, indeed, the victimization of group members. Because groups, too, must abide by the consequences of their actions, the existence of such groups seems logically unlikely.

How much easier it would be to assume that the "delinquent peer group" is a creation of faulty measurement and the tendency of people to seek the company of others like themselves. The faulty-measurement hypothesis can be illustrated by the analytical procedures used by Elliott et al. (1985) to investigate the causal status of the relation between delinquency and the delinquency of one's peers. Using two waves of their cohort data, Elliott et al. first regress current delinquency on prior delinquency and then ask whether contemporaneous "peer delinquency" is related to "delinquency." It is related. The interpretation problem is, however, not resolved by the pattern of correlation alone. For example, one interpretation for these results is simply that delinquency is correlated with delinquency; that is, the variable—self-reported peer delinquency—may merely be another measure of self-reported delinquency. This measurement interpretation of the results seems to us to be consistent with the actual content of the Elliott et al. "peer delinquency" variable.

The Elliott et al. measure of peer delinquency is composed of answers to two sets of questions. The first measures time spent with other people. The second measures the respondent's estimate of the proportion of his or her close friends who have engaged in specific delinquent activities during the previous year. The delinquent activities reported for friends are the same delinquent activities previously reported by the respondent for himself. The method overlap in the two measures of delinquency could hardly be greater.

One might reasonably ask the basis of the respondent's answers to questions about the delinquency of his friends. Several possibilities come to mind: (1) the respondent may have been at the scene, himself engaging in the activity; (2) the respondent may impute his own qualities to his friends; (3) the respondent may impute friendship to people like himself; (4) the respondent's friends may have told him about delinquencies he did not himself witness; or (5) the respondent may have heard about his friend's delinquencies from people who witnessed or heard about them. If "delinquency of peers" is really "delinquency of respondent" (see points 1, 2, and 3), the causal-order question is hardly resolved by this research. If "delinquency of peers" is really hearsay or rumor (points 4 and 5), the value of the measure is obviously suspect (and is again contaminated by the characteristics of the respondent).

The Theory Applied to Peer-Group Findings

People who lack self-control tend to dislike settings that require discipline, supervision, or other constraints on their behavior; such settings include school, work, and, for that matter, home. These people therefore tend to gravitate to "the street" or, at least in adolescence, to the same-sex peer group. Yet individuals with low self-control do not tend to make good friends. They are unreliable, untrustworthy, selfish, and thoughtless. They may, however, be fun to be with; they are certainly more risk-taking, adventuresome, and reckless than their counterparts. It follows that self-control is a major factor in determining membership in adolescent peer groups and in determining the quality of relations among the members of such groups. We would expect those children who devote considerable time to a peer group to be more likely to be delinquent. We would also expect those children with close friendship ties within a peer group to be less likely to be delinquent.

Put another way, adventuresome and reckless children who have difficulty making and keeping friends tend to end up in the company of one another, creating groups made up of individuals who tend to lack self-control. The individuals in such groups will therefore tend to be delinquent, as will the group itself.

This view appears to fly in the face of the widely reported "peer pressure" phenomenon, where adolescents are heavily influenced by the wishes and expectations of their friends, often in a direction contrary to their own inclinations (or to the desires of their parents). However, the evidence also flies in the face of this interpretation; for example, adolescents who commit delinquent acts show less rather than more inclination to live up to the expectations of their peers. In matters of fashion in dress, speech, and music, they appear to be generally unfashionable or to take peer fashions to such extremes that they become objects of derision rather than admiration. (If the current fashion calls for short hair, they will tend to shave their heads; if long hair is in style, they will wear very long hair; and so on.) In these matters, then, delinquents do not appear ordinarily concerned about the expectations and approval of others. Concern for the opinion of peers ("peer pressure"), it turns out, promotes conformity; adolescents who care what other adolescents think of them in terms of their choice of dress, speech, and music are less rather than more likely to be delinquent.

Delinquency Is a Group Phenomenon

Sociological researchers (e.g., Erickson and Jensen 1977; Zimring 1981; Reiss 1988) frequently argue that delinquency appears to be more common among adolescents because they tend to commit their delinquencies in groups. Adolescents do tend to commit delinquent acts in the company of others. This fact is traditionally taken as consistent with a group-support hypothesis and inconsistent with a control perspective. The delinquent commits delinquent acts because he is in a gang; breaking up the gang would therefore reduce the likelihood of delinquent acts.

The theory advanced here is compatible with the idea that some criminal acts are facilitated by group membership or a group context. Facilitation is another word for reduction of difficulty, for the "ease" with which an act can be performed. Adolescents clearly use groups to facilitate acts that would be too difficult or dangerous to do alone (such as robbery), but this does not mean that they *learn* lack of self-control in such groups. On the contrary, participation in such groups is itself indicative of a lack of self-control, of unconcern for long-range goals or benefits. After all, the delinquent group is characterized by weak rather than strong friendship ties, and it has no organizational duties or organized purpose (such as athletic teams or hobby groups). The very existence of such groups is therefore problematic: they clearly do not have the properties ascribed to them by traditional gang theories. On the contrary, they are short-lived, unstable, unorganized collectivities whose members have little regard for one another (Yablonsky 1962; Short and Strodtbeck 1965; Suttles 1968).[1]

The School

If one asks an ordinary citizen, a probation officer, or a prison counselor which American institution is most responsible for crime and delinquency, he or she will typically answer "the family." If, on the other hand, one asks a delinquency theorist or researcher which American institution is most responsible, he or she will usually reply "the school." This perception follows from the major theories of delinquency and from the dominant research traditions of the field.

Perhaps the first theory to implicate the school (and the theory that remains most concerned with what happens there) was labeling theory. The labeling theorist starts with the assumption that differences between individuals in the likelihood that they will commit criminal acts are created by social reactions to morally neutral behavior. Thus, in the first explicit, full-scale labeling theory of delinquency, Frank Tannenbaum (1938) found the beginning of delinquency in the reaction of parents, teachers, and other adult authorities to children who for some good reason do not like school. The child who does not like school does not do well in that setting and is further punished by his participation in it. This leads to truancy, which was, to Tannenbaum

---

[1] The group context of much adolescent behavior probably inflates the number of delinquents relative to the number of delinquent acts committed. For example, if one member of a group spray paints a car or throws a brick through a window, each member of the group may be thought of as having committed the act and indeed all of them may be recorded as having done so. This problem is thought to affect estimates of the age distribution of crime by making it appear that young people commit more offenses than they actually do. However, as is often the case, this methodological "adjustment" is so slight that it has little impact on the age distribution of crime. Differences among offenders in subsequent offending are also unaffected by this adjustment.

(and many others), "the kindergarten of delinquency"—not because the child learns delinquency there but because active dislike of school shown by truancy is reacted to by adult authorities as positive evidence of character deficiency. This reaction is then internalized by the child, who defines himself (after subsequent automatic exposure to the criminal justice system) as delinquent. His future behavior is then shaped by this definition of the self as delinquent or criminal.

According to modern labeling theory, the school causes delinquency by differentiating among students on the basis of presumed differences in academic ability: "The school assumes that students differ in academic ability, that some will succeed and some will fail." These assumptions "are the major foundation upon which school careers and identities are structured, maintained, and perpetuated" (Kelly 1982).

The major focus of the labeling theorist's attention within the school was, until recently, the tracking system. In the days before *Pygmalion in the Classroom* (Rosenthal and Jacobson 1968), which purported to show the ill effects on student performance of low teacher expectations, American schools often tracked students—that is, divided them into equal-ability groupings with such names as college preparatory, vocational, clerical, and technical. Today such groupings are routinely criticized in the academic community, and they tend therefore to be hidden behind euphemistic labels (such as color codes: red, green, bronze, etc.) by teachers who must confront individual differences in academic skills and behavior. To the extent that the practice of ability grouping persists in the school system, it remains possible for the labeling theorist to use it to explain delinquency. To the extent that the practice of ability grouping has been discarded or successfully disguised, the delinquency causation mechanism relied on by labeling theories is no longer operable. However, some labeling theorists argue that the practice of assigning different grades to students is itself a labeling device sufficient to create a delinquent self-image.

Unfortunately for labeling theory, the empirical evidence overwhelmingly contradicts its assumptions and predictions. Whereas labeling theory assumes that the school is the principal cause of behavioral differences, the evidence shows that relevant behavioral differences are clearly established prior to the assignment of the labels identified by labeling theorists. Whereas labeling theory assumes the application of labels independent of behavioral differences, the evidence shows that such labels are highly influenced by actual behavior differences (Gove 1980).

In fact, however, research is not necessary to show the inadequacy of a labeling theory of crime or criminality. According to that theory, the offender acts to fulfill the requirements of a role, a set of expectations others have for his behavior. Although labeling theorists also define themselves as "role" theorists, they are largely silent on what the role of "criminal" entails. Such silence is perfectly predictable, for whatever the content of socially defined roles, they are inconsistent with any meaningful definition of a "crime." Roles are sets of obligations or expectations that require, at a minimum, acting without regard to direct or immediate personal advantage. Crimes, in contrast, involve acting without regard to long-term commitments, without regard to consistency with past behavior, and without regard to the "expectations" of others. (Once again, a theory has been betrayed by the assumption that crime is analogous to an occupation, a career, or an organized way of life.)

But the theoretical tradition that has placed the greatest emphasis on the school is strain theory from sociology. Cloward and Ohlin (1960) make the American educational system responsible for the high rate of delinquency among young, lower-class urban males. At some point, presumably just prior to mid-adolescence, such people evaluate their expectations for success in the American educational-occupational structure and realize that their chances for success through legitimate avenues are remote. Still desiring success, these frustrated young males turn to illegitimate avenues to achieve their goals. Although Merton (1938) first described this process, the emphasis on education as a means to success is stressed most heavily by Cloward and Ohlin and by Cohen (1955).

In Cohen's version of strain theory, the lower-class child is inadequately prepared to meet the demands imposed by the middle-class school. The middle class values ambition, individual responsibility, self-denial, rationality, delay of gratification, industry, manners, control of aggression, wholesome recreation, and respect for property. According to Cohen, the lower class does not have these values and does not attempt to instill them in their young. (If Cohen is correct, the lower class is, in our theory, criminal. We do not think Cohen is correct.) In order to function in an orderly manner, the school insists on adherence to middle-class values by students. Confronted with a system they are unprepared to deal with, yet remaining sensitive to the opinion of middle-class teachers and children, the lower-class child suffers considerable frustration. In an effort to relieve this frustration (strain), lower-class boys seek out others similarly frustrated and, in a group context, redefine the bases of status, turning the middle-class value system upside down.

The strain theorist accepts individual differences in academic competence or class differences in "access" to education and uses these differences to generate motivation to delinquency by juxtaposing them with "universal" desires for affection or achievement. The lower-class boy wants status he cannot attain by conforming. He therefore commits criminal acts to achieve the status he so ardently desires.

This strain "image" of crime could not be farther from the classical image. In the classical image, crime is its own (immediate) reward. It is not used for long-term or indirect gratification. Unfortunately for the strain theories of crime, criminal acts continue to conform to the classical image: they do not provide esteem or status to the perpetrator, they do not provide material goods or material success beyond the bounds of the moment, and they do not solve complex or underlying "psychological" conflicts.

Consistent with the incompatibility of the strain argument with the nature of crime, the strain theory mispredicts the characteristics of offenders. Strain theory predicts that offenders will have high long-term aspirations and low long-term expectations, but the data consistently prove otherwise. Whenever delinquency researchers have sought to measure long-term aspirations, they discover that people committing criminal acts tend to have lower aspirations than others. Researchers also find that expectations for future success tend to be unrealistically high among offenders, rather than extremely low as the strain theory predicts. In short, the disjunction between aspirations and expectations—the critical causal variable of the strain model—has no empirical support (see Hirschi 1969: 162–86; Kornhauser 1978; Elliott, Huizinga, and Ageton 1985).

On inspection, it turns out that both the labeling and the strain theories are constructed from the same empirical material. Offenders do not do well in school. They do not like school. They tend to be truant and to drop out at an early age. As a result, virtually every "school" variable correlates strongly with crime and delinquency.

According to our theory, the school correlations stem from the connections between the school's system of rewards and restraints and the individual's abilities and level of self-control. The school restrains conduct in several ways: it requires young people to be at a certain place at a certain time; it requires them to do things when they are not under its direct surveillance; and it requires young people to be quiet, physically inactive, and attentive, often for long periods of time. At the same time, the school rewards punctuality, the completion of homework, and proper deportment; it also rewards demonstrations of academic competence, providing in return affection from teachers, advancement within the system, and ultimately educational certification and occupational success. All of these punishments and rewards presuppose the existence of a family capable of recognizing and implementing them; that is, the school will have trouble rewarding or punishing children whose families do not attend to the school's requirements.

The school, in other words, is a sanctioning system implicated in the socialization of children. The sanctions available to the school do not affect the behavior of all children equally. In fact, those who do not do well in school will be little restrained by the long-term or potential rewards the school offers, and those with little self-control will have difficulty satisfying the academic and deportment requirements of the school in return for its long-term benefits. The result, of course, is that delinquents will tend to avoid and eventually to leave school in favor of less restricted environments.

The Job

Recent research has undercut the long-held view that unemployment leads directly to crime and that employment insulates against or prevents crime (e.g., Berk, Lenihan, and Rossi 1980; Orsagh and Witte 1981; Zeisel 1982; Freeman 1983). However, the controversy about the connection between unemployment and crime continues, fueled by a variety of theoretical expectations that there should be a negative correlation between employment and crime. There are many reasons for expecting an unemployment-crime relation. First, jobs take time and energy. If the individual is working, he cannot be committing criminal acts. Often referred to as the "idle hands are the devil's workshop" theory, this view suggests that crime and work make incompatible demands on resources of time and energy. Second, jobs provide money and thus reduce the need to commit crime. If material needs are satisfied legitimately, there is no need to steal. Third, jobs provide status and self-esteem, thus obviating the need to achieve them through illegal means. Fourth, crime jeopardizes one's ability to keep a job, a cost not faced by the unemployed. Fifth, jobs build character, teaching the individual punctuality, responsibility, and self-denial.

As a consequence, all theories of crime are comfortable with the expectation of a crime-unemployment relation. Alas, this expectation betrays the fact that no currently popular theory of criminal behavior has attended simultaneously to the nature of crime and its implications for the character of the offender.

It turns out that, from our theoretical perspective, there is little reason to expect employment to be related to crime independent of the character of the offender. First, crime is not a full-time job. In fact, crimes by definition take little in the way of time or energy. (If they did take time and energy, they would not be attractive to offenders. Thus crimes that take much in the way of planning and effort are extremely rare.) As a result, a job and crime can easily simultaneously characterize the same individual. Second, crimes are not a good source of stable income. In fact, they typically provide little in the way of direct monetary compensation and therefore cannot serve as an alternative to a job in the sense of providing food, shelter, and other necessities. (Drug dealers, numbers runners, and the like are often cited as exceptions to these principles. Analysis of these "occupations" reveals, however, that they are short-lived, low-income, risky, and dangerous, and therefore they practically presuppose the existence of more durable sources of income [Reuter 1983].) Third, crimes are not good sources of status or self-esteem. On the contrary, crimes are condemned by virtually everyone, often even by those committing them (Matza 1964).

The empirical relationship between unemployment and crime is too small to be of theoretical import. Apparently, the relation that exists tends to be in the wrong direction. When researchers ask individuals to report their employment status and their delinquent activities, it turns out that those who work outside the home for pay are more rather than less likely to report delinquent acts (Hirschi 1969; West and Farrington 1977). Apparently, money allows people to buy drugs, cigarettes, and alcohol and to indulge otherwise the desires of the moment.

One of the best tests of the employment-crime hypothesis is provided by a natural experiment reported by Glueck and Glueck (1968). At the outbreak of World War II, the Gluecks had identified 500 delinquents and a matched sample of 500 nondelinquents in the Boston area. The Gluecks maintained record contact with this sample through the war years, thus establishing the nature of their employment records with the military forces. In a sense, World War II provided a full-employment treatment program available to all, delinquent and nondelinquent.

The findings are revealing. As compared with nondelinquents, delinquents were much more likely (ten times, in fact) to be found unemployable by the armed services because of "psychiatric impairment" or "moral unfitness." They held military jobs for shorter periods of time (a quarter of the delinquents, as compared with a twelfth of the nondelinquents, lasted less than a year), were much more likely to be "brought up on charges" during their period of military service, and were much more likely to desert or be absent without leave. Finally, delinquents were nearly eight times as likely as nondelinquents to be dishonorably discharged.

Put in other terms, when "full employment" was offered to all young men in the United States, delinquents were less likely to be qualified, were less likely to remain on the job, were more likely to be absent without an excuse, were more likely to quit without telling the boss, and were more likely to be fired for misbehavior on the job. Apparently, then, self-control affects the probability that one will have certain institutional experiences and affects the quality of those experiences as well.

Indeed, in our view, the most significant employment-crime fact is the tendency for people who commit crime to have unstable job profiles—that is, to have difficulty finding jobs and keeping them. The instability of offenders' careers in the legitimate labor market is consistent with the absence of persistence in most ordinary obligations, whether they be interpersonal or school- or job-related. People with low self-control will have difficulty meeting the obligations of structured employment, just as they have difficulty meeting the obligations of school and family. (Moreover, "good" jobs and "meaningful" work will not be the answer, since they too will involve unacceptable restraints.)

Marriage and Family

Conventional wisdom about crime is heavily influenced by the incompatibility of the idea of entrance into a conventional role and the idea of continuation in a criminal career. (Modern defenders of the Gluecks' [1930] career terminology include Blumstein and Cohen [1987].) There is something inconsistent with the idea of being a husband and a father and, at the same time, being engaged in a criminal career. It therefore seems to follow that as men become husbands and fathers they are likely to give up their careers in crime, thus producing a negative causal relation between marriage and crime and an additional negative causal relation between parenthood and crime. David Farrington, Lloyd Ohlin, and James Wilson report complex findings apparently consistent with this view:

Farrington (1986[b]) reported that if a child, up to age 10, had parents who had been convicted, this was one of the best predictors of that child offending at ages 14 through 16 and 17 through 20, but did not predict offending at ages 10 through 13. West (1982) reported that if a delinquent married between ages 18 and 21, marriage had no effect on offending between these ages, while marriage between 21 and 24 (to a noncriminal woman) led to a decrease in offending between these ages. [1986: 27]

Such findings are, in interesting ways, contradictory. They suggest that the criminality of the parent is transmitted to the child (parental convictions predict child criminality). They also suggest, however, that getting married and, presumably, having children are sufficient to suppress the criminality of the parent. To the extent that criminality is so suppressed, the question is how it can be transmitted to those suppressing it.[2]

Conceptual issues aside, it turns out that it is difficult to show a "marriage" or "parenthood" effect on crime. The Farrington et al. "findings" are unpersuasive. Both come from the West (1982) and Farrington (1986b) longitudinal studies of working-class boys in inner-city London. Although it is hard to accept, as do Farrington et al., that the effect of parental criminality ebbs and flows from year to year and produces its effects only after a lag of four to ten years, the general correlation they report is in the *same direction* in all age categories and is consistent with the results of other research (e.g., Glueck and Glueck 1950: 101; McCord and McCord 1959: 93). In fact, Rolf Loeber and Magda Stouthamer-Loeber (1986: 71) report a large number of studies showing a relation between measures of parental criminality and the delinquency of their children. (And, of course, see our discussion of parental transmission in Chapter 5.)

The reported effect of marriage is, in contrast, doubtful. Farrington et al. fail to consider the fact that subjects are not randomly assigned to marital statuses nor to delinquent and nondelinquent wives. On the contrary, it is much more plausible to believe (and there is much evidence to support it) that the subjects and their potential spouses chose each other on the basis of compatible interests, behavior, and lifestyle. As a result, selection of a "nondelinquent" wife is more likely among men whose measured delinquency overstates their delinquent tendencies; that is, men who marry nondelinquent women

---

[2]If parental criminality predicts criminality in the child whereas marriage suppresses its manifestation, the only mechanism of transmission available to Farrington, Ohlin, and Wilson would appear to be genetic. Of course, as we will show, this is only one of the several problems that stem from reporting complex empirical anomalies as though they qualified as "findings."

would be expected to be less delinquent in the follow-up period even if they did not marry.

The tendency to believe numbers that apparently show immediate effects of institutional experiences selected by the individual himself (e.g., dropping out of school, taking a job, marrying, or moving from one community to another) is only possible in the absence of a theoretical scheme that allows characteristics of the individual to influence behavior over time. Since the theory we advance sees self-control as a stable individual difference capable of affecting such decisions, the influence of these decisions on subsequent criminal behavior provides a crucial test of our theory vis-à-vis the standard theories of positive criminology.

Conclusions

Criminologists have long struggled with the problem of separating the effects of individual differences from the effects of situational or structural causes. For the past 50 years, the tendency has been to emphasize situational or structural causes and to deny individual differences. Among researchers who accept the possibility of individual differences—even among those whose work establishes their importance (e.g., West and Farrington)—these differences are not taken into account in assessing the impact of situation and structure. Given the undeniable influence of individual differences on the selection of people into social and institutional arrangements (such as the school, the family, the community, and the work force), it is often easier to use the results of "institutional" or "structural" research as evidence of the effects of individual differences than as evidence of institutional or structural effects. It has been obvious for some time that research capable of isolating institutional or structural effects will be impossible without precise definition and accurate measure of what we call self-control. The only alternative is experimental research in which people are randomly allocated to "natural" institutional experiences. Such research is unlikely. Research that comes close to satisfying the requirements of such experiments—for example, the Glueck and Glueck studies (1968) of the effects of the full employment produced by World War II, and the Berk, Lenihan, and Rossi research (1980) on parolee employment—clearly shows the necessity of taking into account the fact that people do not sort themselves randomly into natural "treatment conditions" before concluding that these natural experiences have had an impact on their behavior.

It is hard to overstate the magnitude of this problem in criminology because of the tendency of people with low self-control to avoid attachment to or involvement in all social institutions—a tendency that produces a negative correlation between institutional experience and delinquency. This gives all institutions credit for negative effects on crime, credit they may not deserve.

Our conceptual scheme provides, we believe, a basis for realistic assessment of institutional effects on crime. For example, the effects of family, school, and friendship patterns are uniformly in the direction of reducing the criminal behavior of those within their sphere of influence. The tendency of people most in need of the restraining influence of family, school, and friendship to be outside of these spheres of influence is a matter of considerable importance. We will return to this topic in the final chapter.

8

Culture and Crime

The problems of cross-national criminology are easily identified: societies differ in what they define as criminal; the popular forms of criminal behavior are not the same from one society to another; and crime-control institutions take markedly different shapes across societies. Moreover, differences in institutional arrangements are often confounded with the definition of crime and the level of criminal activity such that we cannot know whether differences in crime are due to causal factors or to political or cultural factors.

Cross-cultural criminology thus reflects in intensified form the problems of criminology as a whole, a discipline with no clear conception of the phenomenon it wishes to explain. The discipline is therefore beset by endless typologizing of its dependent and independent variables, preoccupied with admittedly minor causes or correlates of crime, and at the mercy of political pressures and the demands of its so-called parent disciplines.

To begin to solve such problems, we must try to understand how they arose. To do this, we must return to the beginnings of scientific criminology. As we pointed out in previous chapters, the troubles of criminology can be traced to the wholesale repudiation of the classical model by the positivists. A summary of their position will be useful here.

The Positivistic Conception of Crime

The classical school defined crime as the use of force or fraud in the service of self-interest. Obviously, self-interested acts of force or fraud are possible everywhere, and it is therefore safe to say that, before positivism came along, crime and criminology were truly and automatically transcultural.

Positivists changed all this. They did so in two ways. First, they argued that crime was not the product of self-interested choice but the product of forces or causes operating in the actor's environment. If crime originates in the environment rather than within the actor, it becomes the product of motives that may vary from time to time and from place to place. With such variability in its causes and consequences, crime could certainly no longer be defined as the pursuit of universally desired ends by the exercise of force or fraud. Second, positivists accepted the state's operational definition of crime (as a violation of law) and of the criminal (as a person in violation of the law). Since laws vary from state to state, criminals also vary from state to state, and the positivistic approach to cross-cultural criminology could only assume that the formal and operational definition of its dependent variable in fact varies from culture to culture. (The typological solution is once again seen to be inherent in the logic of positivism.)

With rejection of the classical definition of crime, positive criminology thus rejected the universalistic conception of its subject matter. Although it retained the generic term, "crime," positivism assumed that because crime was a product of its causes, disciplines should be allowed to define it as they saw fit, that indeed every theory of crime should be free to define crime to suit its own purposes. As a result, crime became, in principle, whatever particular disciplines wanted it to be. Thus some psychological positivists study antisocial personalities (Robins 1966), and others study aggression (Bandura 1973). Some sociological positivists define crime as instrumental behavior directed toward achievement of culturally valued goals (Merton 1938), and others define it as adherence to norms specific to narrow subcultures (Wolfgang and Ferracuti 1967). Economic positivists sometimes view crime as behavior subject to market forces governing entry and exit to all occupations, and at other times they view it simply as the output of the criminal justice system (Becker 1974).

Of course, there are standards by which definitions of crime are judged. Positivists believe that theories should be simple, clear, and testable, that they should strive for broad scope or universality. Although such standards limit the complexity and variety of definitions of crime, strong forces work in the other direction. (And of course the antipositivists deny the validity of the search for parsimonious explanations, arguing that this search is contrary to the nature of society and culture [e.g., Greenberg 1981; Beirne 1983].)

One source of complexity is the positivist principle that one does not ask "What is crime?" but rather "What are the causes of crime?" If we seek the causes of crime before we seek its definition, then the definition of crime is determined by the causes we ascribe to it. Causes are the property of disciplines, and the definition of crime is therefore discipline-specific, depending on the intellectual history and current social affiliations of those studying it. To the sociologist, crime is social behavior. To the psychologist, crime is an individual trait. To the biologist, crime is the manifestation of an inherited characteristic. To the economist, crime is rational behavior. And the list goes on as we add disciplines or identify subfields within them.

Putting the definition of crime under the control of individual researchers makes positivistic criminology vulnerable to the argument that any definition or division of crime is *potentially* useful or meaningful. Thus, when it is said that we need one criminology for juveniles and another for adults, one criminology for boys and another for girls, one criminology for street crimes and another for white-collar crimes, one criminology for murder and another for robbery, and one criminology for Chicago and another for Taipei, then positive criminology has a hard time saying otherwise.

A criminology that cannot control or define its own dependent variable will of course be even weaker in controlling its independent variables, and positive criminology is thus vulnerable to the suggestion that almost everything, from too much chocolate to too little religion, is a cause of crime. If we multiply the number of possible dependent variables by the number of possible independent variables, we have a science so complex that it defies description and so disorganized that it invites ridicule.

For example, suppose we were to come across the following finding: "In the United States, an aggregate increase in unemployment causes an increase in theft among young adults and a decrease in violence among the elderly." As positivists, we would somehow feel we should accept and deal with this "finding" as though it were a legitimate product of serious scientific research. Indeed, given the state of the field, this finding would have to be accorded status equivalent to that granted all the other facts *produced* by research.

Comparative Criminology

If there is no basis (beyond statistical significance and variance explained) for judging facts about crime within a culture, there is even less basis for generalizing them from one culture to another. Indeed, positivism itself is friendly to the view that facts differ from culture to culture and that generalization from one to another is therefore dangerous (Beirne 1983: 34; Johnson and Barak-Glantz 1983: 7).

Faced with chaos, how does a science-oriented discipline proceed? Obviously, it turns to its model, science, and attempts to do better whatever it is science tells it to do (forgetting that science got it into the predicament in the first place). This solution leads to a focus on research methods, and it seems fair to say that comparative criminology devotes a good deal of attention to this issue (see, e.g., Johnson and Barak-Glantz 1983; Archer and Gartner 1984; Block 1984; Mayhew 1987). Unfortunately, science as method cannot solve the problems of science as substantive theory. Bigger samples, better measures, and better statistical technique cannot make meaningful comparison of things that cannot be compared.

Given the limitations of method solutions to comparative criminology's problems, it can only turn for help to one of its disciplines—to sociology, psychology, biology, or economics. Unfortunately, as we have seen, each discipline believes that its conceptual scheme is peculiarly applicable to crime. Worse, all eventually conclude that cultural variability is a major factor in crime, the very conclusion that cross-cultural criminology seeks to rise above.

This point can be illustrated by the work of Cohen (1955). Cohen developed a theory of gang delinquency based on the following logic: lower-class boys are ill-prepared to do well in school, the principal vehicle for status achievement in American society; the school applies middle-class standards in evaluating the behavior of all boys, and lower-class boys do not measure up; as a consequence, they look to alternative means to achieve status; in the course of this search, they encounter other boys with similar problems, and a group solution, the delinquent gang, emerges.

The truth of Cohen's theory as an explanation of American delinquency is problematic. Its applicability to other cultures is, however, even more problematic. Not all cultures have universal compulsory schooling; not all cultures share the achievement values Cohen ascribes to American society; and, at least in some cultures, delinquency does not seem to satisfy the motives Cohen ascribes to it (DeFleur 1970). Any attempt to modify the theory to make it compatible with a different culture must alter the means by which boys achieve status, the ends they seek, or the definition of delinquency itself. Cultural imbalance theories such as Cohen's thus suggest that each and every culture may require its own theory of delinquency, a condition antithetical to a cross-national criminology. If this is true for cultural imbalance theories, it is even more true for so-called cultural deviance theories, theories that see delinquency as a product of positive forces unique to particular cultures and their relations with other systems (Wolfgang and Ferracuti 1967).

Theories that focus on the process of learning criminal behavior rather than on structure or culture may be more general, but they too seem to run into trouble when taken from one culture to another. For example, Wilson and Herrnstein (1985) present a theory derived from general psychological learning theories. This theory points to individual differences in impulsiveness and ability to learn, and it connects these differences to the principle that "the larger the ratio of the rewards (material and nonmaterial) of noncrime to the rewards (material and nonmaterial) of crime, the weaker the tendency to commit crimes" (p. 61). Whatever the truth of this theory, it seems unable to deal with the cross-cultural questions its authors themselves raise: "Each country, perhaps even each locality, places its own stamp on crime as history, culture, and current circumstances act on the individual differences that bear on criminal behavior" (p. 458).

In the end, then, the major disciplines conclude that the conceptual chaos of criminology reflects the natural chaos of a multicultural world. Each therefore concludes that there is no "solution" to criminology's problem, that indeed every culture has its own crime and its unique causes of crime. Ironically, contemporary criminology does not really grant the possibility of analysis or research capable of discovering principles applicable to all cultural settings. As Paul Friday puts it: "Criminologists have been plagued by the inability of the discipline to develop any explanations of criminality that could be considered 'universal'" (1973: 152, as cited in Johnson and Barak-Glantz 1983: 10).

Science typically assumes that proper explanations of phenomena are produced by inductive examination of differences and their correlates. First one determines that, for example, the United States has a higher homicide rate than Japan. Then one locates the cultural (or perhaps structural) differences between Japan and the United States that account for homicide differences. Positivistic explanation normally proceeds in one of two directions. In one, the researcher complicates the configuration of independent variables until it can be said that, were the two cultures alike on these variables, there would be no difference in homicide rates between them. This essentially statistical procedure *could* lead to the conclusion that the causes of homicide in Japan are the same as the causes of homicide in the United States— that is, the homicide rate differs between these cultures only because the ordering or mix of "independent variables" differs between them. We know that it would not, however, lead to this conclusion, but to the contrary conclusion that the causes of homicide are different because their "meaning" differs from one culture to the other. We know, too, that applying the same logic to theft, burglary, robbery, rape, and forgery differences would merely reinforce the idea that "crime" and its causes vary from culture to culture, that a theory capable of dealing with more than one culture is ruled out by the evidence.

The other direction of positivistic explanation attempts to conceptualize the correlates of homicide in the two cultures such that they come under the same "covering laws." Thus if homicide and unemployment are positively correlated in both cultures, one can advance the "law" that "economic deprivation" is a cause of crime that transcends cultural boundaries. This method is more likely to produce the appearance of cross-cultural theory than the statistical modeling approach, but it has problems of its own. For one thing, because the theory starts with empirical correlates of crime, it must conclude with a conception of crime consistent with the meanings it has ascribed to these correlates. Such conceptions of crime are unlikely to travel well from one culture to another. Take, for example, our "economic deprivation" explanation of unemployment. Designed to account for differences in crime rates within a society, it will mispredict crime-rate differences across cultures, suggesting as it does that deprived societies are likely to have higher crime rates than affluent societies.

Interestingly enough, whichever method we use, we usually discover that diverse types of crime and delinquency—such as homicide, rape, robbery, theft, and truancy—appear to have something in common, because they *tend* to have the same correlates and to be explained by the same general principles. Once again, however, positivism seems unable to deal with overlap or redundancy, even when produced by its own methods. It therefore basically repeats itself for each crime, emphasizing minor differences and ignoring substantial similarities.

Application of the Crime and Self-Control Perspective Across Cultures

Since traditional approaches to the problem of cross-cultural criminology have not succeeded and cannot succeed, a new approach is required. Our approach therefore rejects the conventional wisdom of comparative criminology. It assumes instead that cultural variability is *not* important in the causation of crime, that we should look for constancy rather than variability in the definition and causes of crime, and that a single theory of crime can encompass the reality of cross-cultural differences in crime rates. From this it follows directly that a general theory of crime is possible. Let us review briefly the principles of our theory.

The central concept of a theory of crime must be crime itself. We therefore begin with a statement of the nature of crime. We then deduce from the nature of crime the characteristics of people likely to engage in it. At that point, we apply the theory across cultural settings.

Crime

If we want a culture-free theory of crime, we must be careful not to build "culture" into our definition of it. Thus we should not see crime as the achievement of cultural values, whatever these may be. If cultural values underlie crime, and if these values vary from culture to culture, then the meaning of crime will vary from culture to culture. Similarly, we must not define crime in strictly behavioral or legalistic terms. Because the same act (e.g., killing, taking, forcing) may be criminal in some contexts and noncriminal in others, we might then be led to confuse this distinction for an explanation of crime, as subcultural theorists do. (Subcultural theorists assert that people committing criminal acts are guided by "noncriminal" definitions of the behavior.) Likewise, we must define crime such that it includes at least the majority of acts defined as criminal in all societies. If a society defines an act as criminal, our definition should be able to comprehend the basis for that society's definition. Finally, our definition of crime should be derived from a conception of human nature that transcends social groupings (whether within or across societies).

The conception of human nature that satisfies these requirements is found in the classical assumption that human behavior is motivated by the self-interested pursuit of pleasure and avoidance of pain. In this conception, crimes are acts in which force or fraud are used to satisfy self-interest, where self-interest refers to the enhancement of pleasure and the avoidance of pain.[1]

---

[1] It is often argued that general theories of crime are impossible because no particular act is always and everywhere regarded as criminal. The standard example is that willful killing by soldiers during war is not considered criminal. Our conception of crime, which focuses on the self-interested nature of criminal acts, has no difficulty excluding behavior performed in pursuit of collective purposes. (This example illus-

As we have stressed, features of acts that enhance their pleasure or minimize their pain will be implicated in their causation, and should transcend cultures. To be maximally pleasurable, the benefits of acts should be immediate; pleasure is enhanced by the rapidity with which it is obtained. Force and fraud can often produce more immediate results than alternative means; they are therefore obviously useful in the pursuit of self-interest. To be maximally pleasurable, the benefits of acts should be certain; pleasure is enhanced by the certainty with which it can be obtained. Force and fraud can often produce more certain benefits than alternative means, particularly when the benefits sought are immediate and the long-term consequences of the act are of little concern. To be maximally pleasurable, acts should require minimal effort. Force and fraud can often produce benefits with less effort than alternative means, especially when the benefits also have the properties of rapidity and certainty.

Our conception of crime removes the common impediment to cross-national research found in the variation in what nation-states define as criminal. It allows inclusion of entrepreneurialism in a communist society, bid-rigging in a free market economy, truancy in a compulsory education society, and pregnancy in a society with compulsory limits on family size.

Our conception is not embarrassed by large differences in crime rates across societies, but it does not take these rate differences as the sole object of etiological interest, nor does it deny the possibility that a single cause or single set of causes is responsible for the crime rates in all societies. It does assume that the individual's pursuit of self-interest by force or fraud is a problem for all societies, a problem they must deal with if they are to remain true to their own values.

Thus the party worker who trades on the black market, the street mugger who assaults a stranger with a gun, the stockbroker who engages in insider trading, the wife who has love affairs, and the husband who kills his wife in a fit of passion share the pursuit of personal advantage unfettered by concern for long-term interests. They also share membership in societies that try to remind them of their long-term interests (and the interests of others) by invoking the penalties of the law.

Our conception frees societies to define crime as they see fit, but in our view this freedom poses little danger to the theory. Although the ability to "define crime" gives societies the power to criminalize acts

---

trates the tendency of the positivist perspective to begin with a legalistic definition of crime and then to dispute its value by locating cases that meet a behavioral rather than a legalistic criterion.)

that do not produce short-term individual benefits, such laws would be rarely violated or enforced. What, then, accounts for variation across societies in the content and form of law violations and the frequency with which they occur? In our theory, crimes have minimal elements over and above their benefits to the individual: for example, they require goods, services, victims, and opportunity, elements that do vary from time to time and place to place and therefore do much to account for cross-national differences in the rate at which crimes are committed.

Even short-term benefit presupposes opportunity to enjoy the proceeds of crime, and societies differ greatly in the extent to which they provide such opportunity. For example, in societies with few automobiles, auto theft may be doubly rare because it is hard to use or store a stolen vehicle. In societies in which many people share the same living quarters and possess little material wealth, the sudden possession of valuable goods is likely to attract attention. A major factor affecting cross-cultural crime rates is of course the absolute quantity of goods or people available for theft or victimization. Developing countries may simply lack the material wealth to sustain a high rate of property crime, irrespective of the proclivities or tendencies of their populations.

Criminality

As we have stressed, a conception of criminality (low self-control) follows from a conception of crime. It is the tendency of individuals to pursue short-term gratification without consideration of the long-term consequences of their acts. People with this tendency will appear to be impulsive and risk-taking; they will be relatively indifferent to the interests of others and relatively unconcerned about delayed punishment, whatever its source. Because crime transcends national boundaries, criminality does the same.

These individual differences in self-control are established early in life (before differences in criminal behavior, however the state defines it, are possible) and are reasonably stable thereafter. Such stability has been documented in several regions, such as England (West and Farrington 1977), Scandinavia (Olweus 1979), and the United States (Glueck and Glueck 1968).

Fortunately, again, crimes require more than individual tendencies for their performance. They also require goods, victims, physical abilities, and the absence of threats of immediate punishment. Thus tendencies conducive to crime do not *require* crime for their satisfaction.

Many noncriminal acts provide the benefits of crime, such as gambling, having sex, drinking alcohol, smoking cigarettes, and quitting a job. Evidence that these acts and criminal acts are equivalent is provided by the relatively strong positive correlations among them. These positive correlations suggest that "pleasures" do not substitute for one another but tend to come together in bundles or clusters. We would guess, then, that crime cannot be prevented by supplying potential offenders with crime-equivalent pleasures, nor for that matter by denying them such substitute pleasures.

Cross-Cultural Correlates of Crime

So far as we can determine, the important correlates of crime do not vary across cultures. (The data are far from complete with respect to most correlates, and some, such as race-ethnicity, are insuffiently variable within societies to allow confident conclusions. One reason for the lack of good data is the assumption that the correlates of crime *should* vary from culture to culture, an assumption not justified by current evidence.) For example, gender differences are remarkably persistent from society to society, with men greatly overrepresented in the crime statistics of all societies for which data are available (see the data for Japan, Nigeria, Hungary, Poland, Britain, Norway, Finland, the Netherlands, and the United States presented in Adler 1981.) Perhaps even more important, especially for researchers interested in juvenile delinquency, age differences are everywhere the same, with crimes peaking in late adolescence or early adulthood and declining rapidly thereafter (see Chapter 6; see also Ong 1986). Within all societies, family stability appears to be negatively correlated with crime, both at the individual and at the aggregate levels (Rosenquist and Megargee 1969; Toby 1979a; Riley and Shaw 1985). The higher crime rate in urban as opposed to rural areas seems universal, as does the predominance of property crimes among offenses. And cross-cultural rankings of offense seriousness show considerable agreement from one culture to another (Newman 1976).

Individual-level correlates of delinquency that appear everywhere include sexual precocity, limited scholastic aptitude, and drug use (including alcohol and tobacco). The available data are thus consistent with attempts to construct a general—that is, cross-cultural—theory of crime and delinquency, a theory that sees crime as short-sighted pursuit of self-interest and sees criminality as the relative absence of the self-control required to produce concern for the long-term consequences of one's acts.

Self-control is presumably a product of socialization and the current circumstances of life. Individuals in stable families are more likely to be socialized to take into account the long-term consequences of their acts, and they are more likely to suffer from failing to do so. Individuals with limited scholastic aptitude are less likely to have favorable long-term prospects, and their behavior is therefore less likely to be governed by them. In our conception, drugs, tobacco, and alcohol serve more as indicators of limited self-control than as causes of crime, but they can, on occasion, produce criminal acts by reducing the time frame of the user to the immediate situation. With limited time and space horizons, the individual is vulnerable to spur-of-the-moment impulses, impulses that are implicated everywhere in the commission of criminal acts.

Conclusions

In our view, the first goal of cross-national research on crime and delinquency should be to construct two lists of the correlates of crime and self-control: those that are culture-dependent and those that are not. The first list should consist of crime or opportunity variables, variables that affect the ease with which events can occur rather than those that reflect the proclivities of individuals. The second list should consist of the causes and consequences of low self-control, the factors that make individuals more or less willing to risk their long-term futures for the pleasures of the moment. Of course, the construction of such lists requires a general theory of crime. Absent such a theory, cross-national research has literally not known what it was looking for, and its contributions have rightfully been more or less ignored.

9

White-Collar Crime

Nothing in criminology has been more secure than the idea of white-collar crime. No textbook, it seems, is complete without a chapter or set of chapters on the topic. No conference is organized without panels devoted to recent developments in theory and research about crime in the suites. No criminal justice curriculum is constructed without a course on some variant on the theme that much crime is committed by the advantaged class, especially by people in positions of economic power. In fact, no topic in criminology can be discussed without the specter of white-collar crime hanging over it. Theories are constantly tested on the ability of their ideas to comprehend this important portion of the total crime picture. Researchers are regularly faced with the unpleasant fact that the correlates of "crime" they uncover may well be treated as ridiculous examples of the failure of unenlightened criminologists to consider the implications of white-collar crime for traditional work in the area. Outside academia, the notion of white-collar crime has had even more substantial impact; for example, it has fueled prosecutorial efforts directed at white-collar offenders, the creation of regulatory agencies, and even redirection of the efforts of the FBI (Geis and Meier 1977: 2).

Now that white-collar crime is securely established as an important area of inquiry for criminology, and now that much research and thinking have gone into it, the costs and benefits of the idea can be more clearly assessed. In this chapter we apply our general theory to white-collar crime. The thesis of the chapter is that the distinction between white-collar crime and crime in general should be viewed in the same way as distinctions between any particular type of crime and crime in general; that is, the usefulness of the distinction for some purposes has been illegitimately generalized to areas where it is inapplicable and therefore inappropriate. As we have shown, the utility of crime-specific analyses for policy purposes (see, e.g., Cornish and Clarke 1986) is not evidence of the utility of the same distinction for etiological or research purposes. For example, the fact that vandalism may be reduced by banning the sale of paint in aerosol cans cannot be translated to mean that vandals and muggers are produced by different causes. By the same token, the desire to control white-collar criminals should not be confused with the conclusion that they are products of unique causal processes. In fact, our general theory of crime accounts for the frequency and distribution of white-collar crime in the same way as it accounts for the frequency and distribution of all other forms of crime, including rape, vandalism, and simple assault. Given the large amount of literature based on the contrary assumption that white-collar crime poses unique theoretical problems, several conceptual issues must be resolved before we proceed to demonstrate our point.

The Origins of the Concept of White Collar Crime

In classical theory, it was assumed that resort to force or fraud was an ever-present potential in human affairs. Both force and fraud were seen as means of pursuing self-interest, and the distinction between the two was not taken to be of theoretical interest. When the classical school gave way to the positivists, with their assumption that crime is evidence of biological, psychological, or social pathology, force and fraud were no longer assumed to be natural, and some special motive or compulsion was required to explain their use. The major social source of such compulsion was, from the beginning, low social class, poverty, or inequality. This conception explained the high rate of crime among the poor (and suggested that it was really the fault of the rich and powerful). Unfortunately for some political purposes, it also assumed that the poor really did have a high rate of crime as compared to the rich and powerful, who were relatively crime-free.

In this context, invention of the concept of white-collar crime had two desirable consequences: it falsified poverty-pathology theory, and it revealed the criminality of the privileged classes and their impunity to the law.

Those sociological theories that continued to accept the class-poverty-inequality model (e.g., Merton 1938; Cloward and Ohlin 1960; Blau and Blau 1982) were able to do so only by remaining essentially silent on the white-collar crime issue. Those sociological theories that accepted the idea of white-collar crime were forced to move in one of two directions: toward a general theory that denied "pathological" causes (e.g., differential association) or toward theories tailored to particular crimes or types of crime (see, e.g., Bloch and Geis 1970; Clinard and Quinney 1973; Gibbons 1973).

The current popularity of the white-collar-crime concept attests as much to its political attractiveness as to its scientific value (Geis and Goff 1983; Braithwaite 1985: 1). In fact, the major consequence of introducing the idea of white-collar crime has been to complicate the positivistic conception of its dependent variable and to deny the results of positivistic research that does not attend to the idea that crime and its causes are somehow class-specific.

The Existing Theory of White-Collar Crime

A major problem and neglected issue among those who study white-collar crime is to determine the claims or assertions implicit in the concept. On its face, the term assumes that white-collar crimes are indeed crimes, that people of high social standing commit real crimes, that the crimes they commit differ from common crimes, that the causes of their law-breaking differ from those affecting other people, and that the official response to white-collar crime is different from the official response to common crime. (Not obvious from the term itself, but nonetheless commonly encountered in connection with it, is the view that white-collar crime is actually more serious, more dangerous, or more detrimental to social or civic values than is ordinary crime [Sutherland 1983; Will 1987].)

At first glance, these assertions do not seem particularly problematic or unreasonable. On reflection, however, it turns out that the concept of "church crime" would permit the same conclusions. The crimes committed by church leaders are undoubtedly real or true crimes, but they differ from nonchurch crimes (i.e., theft of nontaxable contributions is only possible in a nonprofit organization); the reasons for their crimes may be particular to their culture or economic situation; and, of course, the legal system may respond more leniently or severely to church crime than to crime in other systems.

So, what appears to be a straightforward or useful concept turns out to be a potential source of considerable complexity. If we did not know that the concept of "white-collar crime" arose as a reaction to the idea that crime is concentrated in the lower class, there would be nothing to distinguish it from other ways of reminding us that crime may be found in all groups, even in the low-rate categories of its causes (e.g., intact-home crime; valedictorian crime; female crime; elderly crime; small-town crime). The question is: Does the concept of white-collar crime have virtues or uses that distinguish it from the countless alternative ways of classifying crimes by the characteristics of their perpetrators? The search for such virtues or uses of white-collar crime may be facilitated by considering its assumptions one at a time.

Is White-Collar Crime Truly Crime?

The question of whether white-collar offending is part of the domain of criminology could not have arisen in classical theory, which did not attend to the characteristics of the offender, to the form of the crime, or to the likelihood that the crime would be met with legal sanction. Since crimes were attempts to gain personal advantage by force or fraud, they could obviously be committed by the rich and powerful and they could clearly be committed without punishment by the state.

Positive criminology made the concept of crime problematic in all respects. Essentially, offenders were people unable to learn civilized behavior, or people compelled to misbehave by forces over which they had little control. As a result, the law and its punishments were themselves concepts or institutions at odds with scientific knowledge of human behavior. In this sense, the concept of white-collar crime is again a reaction against positivism, an assertion that something must be wrong with a worldview that denies the possibility of the obvious: the fact that intelligent, powerful people use force and fraud to secure their own ends.

The evidence, it seems to us, clearly supports this element of white-collar theorizing. There is no good reason to restrict the notion of crime to the lower classes (cf. Merton 1938; Cloward and Ohlin 1960; Blau and Blau 1982). On the contrary, the evidence suggests that, when it comes to the use of force and fraud, crime is possible at all social levels, and white-collar crime is clearly crime. In fact, we would suggest that any theory of crime making claim to generality should apply without difficulty to the crimes of the rich and powerful, crimes committed in the course of an occupation, and crimes in which a position of power, influence, or trust is used for the purpose of individual or organizational gain (Reiss and Biderman 1980: 4).

Do People of High Standing Commit Crimes?

According to those promoting it, a major value of the concept of white-collar crime is that it reminds us that actual crime is not restricted to the lower class: "This study has attempted to . . . present evidence that persons of the upper socioeconomic class commit many crimes. . . . [This objective] has been realized in that a sample of large corporations is found to have violated laws with great frequency" (Sutherland 1983: 264).

So, white-collar crime truly is crime, and white-collar crime does indeed occur. Some doctors commit murder, and doctors sometimes cheat on Medicare (Geis, Pontell, and Jesilow 1987); lawyers have been known to misuse funds entrusted to them by their clients; business executives sometimes engage in bid-rigging; labor union executives sometimes embezzle funds from pension plans; and manufacturers sometimes dispose of toxic chemicals in ways contrary to law.

Obviously, one need not introduce the distinction between people and organizations to conclude that white-collar crime is an empirical reality as well as a conceptual possibility. One also need not introduce motivational elements to distinguish white-collar crime from other forms of crime. As with common crime, the white-collar offender clearly seeks personal benefit. This benefit may come directly to the offender or indirectly to the offender through the group or organization to which he or she belongs. As with other crimes, miscalculation of benefits is not evidence that benefits were not sought. In addition, one need not introduce unit-of-analysis issues (e.g., Do organizations commit crimes?) to document offending by persons of high social standing.

Do White-Collar Crimes Differ from Common Crimes?

In order to explore the differences thought to exist between white-collar and common crimes, it is necessary to examine a sample of definitions of white-collar crime and derivative or analogous concepts:

White-collar violations are those violations of law to which penalties are attached that involve the use of a violator's position of significant power, influence, or trust in the legitimate economic or political institutional order for the purpose of illegal gain, or to commit an illegal act for personal or organizational gain. [Reiss and Biderman 1980: 4]

[White-collar crime is] crime committed by a person of respectability and high social status in the course of his occupation. [Sutherland 1983: 7]

An illegal act or series of illegal acts committed by non-physical means and by concealment or guile, to obtain money or property, to avoid the payment or loss of money or property, or to obtain business or personal advantage. [Edelhertz 1970, in Braithwaite 1985: 18]

Occupational crime consists of offenses committed by individuals for themselves in the course of their occupations and the offenses of employees against their employers. . . . [Corporate crimes are] the offenses committed by corporate officials for the corporation and the offenses of the corporation itself. [Clinard and Quinney 1973: 188]

Obviously, advocates of the concept of white-collar crime believe they have identified a significant distinction among types of crime and types of criminals. The value of these distinctions must be determined by their usefulness in explaining, predicting, or controlling the behavior of offenders, victims, or officials of the criminal justice system. Without such criteria, analysis and evaluation of these concepts would be difficult or impossible. We therefore ask how white-collar crimes and white-collar criminals differ from other crimes and other criminals in terms relevant to explanation, prediction, and control. We begin with the "criminals" question.

How Do White-Collar Criminals Differ from Other Criminals?

One way to approach the white-collar-crime issue is to note that it takes a fresh view of the relation between crime and employment. In fact, the white-collar-crime notion challenges the traditional assumption that the *absence* of an occupation (unemployment) is conducive to crime and that an occupation (employment) is conducive to noncrime. The traditional assumption (unemployment theory) stresses motivation, suggesting that crime is a consequence of the deprivation resulting from relative poverty. In contrast, employment theory or "occupation theory" (Clinard and Quinney 1973) stresses opportunity for crime, suggesting that it is a consequence of on-the-job access to money and goods. Neither view is much concerned, however, with the social status or other properties of the offender. In fact, both views suggest that different individuals will respond similarly to the stresses of unemployment and to the opportunities of employment.

Clearly, then, research on the actual impact of employment on crime does not require a distinction between ordinary or common criminals and white-collar criminals. The two views appear to accept the same criminal acts as the focus of inquiry. They differ only on the direction of the predicted impact of a specific independent variable. This difference is consistent with our earlier characterization of "white-collar-crime theory" as a reaction to "positivistic" (force or pressure) theory. Although research favoring employment theory over unemployment theory would say something about the status of the independent variable, it could not demonstrate the need for a special category of criminal (the white-collar offender). Employment theory can be consistent with the evidence without requiring the notion that crime accompanying employment is the product of distinct causes.

In short, a finding that the employed are more likely to steal because of their employment no more justifies a unique theory of theft (white-collar crime) than a finding that the unemployed are more likely to steal justifies a theory focusing exclusively on the lower class (deprivation or strain theory).

Perhaps because the focus on "occupational crime" blurs the distinction between white-collar and other forms of crime, advocates of the white-collar-crime concept sometimes favor restricting it to crimes committed by wealthy, high-status, or respectable people in positions of power or trust (Sutherland 1983; see also Reiss and Biderman 1980). With white-collar crime so restricted, the research question becomes more difficult: Where do we find an appropriate comparison group for white-collar criminals?

Researchers who adopt this restrictive definition of white-collar criminals traditionally continue to compare them with ordinary offenders and to ignore people with low social status who commit white-collar offenses. This allows them to use the same terms to describe common criminals and offenders of high status. For example, Sutherland goes to some length to show that the acts of white-collar criminals are "deliberate," that the offenders often "recidivate," and that they are difficult to "rehabilitate." This comparison also allows expressions of concern about the credibility of high-status-white-collar-crime statistics that are traditionally reserved for ordinary crime statistics. Thus, according to Sutherland, official statistics vastly underestimate the extent of the criminal activities of high-status white-collar offenders, just as they underestimate those of ordinary offenders (1983: 227–28). According to contemporary scholars, such underestimation and disarray in the relevant white-collar-crime statistics continues (Reiss and Biderman 1980).

Comparing high-status white-collar offenders with low-status ordinary offenders loses a large segment of the criminal population, but it allows people in high positions to be described using terms usually reserved for people at the bottom on the social ladder—for example, "White-collar criminals possess a pimp's mentality" (Bequai 1987). It also allows the suggestion that the revealed rot at the top is only the tip of the iceberg. But the comparison has little else of positive value (Toby 1979b). In fact, it forces a separate theory of criminal behavior by suggesting but not demonstrating that the causes of such behavior among the rich and powerful are different from the causes of such behavior among the poor and weak. Some other comparison would seem to be required.

One possibility is to compare high-status offenders with nonoffenders in the same positions. Before making this comparison, let us briefly examine its logic. Offenders are first identified by their social location and then compared with nonoffenders in the same location. This is analogous to comparing lower-class people who commit crimes with lower-class people who do not, or, better, to comparing good students who commit delinquencies with good students who do not (since good students, like white-collar workers, may be expected to have low rates of crime). Given that both groups in the comparison share the locational attribute, that attribute cannot account for the differences in their behavior. Therefore, this comparison directs attention away from social location and toward microlevel or individual-level attributes such as strain, opportunity, or pathology. Since the same microlevel attributes may account for differences between offenders and nonoffenders among good students *and* among lower-class people, we are once again led to question the unique contribution of the concept of white-collar crime to crime theory. (It is ironic that the concept of white-collar crime, designed to introduce macrolevel distinctions into crime theory, actually forces the explanation to a lower or psychological level.)

A third mechanism for distinguishing white-collar criminals from other criminals is found in the work of those who favor a focus on corporate crime (Ermann and Lundman 1982; Braithwaite 1985). According to John Braithwaite, "Corporate crime, as the core area of concern, is . . . a broad but reasonably homogeneous domain for coherent theorizing. While useful theories of white-collar crime have proved elusive, influential corporate or organizational crime theory is a possibility" (1985: 19).

Whatever the potential value of the concept of *corporate* crime, it has not yet generated empirical data that require the concept for their interpretation, nor has it proved useful in identifying an important type of crime that would be missed otherwise. Researchers who suggest that the unit of study can or should be the organization, rather than the individual, do not stay long with this idea when it comes to collecting or interpreting their data. Thus, although Sutherland tabulated his crime data on firms (referring to some large portion of them as "habitual criminals") and ridiculed explanations of their behavior based on individual pathology, he continued to explain corporate crime with the theory of differential association, and he consistently equated the behavior of the corporation with the behavior of the people in positions of power within it (Cohen, Lindesmith, and Schuessler 1956; Geis and Meier 1977: 84). Braithwaite's own review of the research on company executives who violate the law reaches the conclusion that "it is top management attitudes, most particularly those of the chief executive, that determine the level of compliance with the law in a corporation. . . . Moreover, middle managers are frequently reported as squeezed by a choice between failing to achieve targets set by top management and attaining the targets illegally" (1985: 17).

Whatever the validity of these assertions, it seems to us that they take the corporation as a setting in which crimes may or may not occur, but they do not treat the corporation as the criminal actor. In this sense, then, white-collar crime is again no different from other crimes that occur in group or organizational settings where those in authority have more to say about what happens than those in subordinate positions—for example, governments, military units, university departments, and, for that matter, delinquent gangs.

It may be, then, that the discovery of white-collar criminals is important only in a context in which their existence is denied by theory or policy. In Sutherland's time, theory did tend to deny, usually implicitly, the existence of crime among the powerful, and social policy was not so focused on the area as it is today. Today, neither of these justifications is possible. Some other research comparison is therefore required. Perhaps the theoretical utility of the concept can be found in comparisons of crimes rather than of criminals.

How Do White-Collar Crimes Differ from Other Crimes?

White-collar crimes are often defined as crimes that can only be committed by persons occupying positions of power and influence. This approach rules out crimes committed by high-status people that can be committed by low-status people as well. In this definition, murder of one's spouse and rape would not be considered white-collar crime, unless they are a consequence of the offender's occupational power and influence. Thus, bank embezzlement can only be committed by employees of banks; insider trading can only be committed by stockbrokers; Medicaid fraud can only be committed by those who bill their services to the program; only automobile manufacturers can build cars that fail to meet legal standards; and income taxes can be evaded only by people who owe taxes.

This approach appears to identify a distinct class of crimes, one that *could* require a unique explanation. Yet what is the theoretical value in distinguishing a pharmacist's theft of drugs from a carpenter's theft of lumber? What is the theoretical value in distinguishing a doctor's Medicaid fraud from a patient's Medicaid fraud? What is the theoretical value of distinguishing a bank manager's embezzlement from a service-station attendant's embezzlement? The white-collar-crime concept tends to suggest that the pharmacist's theft is more important or serious than, or the product of different causes from, the carpenter's theft. It suggests that the doctor's fraud is more important (socially damaging?) or serious than the patient's, that the causes of one differ from the causes of the other. And so on. It strikes us that these suggestions are problematic at best and really involve two, largely unrelated but often confused questions: Are the causes of various offenses the same? And, Are the offenses themselves equally serious? White-collar theorists and researchers (in common with many criminologists) often assume that the answer to the second question bears on the answer to the first; that is, more serious crimes must have causes different from (more powerful than?) those of less serious crimes. Certainly there is no logical requirement that causes of offenses somehow match their seriousness, and, as we shall show, there is good empirical evidence that they do not and good theoretical reasons why they should not.

If there is no obvious theoretical value in distinguishing white-collar crimes from analogous blue-collar crimes, is there value in the common practice of distinguishing *among* such white-collar crimes as Medicaid fraud, income-tax evasion, insider trading, antitrust violations, bid-rigging, and consumer fraud? For some purposes, distinctions among crimes are clearly useful. For example, the expertise required to uncover and prosecute antitrust violations is different from that required to spot Medicaid fraud or insider trading. And legislation or other crime-control efforts may well require attention to specific offense characteristics (see Cornish and Clarke 1986). But these purposes do not require offender differences across such crimes or unique theories of offending. Students of juvenile delinquency have found no utility in studying specialization in vandalism, arson, rape, or burglary (although they have often been encouraged to do so by ad hoc theories suggesting something special about vandals, arsonists, rapists, and burglars). By extension, there is little reason to think that the idea of specialization in white-collar offenses will bear fruit. On the contrary, there is every reason to think that a single theory will apply to all types of white-collar offenses (and, as we will show, to all other offenses as well). If this is so, then specialized studies of offender motivation for particular offenses (e.g., embezzlement, collusion, polluting the air) will be redundant to the extent that they overlap and will be wrong to the extent that they do not.

The Connection Between Crime Types and Types of Criminals

Exploration of the distinction between crime and criminality easily leads to the conclusion that it makes more sense to talk about types of crime than about types of criminals. Events do have distinct sets of causes (e.g., autos are necessary for auto theft, access to other people's money is necessary for embezzlement, and other people are required for assault, bid-rigging, and rape). At the same time, the evidence seems reasonably clear that offenders seem to do just about everything they can do; they do not specialize in any particular crime or type of crime. Identifying offenders with offenses is therefore misleading. Robbers may have committed robbery, but, in terms of future offending, they are actually more likely to engage in theft than robbery, and they are only very slightly more likely than any other offender to engage again in robbery. If this is so for robbery and rape, which it is, it might also be true for embezzlement, fraud, and forgery. Although embezzlement, fraud, and forgery are distinct events and may therefore have distinct causes, there is no reason to think that the offenders committing these crimes are causally distinct from other offenders. A general theory of criminality is therefore not logically precluded by white-collar crime any more than by robbery or any other specific type of crime. The assumption that white-collar criminals differ from other criminals is simply the assumption, in another guise, that offenders specialize in particular crimes, an assumption for which there is no good evidence.

White-collar crimes satisfy the defining conditions of crime (see Chapter 2). They provide relatively quick and relatively certain benefit with minimal effort. They require no motivation or pressure that is not present in any other form of human behavior.

Since crimes involve goods, services, or victims, they have other constituent properties as well: they all require opportunity, and they are thought to result in punishment of the offender if he or she is detected. Yet such properties cannot account for the general tendency of particular individuals to engage in crime, and they are therefore not central to a theory of criminality.

The central elements of our theory of criminality are, however, easily identifiable among white-collar criminals. They too are people with low self-control, people inclined to follow momentary impulse without consideration of the long-term costs of such behavior.

Application of the General Theory to White-Collar Crime

Low self-control has implications for the likelihood of criminal acts, and it also has implications for selection into the occupational structure. Ordinary occupations require people to be in a particular place at a particular time. They also require educational persistence, willingness and ability to defer to the interests of others, and attention to conventional appearance. These occupational requirements tend to be inconsistent with the traits comprising criminality. White-collar occupations therefore tend to demand characteristics inconsistent with high levels of criminality. In other words, selection processes inherent in the high end of the occupational structure tend to recruit people with relatively low propensity to crime.

Our theory therefore predicts a relatively low rate of offending among white-collar workers, contrary to the now-standard view in the literature (e.g., Reiman 1979; Sutherland 1983). The standard view is based on misleading statistics about the extent of white-collar offending. For one thing, white-collar researchers often take *organizations* as the unit of analysis and do not adjust for their size and complexity when making comparisons with blue-collar *individuals*. For another, the reference period for the organization is often much longer than that applied to individuals (Sutherland 1983). As a consequence, the white-collar-crime literature often compares the number of crimes committed by an organization with many thousands of employees over a period of many years with those committed by single individuals in a single year.

When comparable units (e.g., individuals with the same crime-relevant characteristics, such as age, sex, and ethnicity), comparable reference periods (e.g., one year), and comparable methods of measurement (e.g., self reports or arrests) are employed, rates of crime among employed white-collar workers should be low as compared to those of people in less structured occupations with similar opportunities; the rates should also be low as compared to those outside of the occupational structure with similar opportunities.

Adequate data on this hypothesis are not now available. However, studies of rates of theft among employees are, in our view, consistent with it. Contrary to notions that theft is rampant among employees, John Clark and Richard Hollinger (1983) discovered that 90 percent or more of retail employees report that they have never taken store merchandise of any value, and serious crimes were not uncovered in significant amounts in any of the business sectors (such as hospitals and electronic firms) surveyed.

Note that our distinction between people and events treats white-collar crimes as events that take place in an occupational setting, not as characteristics of people employed in those settings. As a result, it makes problematic the connection between the people and the events, and it allows the possibility that this connection is less strong than the connection between people in other settings and the criminal events unique to those settings. Obviously, only white-collar workers can commit white-collar crimes, but the fact that they do so cannot be taken as evidence of their criminality unless (1) other people are given the opportunity to commit the same crimes in the same setting, or (2) other settings and crimes are construed, for purposes of comparison, to be equivalent to white-collar crime. The latter solution is the one adopted by the criminal law and by most compilations of crime statistics.

In law and in crime statistics, embezzlement, fraud, and forgery are defined without reference to the occupational setting in which they occur. As a consequence, it is possible to study the demographic distributions of crimes typically associated with the white-collar sector of the labor force and to compare them with the same distributions for other crimes. Of course, our general theory predicts that differences in the demographic correlates across crimes should be nonexistent given similar opportunity structures.

Figure 10 shows the *Uniform Crime Reports* arrest rates (U.S. Department of Justice 1981, 1985) for fraud and embezzlement by age. As is apparent, arrest rates for these white-collar crimes peak in the late teens and early twenties, and they decline sharply with increasing age. By about age 37, the rate of embezzlement is half the rate at the peak age. By about age 41, the rate of fraud has declined to half its peak value.

Figure 11 compares the rates of embezzlement of males and females and of whites and blacks/others. As is obvious from the figure, the rates of embezzlement in 1981 for males and females are much closer than for most crimes, especially crimes of violence. (In fact, it is widely reported in the literature that the male/female rates of white-collar crimes are converging.) Figure 11 also shows smaller race differences than are found for ordinary crimes. Although the black/other rates for fraud and embezzlement are higher than those for whites, the differences are not as great as those typically encountered.

Figures 12 and 13 repeat the data shown in Figures 10 and 11,

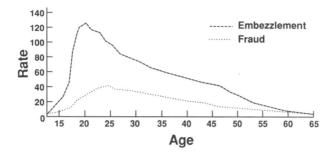

Fig. 10. Fraud (1980 per 10,000) and Embezzlement (1984 per 1,000,000). From Hirschi and Gottfredson 1987: 962; Data Obtained from *Uniform Crime Reports* (U.S. Department of Justice 1981, 1985).

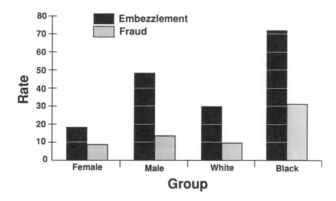

Fig. 11. Arrest Rates by Sex and Race for Embezzlement (1981 per 1,000,000) and Fraud (1981 per 10,000). From Hirschi and Gottfredson 1987: 963.

providing often-overlooked comparisons with ordinary crimes. Figure 12 shows the age distribution of murder along with the age distributions of embezzlement and fraud. The similarity of these distributions is remarkable. The figure presents the rates for embezzlement, fraud, and murder using denominators designed to stress the comparability in the shapes of the distributions at the expense of differences in the level of these crimes. Actually, fraud arrests are much more common than murder arrests (about 13:1), whereas embezzlement arrests are even less common than murder arrests (about 1:2). But what is clear is that a major correlate of ordinary crime is similarly correlated with "white-collar" crime.

In Figure 13 we have adjusted for differences in opportunity to commit white-collar crimes across sex and age groups. We have done

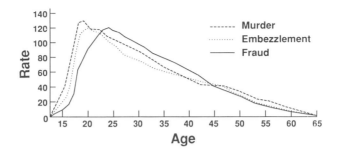

Fig. 12. Arrest Rates by Age for Murder (1983 per 500,000), Fraud (1980 per 30,000), and Embezzlement (1984 per 1,000,000). From Hirschi and Gottfredson 1987: 964.

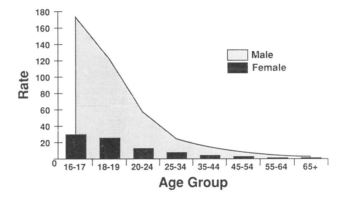

Fig. 13. Embezzlement Rates (1984 per 100,000 White-Collar Workers) by Sex. From Hirschi and Gottfredson 1987: 965.

so by standardizing to the white-collar labor force for the respective categories. These differences are usually taken as the major justification for separate treatment of white-collar crime. In fact, age-sex-race differences in opportunity do not reveal differences in the correlates of white-collar and ordinary crime. On the contrary, they tend to conceal the fact that their correlates are of the same order of magnitude and direction. When opportunity is taken into account, demographic differences in white-collar crime are the same as demographic differences in ordinary crime.

Studies of tax evasion, an offense typically construed as a white-collar crime, lend additional support to our hypothesis. Robert Mason and Lyle Calvin (1978: 84) report that "young people are significantly more likely to report underreporting of income than are older people." (Additional support for the standard age effect on tax evasion may be found in Rowe and Tittle 1977; Clotfelter 1983; and Witte and Woodbury 1985). With respect to property theft by employees, Clark and Hollinger (1983: abstract) write: "the highest levels of property theft were reported by the younger (16 to mid-twenties), unmarried, and male employees."

Individual Differences and White-Collar Crime

Research and theory relating characteristics of individuals to involvement in crime are often held up to ridicule on the grounds that individuals involved in white-collar crime have traits "opposite" to those said to cause crime. In fact, the white-collar-crime literature in one sense owes its origins to precisely this logic:

Quite obviously, the hypothesis that crime is due to personal and social pathologies does not apply to white-collar crimes, and if it does not explain these crimes such pathologies are not essential factors in crime in general. In contrast with such explanations the hypothesis of differential association and social disorganization may apply to white-collar crimes as well as to lower-class crimes. [Sutherland 1983: 264]

Trait theorists were particularly vulnerable to this criticism, since most of the traits they believed to be conducive to crime (such as aggressiveness, risk-taking, activity level, mesomorphy, and sociability) could also be said to be conducive to business success. (If aggressiveness causes crime it also causes business success. Therefore, it cannot cause crime. Or, so the logic goes. As we have shown in Chapter 3, the tendency of aggression researchers to equate aggression and crime makes all such discussions pointless anyway.) The problems with this argument against trait theory were threefold. First, it assumed facts not in evidence. There was no empirical reason to believe that "traits" positively correlated with ordinary crime were negatively correlated with white-collar crime. On the contrary, as we have shown, there is good reason to think otherwise. Second, it denied the obvious fact that a single cause (or set of causes) may have differential manifestations. All things being equal, an active person may be more likely to succeed in business and more likely to engage in criminal acts. All things being equal, an impulsive person may be more likely to shoplift and more likely to embezzle from the firm. Third, the argument confused location in the business world with success in business. It assumed that white-collar criminals are successful at white-collar occupations, an assumption exacerbated by the tendency of white-collar-crime researchers to rely on anecdote and on particularly notorious cases. Although by definition one must be in the white-collar world to be a white-collar offender, not all white-collar workers enjoy the power, income, and prestige to be found at the top of this world. In fact, most have little power, not much income, and only moderate prestige. However, this erroneous assumption leads to the expectation that the correlates of white-collar crime will be opposite to the correlates of ordinary crime. After all, it takes a while to be successful in the business world, and while this is happening one is growing older, a fact that should reverse the usual negative relation between age and crime: obviously, whites have an advantage over blacks in the white-collar world, and therefore here, at least, whites should have a higher rate of crime; and it is obvious that intelligence is positively related to white-collar success and it should therefore be positively related to white-collar crime. In all cases where data are available, however, those data suggest that the reverse of these assumptions is more nearly correct.

Experimental tests of our hypotheses could be achieved by distributing credit cards to junior high school students or by using banks for prison work-release programs. Without such tests, it is difficult to document the relatively low level of criminality among white-collar workers. Absent such tests, scholars will continue to argue that the criminal justice system favors white-collar workers, that businesses protect them to maintain their own reputations, and that white-collar crimes are relatively easily concealed. A case could be made that these arguments are themselves relics of a bygone age. The Bureau of Justice Statistics (1986) reports that in 1983 the probability of incarceration for white-collar offenders was as high as that for violent offenders. And good research shows that criminal justice–system punishments for white-collar offenses are governed by the same criteria governing punishments for other crimes (Wheeler, Weisburd, and Bode 1982).

The Value of White-Collar Crime for Crime Theory

The concept of white-collar crime is usually seen as incompatible with most theories of crime, particularly theories that focus on differences in the biology, psychology, or social position of offenders and nonoffenders. Other theories have gained considerable advantage from appearing to be peculiarly compatible with the concept. It is universally agreed that the more general a theory, the better it is, and theories that can encompass white-collar crime along with common crime must, it seems, be very general and therefore superior to theories that deal only with ordinary crime or, more narrowly, only with "juvenile delinquency." Indeed, the objection most frequently raised to explanatory efforts in criminology is typically phrased as: "Yes, but what about white-collar crime?"

The theories that gain most from the white-collar-crime concept are those that focus on learning, especially on the learning of cultural values, such as Sutherland's own theory of differential association. In his early work, Sutherland asserted that white-collar crime could only be understood as a consequence or natural extension of ordinary business values (1983: 240–64; see also Cressey 1986). People socialized within the business world could come to define their criminal activities as required by the needs of profit-making and as generally supported in the business community by "neutralizing verbalizations" (Cressey 1986: 200). Additionally, they could there find training in the techniques required to commit crimes of such complexity.[1] Modern variants of this perspective seek to answer similar questions: "In what ways is society organized that it may encourage the very phenomenon it seeks to control?" (Vaughan 1983: 19).

The survival of such theories of crime is directly attributable to their apparent generality, their apparent ability to account for phenomena beyond the reach of theories that focus on individual differences. Ironically, although these theories owe their current popularity and even survival to their connection to white-collar (or organizational) crime, white-collar crime has done more for them than they have done for the understanding of it.

Consider the causal mechanisms used to understand crime in the cultural theory tradition. In this tradition, the individual learns that crime is condoned by the values of the organization or is required as a natural byproduct of its pursuit of profits. In some versions, the organization creates expectations of performance that may be met only by law violation (Vaughan 1983; Braithwaite 1985: 17); in others, the techniques and rationalizations required for white-collar crime are simple extensions of routine business practices. In either case, criminal activity is seen as consistent with—rather than contrary to—the values of those engaging in it.

[1] Cressey falsified Sutherland's theory of white-collar crime by talking to a sample of embezzlers. These embezzlers reported that they had not learned embezzlement from a "business culture" but that, in fact, their criminal behavior resulted from efforts to cover problems created by their own prior misbehavior (Cressey 1953). Cressey's findings are often ignored in the white-collar crime literature, as is the irony of the fact that Cressey found his subjects in prison, an unlikely location for criminals whose crimes are "ignored by the criminal justice system."

The first difficulty encountered by such theories is the relative rarity of white-collar crime. Contrary to the expectations of these theories, white-collar offenses must be relatively rare. If the white-collar work force is actually socialized to the virtues of embezzlement, bid-rigging, and fraud, what accounts for the extraordinarily high level of law-abiding conduct among white-collar workers? It is easily shown that crime by partners or employees may increase the cost of doing business to the point that business is no longer profitable. The limits on white-collar crime set by the requirements of profits and survival are rarely recognized by white-collar-crime theorists. (These limits have, however, been noted by students of "organized crime" [see Reuter 1983].)

A second difficulty for such theories is suggested by the routine finding that white-collar offenders tend to receive little support for their criminal activities from the organization or from other white-collar workers. Indeed, the evidence suggests that they are especially concerned with concealing their crimes from coworkers and management (Cressey 1953; Vaughan 1983; Lasley 1987). The reason for such concern is revealing: the victim of white-collar crime is typically the organization itself, not in a direct way the general public. Since white-collar offenders share the general propensity of offenders to pursue self-interest, they naturally take advantage of the most readily available opportunities. By ascribing larger purposes to white-collar criminals, cultural theories tend to mispredict the nature of white-collar victimization.

A third difficulty with the cultural theory of white-collar crime is that it mispredicts the correlates of the phenomena, suggesting that the longer the exposure to the business culture, the higher the level of criminal activity (contrary to the age distribution of white-collar crime). It also suggests that opportunity itself is sufficient to overcome ordinary differences in the likelihood of criminal activity (contrary to the sex, race, and age differences reported earlier) and that white-collar crimes are so complicated that unusual training or skill is required for their performance (contrary to evidence showing that most white-collar crime involves such activities as transferring funds from one account to another, dumping barrels of chemicals in remote areas, or altering routine billing practices [Vaughan 1983]). To say that such practices are consistent with the offender's profit motive (self-interest) is obviously true, but to say that they are consistent with the generally accepted values of the business world is wrong.

A fourth difficulty with these theories is frequently noted by students of common crime: they all fail as explanations of ordinary crime and delinquency (Kornhauser 1978). The white-collar crime area thus falls prey to its own critique of criminological theories. The generally accepted white-collar-crime theories cannot explain ordinary crime and are thus, by their own logic (see Sutherland 1983), incapable of explaining crime, whether white-collar or ordinary.

One of the sources of difficulty for the white-collar-crime research tradition is that it fundamentally misconstrues the nature of crime. Starting with an image of crime as a complex, highly sophisticated, high-stake enterprise driven by large potential profits within the context of ambiguous moral codes, it is little wonder that the white-collar-crime tradition came up with a white-collar offender distinct from ordinary offenders. Alas for this tradition, modern research on white-collar crime depicts an enterprise decidedly closer to (even identical with) the conception of crime used throughout this book. Stanton Wheeler and his colleagues (1988) investigated this question directly. They "selected eight specific statutory offenses . . . that [they] believed would be included in almost every major conceptualization of white-collar conduct" (p. 332) and that "provide a broad and heterogeneous view of the white-collar criminal activity that is prosecuted in the federal judiciary" (p. 334). Wheeler et al. then say:

> After reading hundreds of presentence investigation reports describing such offenses, we emerged with a strong sense of the banal, mundane quality of the vast majority of white-collar offenses. . . . Consider what some would regard as the most elite form of white-collar crime, namely antitrust offenses. . . . The vast majority of cases in our sample are characterized by low-level, local or narrowly regional offenses that are hardly of major significance. . . . Our point . . . is not that these are inconsequential offenses, only that they are common, for the most part requiring little sophistication. And if that is true for antitrust, it is surely true for many offenses in our sample. [1988: 348–49]

Our theory avoids these problems. It begins with an image of crime that is consistent with good research. It predicts variation in rates across social settings, with white-collar crime rates being relatively low, depending on the process of selection into the particular white-collar occupation. Our theory directly disagrees with traditional "white-collar" theory on the rate issue, and thus it leads to a directly testable empirical question. Our theory is of course not bothered by the fact that people can pursue criminal activities without social support. On the contrary, it explicitly predicts lack of social support for most white-collar crimes since they are both contrary to general social norms and against the interests of the organization itself. We therefore have a second empirical issue of direct theoretical relevance.

Earlier we asserted that our general theory expects the properties of those committing crime to be similar regardless of the type of crime. It therefore asserts that the distinction between crime in the street and crime in the suite is an *offense* rather than an *offender* distinction, that offenders in both cases are likely to share similar characteristics. We therefore have a third directly testable distinction between our general theory and the commonly accepted view of white-collar crime.

The cultural theory's difficulty with ordinary crime provides another empirical test of the relative value of these competing perspectives. Our theory was constructed with common offenses and offenders in mind. It is meant to predict and explain ordinary crime, juvenile delinquency, drug abuse, serious crime, "organized" crime, and status offending as well as white-collar crime. Since our theory permits no propensity distinctions among types of offenses, it is perfectly general and is once again directly contrary to cultural theories, which view crimes as having unique, specific cultural motives.

Summary

We have shown that the typological approach inherent in the concept of white-collar crime was a mistake. One of the causes of this mistake is the enduring tendency of those who study crime to subordinate the topic to the interests of their parent discipline. This tendency is particularly marked among sociologists, who see in white-collar crime an opportunity to save conceptual schemes that have not proved useful with ordinary offenders. It is also present among economists, who see in white-collar crime an opportunity to explicate once again the grand scheme of their discipline. Psychologists, comfortable with the idea of typologies, endlessly divide offenders into groups thought to be "relatively homogeneous" with respect to the meaning of their offenses. And quantitative analysts of all disciplinary persuasions see white-collar crime as one more opportunity to specify a formal model. All of these disciplinary interests are served by acceptance of the received view of "white-collar offending." This chapter questions the received view and reasserts that crime is a unitary phenomenon capable of explanation by a single theory, a theory that seeks first the features common to all crimes and deduces from them tendencies to criminality in the individual.

Such a theory is then in position to outline the causes of such tendencies and to consider their differential manifestations. Such differential manifestation is of course a function of the opportunities available to people and of the circumstances in which they find themselves. To think otherwise is to confuse social location with social causation.

10

Organization and Crime

The general public, the law enforcement community, and many academic criminologists see organized crime (such as La Cosa Nostra, the Mafia, the syndicate, and, for that matter, the Hell's Angels) as evidence contrary to the view advanced in this book. The idea of *organized* crime argues against our view in at least four ways: (1) it challenges the notion that self-control is a general characteristic with multiple manifestations (i.e., it contradicts the conclusion that offenders engage in a variety of criminal and analogous activities); (2) it challenges the notion that characteristics reliably accompanying the low self-control of offenders make their long-term participation in cooperative activities unlikely or problematic; (3) it challenges the notion that crime involves easy pursuit of immediate pleasure without concern for long-term values; and (4) it suggests that a complete theory of delinquency among adolescents and crime among adults must take into account the causal influence of the group or organization.

In fact, none of these objections is valid. The theory we have advanced can account for the facts claimed by theories constructed to deal with the "organized nature" of criminal activity. Here, as elsewhere, it is necessary to separate facts stemming from disciplinary interests from those stemming from observation of the phenomenon. If indeed some crime is the product of formal organization, or if the mob is indeed structured like a legitimate firm, then there may be merit in invoking principles of organizational behavior to explain some criminal behavior. But the first order of business is to determine the extent to which this media / law enforcement / political / social scientific image of crime and criminality is consistent with the evidence. Here too we must be careful to distinguish observation from the demands of positivistic theory.

The crime and criminality perspective applied to organized crime suggests that whatever organization may be found among offenders is likely to be imposed and maintained from without—that is, the apparent pursuit of long-term goals by offenders is post hoc interpretation by scholars or law enforcement officials to account for a series of events that otherwise has no inherent structure or coherent purpose. The fact that captured mobsters and gang members paint their activities as part of a large and powerful syndicate is perhaps understandable. The ready acceptance of this picture by social scientists is more puzzling, but it can be traced to their natural attraction to the idea that organization underlies all human activities.

Sociological positivism initially reacted against the classical notions of choice and free will, positing instead a social animal living naturally in society. The task of sociological theory was to explain how a social animal can be caused to commit antisocial acts. We have addressed earlier (Chapter 4) the standard solutions to this problem under "strain" and "cultural" theories. These theories were designed to provide sociological explanations of the behavior of individual offenders. For example, the strain theory argues that lower-class males are more likely than middle-class males to commit criminal acts because they are denied access to legitimate means of attaining conventional success. This theory explains differences in *rates* of crime between groups. When pressed for explanation of differences within groups (e.g., why are most lower-class males law-abiding?), the strain theory is forced to accede to a "lower level" of explanation, to grant a role to the family, psychology, or even biology in crime causation.

As initially formulated, cultural theories too were forced at some point to move to another level of explanation. For example, these theories argue that lower-class males are more likely than middle-class males to commit criminal acts because they have been socialized into a culture with definitions favorable to the use of force and fraud. When pressed for explanation of intra-group variation in crime (again, why are most lower-class males law-abiding?), the cultural theory is forced to accede to a lower level of explanation, to grant a role to family, psychology, or even biology.

This state of affairs did not sit well with sociological positivism (recall the tendency of disciplinary positivists to claim ownership of all of the important variables in an area, whether independent or dependent). It therefore sought, in the terms of unabashed disciplinary imperialism, a *fully social* interpretation of the causes of crime. In the present context, this implies conceptualization of the independent variables (and of the forces they exert) as group-level phenomena. The strength of this urge to conceptualize crime in a manner compatible with the interests of the discipline of sociology is perhaps captured by the following effort to distinguish it from other "levels" of explanation:

> The macrosocial level addresses a very different set of questions. It asks, what is it about social systems, cultures, and subcultures that accounts for variations in the types and rates of behaviors found in those systems and cultures? This level of explanation embraces a variety of functionalist, conflict, and Marxist theories of crime. These types of theories are concerned to explain why different social systems and structures, cultures and subcultures, produce different types and rates of crime, and why crime in a particular social system, culture, or subculture, or in particular locations in social structures, is patterned in characteristic ways. [Short 1987: 2]

"Fully social" alternatives to standard sociological theories of the crimes of individuals do not make reference to the properties of individuals. They attend only to the properties of the environment. Typically, the major aspect of the environment of interest to sociologists is "other people" or "the group." All of this led more or less directly to the modern tendency of sociologists to focus on *organization* (aka "group") as the theoretical embodiment of the interests of their discipline.

As sociologists came to distinguish between formal and informal, simple and complex, and crescive and enacted groups, they came to see that the distinction between organized and disorganized groups was in fact a device for reintroducing individual-level explanations of behavior. (In the "disorganized" group, the individual is thrown back on his own devices and reacts as his own makeup requires.) In the interest of disciplinary purity, they therefore rejected "disorganization" as an explanatory concept. Thus the idea of disorganization, so prominent in the early days of sociology (Thrasher 1927; Shaw and McKay 1931), eventually fell into disfavor, whereas its counterpart, organization, came to occupy a central role in sociological thinking.

A fully social theory of crime is easily realized by combining the idea that social behavior takes place in groups or organizations with the idea that crime itself is social behavior. This combination produces the standard concepts of contemporary sociological criminology, such concepts as "criminal organization," "organized crime," "organizational crime," "corporate crime," "criminal subculture," and "gang delinquency."[1]

---

[1] Most of the types of crime acknowledged by sociological theory appear to have been produced by similar logic. Thus "lower-class crime," "British crime," and "rural

Sociological criminology initially inherited a research tradition that focused on juvenile delinquency. As a result, sociologists too initially focused on the behavior of children. Pre–sociological positivism only rarely alluded to "delinquent companions," treating gang membership as a collateral consequence of the causes of delinquency. Sociological positivism, in contrast, quickly came to regard group involvement as the *sine qua non* of juvenile crime and produced a large research literature on gangs, group delinquency, and the companionship factor, an emphasis that persists to the present day (Erickson and Jensen 1977; Zimring 1981; Elliott, Huizinga, and Ageton 1985; Reiss 1988).

The first large-scale study from this perspective was Frederic Thrasher's *The Gang: A Study of* 1313 Gangs (1927). Thrasher believed that juvenile gangs were an organizational response to the lack of organization in the lives of young people in city slums (a standard assumption of sociology). He believed that gangs took on the attributes of "primary groups," groups in which the individual could find personal comfort and where he could be socialized. In Thrasher's view, gangs eventually became highly and complexly organized, such that they were able to perpetuate themselves in the face of external threat.

Thrasher's definition of the gang followed directly from such assumptions: "The gang is . . . originally formed spontaneously, and then integrated through conflict. It is characterized by . . . meeting face to face, milling, movement through space as a unit, conflict, and planning. The result of this collective behavior is the development of tradition, unreflective internal structure, esprit de corps, solidarity, morale, group awareness, and attachment to a local territory" (1927: 57).[2]

The features Thrasher thought he had identified in delinquent gangs are of course the features of formal organizations: rational purpose or goal-directed activity, internal stratification, exclusivity, commitment to the group, and a stability that does not depend on the particular individuals occupying roles in the organization. Indeed, in Thrasher's view, the gang was an entity capable of action, influence,

---

crime" are assumed to possess peculiar properties derived from the groups in which they occur.

[2] A modern version of Thrasher's definition is provided by Short: "(1) recurrent congregation outside the home; (2) self-defined inclusion/exclusion criteria and continuity of affiliation; (3) having a territorial basis consisting of customary hanging and ranging areas, including self-defined use and occupancy rights; (4) a versatile activity repertoire; and (5) organizational differentiation, e.g., by authority, roles, prestige, friendship, or special-interest cliques" (1987: 16).

and culture, not unlike a modern corporation, educational institution, or criminal syndicate.

If the adolescent gang can be described as a complex organization, it is not surprising that the same "formal group" assumptions have been applied to crime by adults, producing fully social explanations of white-collar crime, organized crime, and corporate crime.[3] This chapter examines the applicability of such assumptions to crime and criminality. It does so by tracing the history of research on gang structure, tracing the history of research on organized crime, and applying, in systematic fashion, our ideas of crime and self-control to the assumptions of the theory of complex organizations and the data on organized crime.

The Gang

The media are typically full of references to gangs. Although much coverage is devoted to gang killings, gangs in prisons, and the operations of gang units in police departments, the "natural" connection between criminal organization and the drug market is a major stimulant of interest in gang activity. The idea of an organized adversary has always appealed to the law enforcement community and, in turn, to the media, whether the organization be bootleggers in the 1930's, motorcycle gangs in the 1950's and 1960's, or drug dealers in the 1970's and 1980's. Unfortunately for the cause of truth and sound public policy, the idea of organized criminal gangs toiling long and hard with extraordinary competence derives more from politics and romance than from the results of research. In fact, research routinely fails to find more than anecdotal support for it.

Let us begin by analyzing the argument that juvenile gangs are organized in the ways suggested by sociological theory, the popular media, and the law enforcement community. We will also study the corollary conclusion that such organization has a direct effect on crime and delinquency.

Internal Stratification

The keystone of the sociological view is Thrasher's argument that gangs have "authority, roles, prestige, friendship, or special interest

[3]Our discussion of white-collar crime in Chapter 9 focused on the sociologists' rejection of individual pathology as an explanation of crime rather than on its connection to organizational assumptions. The reason for this focus is that sociological development of the theory of white-collar crime has been so rudimentary that it is more easily seen for what it rejects than for its positive contributions.

cliques" (Short 1987: 17). In this view, leaders are people with particular skills or qualities, people who set the direction and long-term orientation of the organization, define its goals, decide its daily activities, assign individuals to roles, control membership, and generally reap the major benefits of goal achievement. Moreover, in this view, the leadership role is supported by a hierarchical role structure that involves a system of internal stratification and a specialized division of labor. (Descriptions of the role structure of specific delinquent gangs are hard to come by, even in the classical literature. Apparently, it is easier to assume structure than to document it.)

Serious studies of gang leadership and role structure have failed to substantiate the classical image of the gang. In fact, these studies reveal that gangs of adolescent males are better characterized as unorganized than as organized. They are typically unable to identify their own "leaders," they resist attempts by others to identify them, and those identified as leaders by whatever process typically refuse to accept the position when offered. It is reported that when social workers try to organize gangs—asking them to elect officers—they are usually unsuccessful (Suttles 1968; Klein 1971). Lewis Yablonsky (1962), studying an atypical gang, reports that it was created by its "leaders" as a figment of their "psychotic states"—suggesting that "gangs" serve purposes for boys as well as for law enforcement and reminding us that the reports of juveniles themselves are suspect as a source of information about the structure of gangs. In short, gangs are not structured in ways suggested by the classical image. There is, at best, an informal structure of friendship (Suttles 1968) but no hint of formal organization.

Exclusivity and Commitment to the Group

The popular image and the law enforcement view show the gang as a tightly knit group that places great emphasis on membership and loyalty. Evidence of such concern is said to be shown by such things as uniformity in dress (e.g., black leather jacket), speech, and methods of grooming (e.g., spiked haircuts). The image suggests further that gang members spend the bulk of their time with other gang members ("interact frequently and regularly") and are highly attracted to one another ("cohesive"). Academic theorists who emphasize the causal influence of the gang make similar assumptions. After all, it is hard to see how a group toward which one feels little affinity, whose members are unattractive, and with whom one spends little time could exert a powerful influence on (or be blamed for) one's behavior.

Again, research does not support the classical or organizational image. Gang members do not care much for one another. They do not trust one another and do not themselves recognize much in the way of an internal stratification system. Gerald Suttles (1968) reports that gang members will not contribute money for mutual enterprises unless the group worker agrees to hold it. Malcolm Klein (1971) reports that gang members tend to know each other on a first-name or nickname basis, suggesting little knowledge of or interest in each other's past or future.

These facts are consistent with another fact frequently reported in gang research. The membership of the gang is highly variable from day to day, and rules of attendance do not apply. (Most gang members are, after all, dependent on adults for room and board; most are required to make some accommodation with the school system; and many have some sort of employment, at least intermittently.) But much of the infrequency of interaction of gang members can probably be attributed to the general lack of friendship, affection, or trust among them. As Klein (1971) points out, gang members do not come together because they share positive interests or values, but because they share poverty, unhappy homes, and social disabilities (see also Short and Strodtbeck 1965). Since sustained social interaction requires mutual interests, the ability to reciprocate benefits, reliability, and some concern for others, the transitory nature of gang attachments is easily predicted.

Organizational Goals

Classical theory assumed that gangs perform two functions for their members: they facilitate the commission of delinquent acts, and, in so doing, they confer status on or enhance the self-esteem of their members. In fact, however, the gang is not particularly suited to the commission of delinquent acts. The typical criminal acts described in Chapter 2 are, in many cases, made more rather than less difficult by the participation of large numbers of boys. Burglary may be easier with two or three boys, but certainly more than that become a liability. The same is true of robbery, auto theft, and the acquisition of drugs. We pointed out in Chapter 2 that some events are made easier and more certain in outcome by the presence of confederates, but these events are typically not characterized by planning or organization. There can be no doubt that many criminal events virtually presuppose the presence of several adolescents at the same place at the same time. Sociological theorizing has, however, mistaken the connection between multiple adolescents and offending for a connection between group activity and offending. If a boy in the company of other boys pops the antenna off an automobile, sociological theory would say that the organization (peer group) caused the behavior by providing the motivation (i.e., it required the act as a condition of membership or it rewarded its performance through status enhancement).

Another interpretation, consistent with the facts and with our theory of crime, focuses on the features of events that make them more likely to occur. Those features that appear to reduce the certainty or rapidity of sanctions increase the likelihood that the events will occur, whether or not the features are accurately perceived. In this respect, groups imply immunity from sanction; they diffuse and confuse responsibility for the act, and they shelter the perpetrator from immediate identification and from long-term risk of retribution. In some cases, they prevent sanctions through threats of retaliation. Groups, then, act as a mask and a shield, as a cover for activities that would not otherwise be performed.

Occasionally huge police "sweeps" of gang members are reported in U.S. cities. These sweeps presuppose gang activity. They are typically reported so as to appear to confirm this presupposition. Thousands of arrests follow, and the reader is left to conclude that they were of gang members. Unfortunately, the details of these arrests are only sketchily reported. Usually, in fact, they are for motor vehicle violations, driving under the influence of alcohol, or possession of relatively small amounts of drugs—crimes that do not suggest gang connections. Usually, too, those arrested in such sweeps are not adolescents but adults too old to be credible candidates for gang membership.

Given the large numbers of adolescents with relatively low self-control living in close proximity, and given the relatively low level of supervision exercised over them, it is inevitable that from time to time they will congregate on the streets of U.S. cities. Given these facts, it is also inevitable that these "gangs" will occasionally engage in delinquent and criminal activities, ranging from shoplifting cigarettes and intimidating the elderly to using heavy drugs and participating in drive-by shootings directed at no one in particular. To call these collections of individuals "gangs" and to suggest that confederations of them transcend national boundaries has undeniable appeal to politicians of all persuasions. On the left, these massive organizations of offenders can be linked to the organization of capitalist society. On both the right and the left, they can be used to justify equally massive expenditure for the criminal justice system.

Even if juvenile gangs can be explained readily by the crime and criminality perspective, we are still left with the problem of the Mafia, La Cosa Nostra, the syndicate, and other highly organized criminal activities of adults. American criminology has devoted considerable attention to describing the structure and influence of organized crime. In fact, at any given time, organized crime is likely to dominate media and congressional interest in the crime problem.

Organized Crime

In the traditional sociological view, the gang acted as a training ground for adult careers in organized crime (Cloward and Ohlin 1960). The idea of apprenticeship made plausible the idea that the organization of adult crime is analogous to the organization of legitimate corporations. Beginning with the earliest days of the FBI, the law enforcement community has repeatedly pushed the idea of organized crime.[4] This perception is reinforced by periodic reports of prestigious, government-financed commissions and investigatory bodies. Witness the statement of the President's Commission on Law Enforcement and Administration of Justice:

Organized crime is a society that seeks to operate outside the control of the American people and their governments. It involves thousands of criminals, working within structures as complex as any large corporation, subject to laws more rigidly enforced than those of legitimate governments. Its actions are not impulsive but rather the result of intricate conspiracies, carried on over many years, and aimed at gaining control over whole fields of activity in order to amass huge profits. [1967: 1]

The organized-crime portion of the President's Commission report was in large part authored by the sociologist Donald Cressey, who argues that:

There is a broad range of formal and informal organization among criminals, just as there is a broad range of organization among businessmen, government officials, and other citizens. One kind of organization is simply a stabilized pattern of interaction based on similarities of interest and attitudes,

[4] The benefits (and costs) of the idea of organized crime extend to politicians as well. The 1988 impeachment trial of Governor Evan Mecham of Arizona focused considerable public attention on the governor's stance toward organized crime. Mecham's supporters took the position that his conviction would remove the last obstacle to the domination of the state by organized crime. His opponents were clearly made uneasy by the suggestion that they were not equally dedicated to opposing the forces of organized crime threatening the state.

and on mutual aid. . . . In other cases, organization means a particular set of roles that has come to be seen as serving express purposes by the persons playing the roles. An enterprise of this kind qualifies as an organization because specific tasks are allocated to individuals, entrance into the organization is limited, and survival and maintenance rules are delineated. More specifically, such units have three important characteristics. First, a division of labor is present. . . . Second, the activities of each person in the organization are coordinated with the activities of other participants by means of rules, agreements, and understandings which support the division of labor. Third, the entire enterprise is rationally designed to achieve announced objectives. [Sutherland and Cressey 1978: 282–83; see also Cressey 1969]

Obviously, the law enforcement / political / media view of crime is supported by the assumption that here, as elsewhere, the fundamental premises of organizational sociology apply. Within criminology, the idea that the principles of formal organization explain crime as well as noncrime is supported by the conception of offenders as professionals pursuing careers in their chosen occupation. If criminals are professionals, they of course operate within a context of routine and predictability. In fact, in Sutherland's *The Professional Thief* (1937), one finds the view that professional criminals operate in concert with one another, influence law enforcement activities, bribe judges, develop elaborate fencing networks, and create an internal prestige hierarchy, all in order to maximize their profits and minimize their risks. Thus, whether one starts from the idea of organization or from the idea of a profession, one comes to the conclusion that crime is like other rationally structured forms of human activity and can be explained in the same way: people organize to increase their safety and profit, whether they are burglarizing homes or disposing of toxic wastes. (Cressey's description of the functions of criminal organization is identical to standard descriptions of the functions of conventional corporate organization; Sutherland's description of the profession of thievery is virtually identical to standard descriptions of conventional professions, such as medicine or social work.)

Research on organized and professional crime paints a picture at odds with the standard social scientific / media / law enforcement view. Competent ethnographies of fences, the key players in the game of theft, reveal several facts inconsistent with the view that it is staffed by professionals. First, thievery is largely petty, unplanned or spontaneous activity that involves shoplifting or the taking of unattended materials. Second, thieves usually do not know the value of the goods they have stolen. In fact, they often part with goods for a fraction of their value. Third, there is little honor among thieves. The fence is most afraid of the thief who will turn him in as part of a plea negotiation with authorities. Fences may have reason to fear thieves, since they routinely cheat those they deal with. And finally, there is little evidence that the competency of law enforcement requires bribery (Klockars 1974).

Characteristics of thieves may also be inferred from the nature of the materials purchased and offenders arrested in police sting operations, "wherein police pose as thieves and as dealers in stolen property, fences, in order to induce thieves to bring stolen property to them" (Klockars 1988: 85). Because these stings are reported by the police, it appears that a large and thriving market for stolen property of all sorts exists in all metropolitan areas. In fact, however, this market appears to be largely police-generated, since it involves items for which no market, legitimate or illegitimate, ordinarily exists. As a result, the "thieves" captured by sting operations are often so naive or unskilled that they have no conception of the value of anything, let alone the value of labor. Carl Klockars's description of people "swept up" in such operations is revealing:

Others steal whatever is available when the opportunity presents itself, coming up with some quite unusual things for which finding a buyer is no small problem. Consider the predicament of the thief who steals three 1977 Ford Pinto carburetors. This thief is unlikely to know three people who own such vehicles, much less three who are having or anticipate carburetor problems. Even so, tracking them down, showing them the wares, and getting any sort of decent price, even if it was "good luck" that gave the opportunity to the thief, is simply not worth the effort. . . . Consider the thief who steals a truck, car, or a van. . . . Few people are willing to buy a stolen car. . . . So, while the streets are filled with vehicles in the $8,000 to $10,000 range, and many costing more, most of which are simple to steal, the vast majority that are stolen are found abandoned. However, should a budding young car thief find a fence [i.e., a police sting operative] who is foolish enough to pay 7 cents, or even 3 cents, on the dollar for stolen cars, trucks, or vans, the thief can, in short order, make a fortune. [1988: 109]

Organized Crime from the Perspective of a General Theory of Crime and Criminality

How could our theory account for criminal syndicates organized along the lines proposed by Cressey (1969) and by others too numerous to mention? The Cressey view suggests a large number of tightly knit, hierarchically organized individuals acting in concert over an extended period of time in an organization that persists beyond the membership of particular individuals. This organization is held together by a rigid code of conduct that includes such rules as "be loyal to the organization," "be a man of honor," "don't talk to the police," and "respect womanhood and your elders."

Clearly, our theory disputes the idea that this characterization could account for a significant amount of criminal activity. Our view of the existence of organized crime is the same as that of Norval Morris and Gordon Hawkins (1970). We reached this view from a rather different route, however. Whereas Morris and Hawkins were (rightly) impressed by the flimsiness of the evidence favoring the existence of organized crime (comparing it to the evidence for the existence of God), we are impressed by the incompatibility of the idea of organized crime and the ideas of crime and self-control.

Conclusions

Sometimes people work together to commit a crime, and sometimes people hire other people to commit crimes for them. The "drug market" is a good example of both phenomena. Still, the idea of crime is incompatible with the pursuit of long-term cooperative relationships, and people who tend toward criminality are unlikely to be reliable, trustworthy, or cooperative. This is not to say that some individuals do not make enormous profits from crimes that require cooperative effort over a period of time. But these "organizations" are comparatively ephemeral, and a good guess would be that for every one that survives long enough to be noticed, there are hundreds that fail to realize their immediate goal. Given a relatively restricted pool of people who tend toward criminality, and given their willingness to engage in a wide variety of criminal enterprises, on occasion the same individuals will be found working together off and on over a period of time. An illusion of organization and continuity will thereby have been created.

The "careers" of organized crime figures (as typically told by themselves) are consistent with the general theory of crime and criminality. Although these people weave a thread of organization and affiliation through the criminal events they participated in, they typically describe participation in a wide variety of criminal activities, some in concert with others (typically via accidental contact), many as solitary acts. Even those with reputations for participation in big-time swindles (see, e.g., Teresa 1973) report involvement in such mundane crimes as house burglary, car theft, and robbery. They also typically report involvement in gambling, where they do not control the outcome. As with ordinary offenders, then, so-called organized-crime figures often report engaging in high-risk, low-profit crimes, the detection of which would effectively bring to an end any organization dependent on them. In other words, on the testimony of those staffing it, organized crime is incapable of perpetuating itself.

We do not believe that our argument will change the law enforcement or media image of organized crime as a sophisticated enemy responsible for the distribution of vice and justifying massive law enforcement response and perpetual media attention. We do believe, however, that there is no need for theories designed specifically to account for gang crime, organized crime, or professional criminals. The theory of crime and self-control is capable of accounting for the facts about "organized" crime once they have been stripped of the social-organization myth.

IV

RESEARCH AND POLICY

11

Research Design and Measurement

Conceptions of crime and criminality suggest research designs and measurement procedures. If our concepts are truly new, they should cast design/measurement issues in a new light. They should have something to say about whether self-reports of offenders are adequate for measuring crime and delinquency, about the relation between "serious" and "nonserious" crime, about preferences for different counting rules (i.e., incidence or prevalence), about the utility of scales for crime and delinquency, about the desirability of longitudinal research, and about the promise of experimental or quasi-experimental research designs. As is too often forgotten in criminology, substantive ideas and theoretical preferences should structure research design and measurement, not vice versa.

Ideal Design

All else being equal, the ideal design in scientific research is the true experiment, where subjects are randomly assigned to treatment conditions and the effects of the various treatments are then compared (see Campbell and Stanley 1963: 3, who refer to experimentation as "the basic language of proof, as the only decision court for disagreement between rival theories"). This design, with sufficient replication, uniquely satisfies the three criteria of causation: association between cause and effect; temporal precedence of cause over effect; and nonspuriousness (Hirschi and Selvin 1967; Cook and Campbell 1979). All other designs are inferior, but some are better than others. For example, Thomas Cook and Donald Campbell (1979: 9) persuasively argue that next to the true experiment in scientific adequacy is the quasi-experiment, a design involving some of the active intervention of the true experiment without its control over extraneous conditions. (This design satisfies the first two criteria of causality and sometimes, if one is lucky, the third as well.) Farther down the list of scientific adequacy, one finds passive observational designs, where the investigator takes what nature gives and attempts to infer the elements of causation through correlational or similar statistical methods. Passive designs are able to establish correlations between variables, but they have difficulty distinguishing cause from effect, and they can only weakly approximate the experiment by statistically controlling for other variables that may be producing the correlations of interest. These difficulties are likely to remain in spite of advances in multivariate statistics, since such statistics remain ambiguous substitutes for manipulation and randomization.

In criminological research informed by our conceptual scheme, the researcher would be studying one of two dependent variables, crime or self-control. The ideal research design will depend on whether crime or self-control is the focus of attention, and on the assumed interaction between them. Let us begin with crime.

Crime and Research Design

It is often said that experimentation is not possible in criminology because we "cannot make people criminal" in order to test our theories. This conclusion confuses crime with criminality. In fact, we experiment every day in an effort to control crime, and there is no reason whatsoever, ethical or otherwise, for refusing to conduct such experimentation in a systematic, rigorous, or scientific manner.

For example, people do and do not buy lighting systems for their yards, bars for their doors and windows, and locks for their valuables; they lock and forget to lock their cars and houses; they sometimes avoid and at other times venture into sections of the city thought to be dangerous; they sometimes go out alone and at other times go out in groups; they form and do not form neighborhood-watch associations; they sometimes live on busy commuter routes and at other times in secluded cul-de-sacs; they sometimes accept rides from strangers and at other times do not; they sometimes spend much time with friends and family and at other times much time among strangers. In all such cases, people engage in natural experiments capable of shedding light on the causes of crime.

Consistent with our terminology, such experiments do not require the identification of "criminals" or, for that matter, of specific victims. They involve variation in the ordinary or routine risks of life and are therefore ethically neutral. They call for no particular research design beyond the most efficient sample size and methods of controlling for the effects of extraneous variables.

Crime, therefore, is relatively easy to study, and it requires nothing in the way of exceptional design considerations. Recent research from the routine-activities or criminal-opportunities perspective suggests the range of work possible when crime is the focus of inquiry (Newman 1972; Mayhew et al. 1976; Waller and Okihiro 1978; Cohen and Felson 1979; Clarke and Cornish 1983; Hope 1985; Felson 1987). As described in Chapter 2, features of the target or victim are important determinants of crime, features such as the ease with which buildings can be entered, the accessibility or convenience of the target to the potential offender, the portability and disposability of available goods, and the presence of obvious deterrents.

In the studies cited just above, the dependent variable is simply a count of specific types of criminal events, burglaries, robberies, or rapes, where no effort need be made to add events together or to connect them to specific individuals, either as offenders or victims.

Of course, it is always possible that apparent variation in opportunity is in fact variation in the availability of offenders. Television sets may be getting lighter at the same time people are becoming more interested in stealing them; people may be leaving the house at the same time other people are becoming more interested in its contents. To study the effects of opportunity on crime, we should therefore make some effort to "control" the propensities of individuals.

Self-Control and Research Design

In traditional criminology, the count of crimes is used to provide a measure of some characteristic of the offender. In early research, those committing one or more crimes were classified as criminals or delinquents, and those committing no crimes were classified as noncriminals or nondelinquents. This tradition lasted until quite recently (see, e.g., Glueck and Glueck 1968). In more recent research, there is a tendency to try to make offending a continuous variable by ascribing to all persons in the sample a score—often a count of the number of offenses they have committed (see, e.g., Wolfgang, Figlio, and Sellin 1972).

In our theory, both of these traditions overlook the fact that criminal acts are problematically related to the self-control of the actor: under some conditions people with low self-control may have few opportunities to commit crimes, and under other conditions people with high self-control may have many opportunities to commit them. If such people are mixed together in the same sample, differences in opportunities to commit crime will be confounded with differences in self-control such that the researcher may mistake the influence of one for the effects of the other.

One solution to this problem is to attempt to measure criminal tendencies independent of opportunity to commit criminal acts. This may be done in several ways. For example, tendencies may be assessed *before* crime is possible; that is, the measure of criminality is constructed from information available in the preadolescent years (and validated by its ability to predict subsequent behavior). Opportunity may also be held constant through assignment to conditions of varying opportunity, by natural variation, or by restricting attention to people sharing identical crime-relevant characteristics. Differences in criminal activity can then be ascribed to differences in tendency, since there are no differences in opportunity.

Of course, the best way to distinguish crime from self-control is through experimentation, where the researcher controls the assignment of individuals to conditions and is able to vary the level of opportunity and to measure self-control independent of opportunity. Such experimentation, even quasi-experimentation, is not often possible with phenomena such as crime, and researchers are forced to do the best they can with the less-than-ideal designs available to them. (It should be noted that designs ideal in theory are themselves often less than ideal in practice. Thus many true experiments are simply uninformative, and others are more trouble and expense than they are worth.) Nonexperimental designs also differ among themselves with respect to the extent to which they satisfy the criteria of causation, with respect to other valid scientific criteria such as external validity of their results and their compatibility with the phenomenon at issue, and with respect to such nonscientific but important criteria as cost in time and money. The currently fashionable solution to these problems is the longitudinal design. The extensive research based on the longitudinal method and the strong claims made on its behalf provide an opportunity to assess its methodological and substantive virtues. Such an assessment will allow us to investigate in some detail the proper connection between criminological theory and research design.

Is longitudinal research consistent with the nature of crime and self-control? Do the methodological strengths of longitudinal research compensate for its methodological deficiencies? Do its efficiencies outweigh its costs? Answers to these questions should lead to designs consistent with or appropriate to further development of the crime and self-control distinction.

Early Longitudinal Research

Systematic empirical research on crime in the United States is perhaps best traced to the pioneering work of Sheldon and Eleanor Glueck. The Gluecks' early work (1930, 1940) was primarily longitudinal, following large numbers of offenders over long periods of time. In the Gluecks' conception, offenders commit crimes and nonoffenders do not. Variation in criminality is therefore virtually identical to variation in crime. Once identified, nondelinquents can for all practical purposes be ignored because they will remain nondelinquents. Delinquents, however, vary among themselves over time. Some undergo maturational reform, others recidivate, and the factors producing these outcomes are worthy of sustained investigation. Thus the Gluecks typically began by locating a sample of offenders. They then followed them over time to document changes in their behavior, with the aim of discovering "the effectiveness of various forms of peno-correctional treatment" (1950: ix).

The Gluecks eventually shifted their attention to the study of causation. With causation at issue, a major problem with their research design was that it did not include reasonable comparison groups. For comparisons, the Gluecks typically relied at the beginning of their longitudinal studies on statistics from the general population. Later, when data became available, offenders could of course be compared with themselves at earlier ages. But none of this was completely satisfactory to the Gluecks, or to their critics, and they eventually turned to comparisons of matched samples of offenders and nonoffenders (on such things as age, IQ, and neighborhood) in a standard cross-sectional design. Their major cross-sectional study was published in 1950 as *Unraveling Juvenile Delinquency*.

The Gluecks continued to follow over many years the 500 delinquents and 500 nondelinquents first identified for *Unraveling*, publishing the results in 1968 under the title *Delinquents and Nondelinquents in Perspective*. As a result, the Gluecks have provided us with a large-scale, cross-sectional study to compare with an equally large-scale, longitudinal study, both studies based on the same subjects.

Without a doubt, the Gluecks' major contributions to the empirical literature on crime may be found in their 1950 cross-sectional study. Marvin Wolfgang, Robert Figlio, and Terence Thornberry (1978) report that, as of 1972, *Unraveling* was the most heavily cited book in criminology. In the sixteen years following publication of the 1968 longitudinal work, the cross-sectional study was cited four times more often than the longitudinal study (*Social Science Citation Index*, 1966–1984). Given the tremendous overlap in measurement, conceptualization, and analysis, the disproportionate influence of the cross-sectional study contradicts the idea that, all else being equal, longitudinal research is more important or valuable for criminology. Despite the claims of those favoring longitudinal designs (Farrington, Ohlin, and Wilson 1986), other comparisons of longitudinal and cross-sectional research lead to the same conclusion: the common assumption that longitudinal research, study for study, has had greater impact than cross-sectional research is not supported by the evidence.

What, then, accounts for the widespread view that longitudinal designs in criminology should be preferred to cross-sectional designs? (The list of proponents of longitudinal research is lengthy; see, e.g., Elliott, Huizinga, and Ageton 1985; Blumstein et al. 1986; Farrington, Ohlin, and Wilson 1986; Reiss 1988). We see three answers to this question: alleged methodological superiority, according to which longitudinal research solves causal questions beyond the reach of cross-sectional designs; alleged substantive superiority, according to which the facts of crime and criminality require longitudinal designs for their explication; and alleged policy superiority, according to which longitudinal research is uniquely capable of assessing the operations of the criminal justice system.

The longitudinal design involves repeated measures of the same subjects, where the frequency and duration of the "follow-up" is a function of the phenomenon in question. In longitudinal studies of crime, the researcher sometimes collects data every year (e.g., Elliott, Huizinga, and Ageton 1985) and sometimes every two years (West and Farrington 1977), but usually at longer intervals (e.g., McCord and McCord 1959; Glueck and Glueck 1968; Wolfgang, Figlio, and Sellin 1972). The longitudinal design does not entail any particular method or frequency of data collection, sampling strategy, method of analysis, or project duration.

When all subjects share a common experience (e.g., are born in a single hospital or in a single year), longitudinal studies are called "cohort" studies. When the sample includes people from more than one cohort (e.g., people born in two different years), longitudinal studies are called "multicohort" studies. When such a study completes a second wave of data collection, it becomes a multiwave, multicohort study. The multiwave, multicohort study is designed to allow separation of the effects of age, period, and cohort. It is designed to determine whether it matters that the subjects were born in a particular year (or hospital), that they are a particular age, and that the study was conducted at a particular period of time. Obviously, the multiwave, multicohort study is typically thought to be better than the single-wave, single-cohort study and, of course, better than the cross-sectional study, which, in the terms thus far introduced, is a retrospective, single-wave, multicohort study with minimum frequency of data collection.

One of the purported strengths of the prospective longitudinal study is that it entails a lack of knowledge of "outcome" variables. For example, the longitudinal researcher does not know which subjects are going to be delinquents and which are going to be nondelinquents. The disadvantage entailed by this strength is that it rules out efficient sampling procedures. One such procedure is to stratify the population on variables known to be closely associated with the dependent variable and to oversample subjects likely to be delinquent (a strategy that assumes stability in the correlates of crime or in the tendency to commit criminal acts). Because they find the assumption of stability or long-term predictability problematic, longitudinal researchers in crime and delinquency tend not to adopt this common procedure (e.g., Wolfgang, Figlio, and Sellin 1972; Elliott, Huizinga, and Ageton 1985; Tracy, Wolfgang, and Figlio 1985).

Causal Order

In the criminological literature, it is frequently asserted that the longitudinal design is superior to the cross-sectional design when one is interested in the problem of causal order. Delbert Elliott and Harwin Voss say:

> Because of the difficulty involved in establishing the temporal order of variables, causal inferences are difficult to derive from cross-sectional data. Data gathered at one point in time generally preclude insight into developmental sequences or processes that lead to delinquent behavior or dropout. . . . The availability of data gathered at different points in time permits assessment of the direction and amount of change in these scores during the course of the study and enables us to derive causal inferences. [1974: 7–8]

David Farrington makes the same claim: "Another advantage of a longitudinal study is its superiority over cross-sectional research in establishing cause and effect, by showing that changes in one factor are followed by changes in another" (1986a: 212). Joan Petersilia claims that longitudinal research is "superior to cross-sectional if one is primarily interested in drawing causal inferences" (1980: 337). And Alfred Blumstein et al. provide a list of substantive areas in which the longitudinal design is "required":

Many issues about criminal careers cannot be adequately addressed in cross-sectional research: the influence of various life events on an individual's criminal career; the effects of interventions on career development; and distinguishing between developmental sequences and heterogeneity across individuals in explaining apparent career evolution. Answering these and related questions requires a prospective longitudinal study of individuals of different ages. [1986: 199]

Such statements illustrate the extent of the *belief* that longitudinal designs solve the problem of causal order (although they suggest that faith in the design extends beyond the causal-order question). They do not, however, provide evidence or even illustration of the actual ability of the design to produce such solutions. Nor, for that matter, do these proponents of longitudinal research show that causal order is an especially difficult problem for criminology.

Is causal order especially problematic in crime and delinquency research? Recall that, in our definition, crimes are events that provide immediate gratification. As a result, they are not temporally ambiguous. Typically, in fact, they can be pinpointed to the minute or hour. When was the liquor store robbed? When did the assault or burglary or homicide or arson take place? These are not inherently difficult or ambiguous questions. Some crimes or delinquencies are of course more difficult to locate precisely in time. When did the child begin to use cigarettes or drugs? When did the child become incorrigible? But even these more ambiguous offenses can be located in time with sufficient precision to allow unambiguous conclusions about temporal sequence, at least with respect to most nontrivial causal variables.

It would appear, then, that if causal order is a problem it must stem from difficulties in establishing the order of crime and its potential causes. Since crime is, in these terms, relatively nonproblematic, we are led to infer that the potential causes of crime are especially problematic in terms of when they occur.

What causes of crime are, in these terms, problematic? From the discussions of proponents of longitudinal research, we can infer four classes of independent variables relevant to this issue: (1) age, period, and cohort; (2) standard causal variables thought to be implicated in crime and delinquency causation; (3) treatment and criminal justice intervention; and (4) the effects of ordinary life events. Let us examine each of these classes of variables with the causal order issue in mind.

Age, Period, and Cohort

In standard cross-sectional research, the observation that age is correlated with crime is subject to alternative interpretations. Differences apparently due to age (e.g., higher rates among the young) may be due to recent changes in economic or social factors important in crime causation. They may also be due to conditions present at the time when the high-rate group was born or when it graduated from elementary school. Such suggestions—that apparent age effects may be period or cohort effects—are a major justification for longitudinal research among those urging a greater emphasis on this design (see, e.g., Greenberg 1985; Blumstein et al. 1986; Farrington 1986a). If a single cohort (persons born within a limited period of time) is followed from birth to death, age differences in their criminal activity cannot be ascribed to cohort differences. Unfortunately, they may be ascribed to period effects. It may be that high-rate ages reflect nothing more than high rates of crime in the society when the cohort was at the age in question. Obviously, the cohort design must be complicated to allow resolution of this problem (or the researcher must look at data not collected as part of the cohort design).

But note that none of these inferential difficulties is a consequence of ambiguous causal order, the justification for longitudinal research we are now considering. However complex age, period, and cohort questions may be in terms of determining which of them is responsible for observed differences, there can be little controversy about whether they precede or follow crime. Crime cannot cause age, period, or cohort. Therefore, longitudinal research is not required to answer causal-order questions involving them.

In our view, the much-touted ability of the complex longitudinal study to separate age, period, and cohort effects could not be of less theoretical or practical consequence. In fact, a good case could be made for the view that concern about this distinction has distracted attention from more interesting crime data and has caused the field to misinterpret data long available on age. For example, longitudinal researchers frequently wonder whether the apparent age distribution of crime could be a "cohort" or a "period" effect rather than an age effect (Blumstein and Cohen 1979; Greenberg 1985; Farrington 1986a; Cohen and Land 1987), when an empirical answer to this question may be had by examining the age distribution of crime for differing periods and cohorts (Hirschi and Gottfredson 1983; Gottfredson and Hirschi 1986). For that matter, the longitudinal study appears to be a grossly inefficient method of discovering period effects. The post–World War II crime wave was well documented by ordinary cross-sectional data long before it was reported by longitudinal researchers (Tracy, Wolfgang, and Figlio 1985).

Concern about cohort effects is even more puzzling. Suppose it is found that a given cohort has a higher crime rate than an adjacent cohort, when age and period effects have been removed. What is to be made of this difference—that is, what life circumstances distinguish one cohort from the other? The answer, alas, is that the number of possible explanatory variables is, for all practical purposes, unlimited. It could be the size or composition of the cohorts, or it could be that they were of different ages when one of many natural catastrophes occurred. (A further irony of interest in "cohort effects" is that they can be identified only long after their occurrence. They are therefore immune to manipulation and devoid of policy significance.)

Standard Causal Variables

Data on some variables are so routinely collected by the criminal justice system and by researchers, whatever their design or theoretical interests, that it is possible to speak with confidence about their relation to crime. Interestingly enough, longitudinal researchers continue to use these variables to justify the promise of longitudinal research. This section looks at some of these standard variables and the arguments offered to justify longitudinal study of them.

Sex. In a work extolling the virtues of the longitudinal design, Blumstein et al. report that "the most consistent pattern with respect to gender is the extent to which male criminal participation in serious crimes at any age greatly exceeds that of females, regardless of source of data, crime type, level of involvement, or measure of participation" (1986: 40; see also Hirschi and Gottfredson 1983; compare Farrington 1986a; Blumstein, Cohen, and Farrington 1988b). If sex differences are sufficiently robust that they survive all these conditions, including age, then longitudinal research is not required to discover them. If the sex difference is the same at every age (see Chapter 6), then examination of this difference at any age will be sufficient to determine its magnitude, and sex differences in crime cannot be used to justify longitudinal research, however crime might be measured or defined.

Race. Longitudinal researchers do not suggest, of course, that the race-crime correlation is problematic with respect to causal order.

What, then, might be the value of a longitudinal design with respect to a race-crime connection? It is possible that race is more important at some ages than at others. In fact, the Wolfgang, Figlio, and Sellin cohort study (1972) suggested that blacks "start earlier" than whites. Our reanalysis of the Wolfgang et al. data (Hirschi and Gottfredson 1983) suggests that "age-of-onset" differences between blacks and whites are in fact merely rate differences in crime, differences that could be easily determined by cross-sectional research at any age. Because blacks have a higher rate of crime than nonblacks at all ages, they automatically have higher rates of crime at very young ages. In cohort studies, this creates the illusion, expressed in cohort terminology, of age-of-onset differences. Because blacks also have higher rates of crime at advanced ages, the same design terminology would suggest "age-of-desistance" differences between blacks and nonblacks. In fact, black offenders do not start earlier or stay longer than non-black offenders, and the cohort finding is therefore simply misleading. The design language that produces this conceptual confusion (career terminology such as "onset," "persistence," and "desistance") is foreign to the crime and self-control model, which does not make distinctions among offenders.

Longitudinal logic goes beyond onset and desistance to suggest further meaningful perturbations in race effects by age. For example, Blumstein et al. (1986: 41) interpret the National Youth Survey, a multiple cohort longitudinal study (Elliott, Huizinga, and Ageton 1985), as indicating that black-to-white robbery ratios fall from 2.25:1 when the cohort members were 11–17 years of age to 1.5:1 when the cohort members were 15–21, four years later. Such facts may or may not be important. One way to find out is to place them in the context of a conceptual scheme. Once this is done, they will turn out to be interpretable or suspect. From a crime and self-control perspective, these particular facts lead directly to concern about the adequacy of the research producing them.

On inspection, the Elliott et al. data on age-race effects might be better used to illustrate the weakness rather than the strength of the longitudinal design. Putting aside the disconcerting overlap in the age ranges compared by Blumstein et al., the cited differences do not appear to be statistically significant at conventionally accepted levels. The large standard errors of these age-, race-, and crime-specific estimates stem from the sample limitations imposed by the National Youth Survey's longitudinal design. In fact, this survey is unable simultaneously to disaggregate by sex in making race comparisons. Since race-sex interactions are routinely reported by cross-sectional research (e.g., Hindelang 1981; Hindelang, Hirschi, and Weis 1981), there would be reason to question the study's findings even were they to survive tests of statistical significance.

Age. As we have noted, one feature of the longitudinal study in criminology is its agnosticism about what it is likely to find (or about what it is looking for). Each longitudinal study begins with the fresh and seemingly scientific stance that all things are equally possible. Thus, after scores of studies of the relation between age and crime conducted over a period of about 150 years, Blumstein et al. could still say that "data are needed for a common sample on crime-specific age distributions of initiation and current participation according to both official records and self-reports" (1986: 42).

Although many criminologists would agree that the age-crime relation is crucially significant for criminological theory and crime-control policy (Greenberg 1979, 1985; Hirschi and Gottfredson 1983, 1986; Gottfredson and Hirschi 1986; Cohen and Land 1987; Shavit and Rattner 1988), only a proponent of longitudinal research would argue that the basic facts about this relation are problematic. In Chapter 6 we described the evidence supporting our view that the age-crime relation is for all practical and theoretical purposes invariant. In the view of those promoting longitudinal research, the evidence suggests that causes of crime vary from one age to another.

Let us make explicit what has been implicit in this controversy. Proponents of longitudinal designs argue that potential age-causal variable *interactions* are of great theoretical and policy significance. We argue that such interactions are trivial compared to the theoretical and policy implications of a large and direct influence of age on crime. Our view is based on research. Their view is based on research not yet conducted. The alleged weakness of our view is that it is based on findings produced by a weak design. The presumed strength of their view is that it *may be* supported by a stronger research design. This situation is not unique; in fact, it is vintage positivism. One of the features of positivism is its tendency to destroy currently accepted facts as a pretext for further research. All that is required to accomplish such destruction is to note that current facts may not mean what they appear to mean. Once doubt about current findings has been established, the positivist modestly points out that knowledge to come will be better than current knowledge and should therefore be taken more seriously.

This position leads, the evidence suggests, nowhere. It makes knowledge we do not have always superior to knowledge we do have, and it allows us the luxury of pretending that all previous research has been for naught. To treat conclusions about age effects as suspect because they derive largely from cross-sectional data is to misunderstand the problematic relation between research and truth. We do not conduct research to find the truth, but to help us find the truth. In the end, we consider the results of any given piece of research, whatever its quality, in the light of what we have learned by other means:

All too often, students of aging now fail to recognize that cross-sectional data, properly analyzed and supplemented with information from other sources, can often provide more nearly conclusive evidence about the effects of aging than can any other one kind of data. Furthermore, the recognition of the hazards of inferring age effects from cross-sectional data was all too often accompanied by an unwarranted enthusiasm for longitudinal data. [Glenn 1981: 362]

Family variables. We have made family variables among the most important factors in self-control. Longitudinal researchers agree that family factors have "a strong and consistent effect on participation [in delinquent acts]" (Blumstein et al. 1986: 43). Because they have no conception of criminality, longitudinal researchers are, however, as likely as not to miss what we would consider the crucial period of life, taking up their longitudinal studies *after* the crucial differences in level of self-control have been established. For example, Blumstein et al. cite the West and Farrington longitudinal study (1977) as exemplary, arguing that "longitudinal studies that relate measures of parenting and family structure when a child is in elementary school to later official records or self-reports of that child's participation in serious or adult criminal behavior are particularly well suited to assess the impact of parenting on criminal involvement" (1986: 43).

In our view, research interested in the impact of family factors on self-control would attempt to determine what the family was like when differences in self-control were established. The crucial period, research indicates, is *prior to* the elementary school grades, since important differences are usually present by this time. Actually, many researchers *have* been interested in the condition of the family when the child was very young, and they have done what they could to study this period. As a result, we do know something about it. In the words of Blumstein et al., the literature on family factors shows that "consistent, strict discipline; close supervision; and strong parent-child relationships including communication, affection, and interest in the child's activities" are associated with low rates of criminal participation (1986: 43).

Unfortunately for the idea that longitudinal research is "particularly well suited" to such questions, the factors listed are precisely those identified in the 1940's by cross-sectional research (Glueck and Glueck 1950). These factors have been replicated by much subsequent cross-sectional research (see, e.g., Patterson 1980) and are not dependent on longitudinal designs for their acceptance. In fact, longitudinal studies are perhaps best seen as having confirmed the results of cross-sectional designs and as having shown that the methodological criticisms of cross-sectional family research were not justified. Once again, then, we must conclude that the idea that a particular method is necessary or sufficient for the generation of truth about crime or criminality is not supported by competent evidence.

Early antisocial behavior. The continuity of the criminal career has been a major focus of longitudinal research. As a consequence, longitudinal research should now be able to tell us whether longitudinal research is required. If there is continuity over the life course in criminal activity (or its absence), it is unnecessary to follow people over time. If there is little or no continuity in criminal activity over the life course, it is again unnecessary to follow people over time. So, the longitudinal design assumes patterned change or *development* over the life course—that is, patterned change or development in criminal activity. What do the results of longitudinal research say about this assumption? Given the large amount of longitudinal research conducted in recent years, we should be able to find many estimates of the stability of delinquency.

Using Jerald Bachman's data (Bachman et al. 1967), Ross Matsueda (1986) reports stability coefficients for delinquency of .75, .81, and .59 for four waves of data collected on boys from ages 15 to 18. Lyle Shannon (1978) reports a correlation of .52 between number of police contacts before age 18 and number of police contacts after age 18 (by the time the subjects reached 32). Elliott, Huizinga, and Ageton (1985) report correlations of .58 and .71 between prior delinquency and delinquency between years in their National Youth Survey. Farrington (1973) reports data reflecting a correlation uncorrected for attenuation of .62 (gamma) between self-reported delinquency at ages 14–15 and self-reported delinquency at ages 16–17 in his London cohort. As Hindelang, Hirschi, and Weis note (1981: 79), such stability is about all that could be expected from a behavioral inventory, even if the underlying personality characteristic did not change over the period in question.

In fact, when an underlying personality characteristic is invoked, the evidence for stability becomes even more impressive. From a review of 24 longitudinal studies of aggression among males, Dan Olweus concludes that "for an interval of five years, the estimated disattenuated stability correlation is .69 and for an interval of ten years is .60" (1979: 866). Blumstein et al. summarize the evidence on persistence in crime, concluding that "while the precise fraction persisting into adult criminal careers varies by jurisdiction, by domain of crime, and by the criterion used for characterizing the adult record (e.g., arrests or convictions), there is strong evidence that the existence of a juvenile delinquency career foreshadows adult criminal careers" (1986: 88).

Thus, according to Blumstein et al. (and virtually all reviews of developmental research; e.g., West and Farrington 1973; McCord 1979; Loeber and Dishion 1983; Hirschi and Gottfredson 1986), differences in self-control remain reasonably stable from the time they are first identified. In the language of the longitudinal researcher, early self-control predicts self-control in adulthood. Given good long-term predictability, short-term predictability should be excellent. This presents something of a problem for those advocating longitudinal research: How can short-term change be the principal focus of study when little change is in fact occurring?

Longitudinal researchers use two devices to deal with this problem. One is to suggest that the continuity thus far observed has not been established over the entire life span. Taken seriously, this justification would lead future longitudinal research to concentrate on the period before ages 8–10 and on the period after about age 50. Longitudinal researchers have not displayed much interest in these periods, however, probably because the theoretical perspectivies under which they operate assume that institutional experiences generate differences in crime propensity (and because they prefer to study "serious" crime). Not much happens to infants or young children that is relevant to theories stressing adolescent gangs, marriage, or the effects of the criminal justice system. Equally obvious, crime by the elderly is so rare that efforts to make something of it are hard to justify.

If this solution to the problem of little short-term change is problematic, the second appears to be much more clever. Despite consistency over the life course, this consistency is not perfect. The task is to explain the inconsistent cases. To quote Blumstein et al.: "There is little knowledge of the factors that reliably identify antisocial preadolescents who do not progress to offending patterns involving serious crime. Furthermore, there is evidence that suggests it is even more difficult to predict eventual serious criminal behavior among persons who first become offenders in young adulthood" (1986: 47).

The idea of concentrating research attention on cases not yet explained is old and obvious. If explanatory effectiveness is to be improved, one must concentrate on cases whose behavior has not yet been explained. For example, if having a low IQ and being poorly supervised by one's parents predicts delinquency, then the puzzling case is the well-supervised delinquent with a high IQ. This problem surfaced early in delinquency research, appearing under several guises. It is the problem of the "good boy in a high-delinquency area," the "middle-class delinquent," the "latecomer to crime," and the "school dropout who makes good."

Pursuing this problem, Glueck and Glueck (1968) systematically followed 500 delinquents into adulthood in an attempt to explain the delinquency of those boys classified as being at "low risk" of delinquency (based on supervision by mother, discipline by mother, and family cohesiveness). The Gluecks' extensive analysis of their longitudinal data (an analysis not cited by those calling for longitudinal research directed at this precise question) failed to uncover variables predictive of delinquency among the sample of delinquents.

In other words, subsequent delinquency could not be predicted among groups homogeneous on current delinquency, an observation previously reported in just these terms (Hirschi and Gottfredson 1983) and repeatedly confirmed by attempts to predict subsequent crime among offenders. For example, the lengthy history of parole prediction demonstrates that the principal factor that reliably distinguishes subsequent offenders from nonoffenders is the extent of their prior records of offending (see, e.g., Gottfredson and Gottfredson 1988). The significance of the results of these longitudinal studies for the idea that change in the level of crime can be explained by longitudinal research has not been appreciated by those calling for more such research focusing directly on the same question.

The fact that crime is by all odds the major predictor of crime is central to our theory. It tells us that criminality (low self-control) is a unitary phenomenon that absorbs its causes such that it becomes, for all intents and purposes, *the* individual-level cause of crime. As a corollary, it tells us that the search for personality correlates of crime other than self-control is unlikely to bear fruit, that short-term institutional experiences (e.g., treatment programs, jobs, jail) are incapable of producing meaningful change in criminality. And, of course, it tells us that theories based on contrary assumptions are wrong.

Our assertion that only crime can predict crime is apparently contradicted by the results of research that claims to predict delinquency when prior delinquency is held constant. Thus Elliott, Huizinga, and

Ageton report that "the only variables having a direct effect on [subsequent delinquency or drug use] are involvement with delinquent peers and prior delinquency or drug use" (1985: 117). However, it turns out that Elliott et al. do not use the longitudinal feature of their longitudinal design to test the theory that justified the design in the first place. Instead, they decide that, with respect to the relation between delinquency of peers and changes in delinquency, "the use of the concurrent measures is not necessarily inappropriate . . . because certain relationships may be expected to operate at more or less the same time" (1985: 107). As a result, the Elliott et al. study merely shows that current delinquency of friends is related to current delinquency when prior delinquency is controlled. This finding may be interpreted as showing that current measures of delinquency are related to current measures of delinquency. It does not contradict the conclusion from longitudinal research that only prior delinquency predicts subsequent delinquency. (It is sometimes argued that the problems we identify are unique to particular studies and therefore say little about the virtues of the longitudinal method as a whole. Such arguments ignore the fact that the studies in question were designed in large part to display the virtues of the longitudinal method. That they fail to do so cannot therefore be dismissed as irrelevant to their justification.)

Substance abuse. After noting a relation between self-reported delinquent acts and self-reported drug use from the National Youth Survey, Blumstein et al. conclude that a "longitudinal study of both criminal involvement and drug use is needed to sort out the causal relationship between substance abuse and criminal activity" (1986: 50–51). Once again, such optimism about future longitudinal research does not appear to be justified by prior longitudinal research, or by the conceptualization of the drug-crime connection advanced by those advocating such research. The question of the causal relationship between substance abuse and criminal activity has been addressed by longitudinal research, with inconclusive results. According to survey data reproduced by Blumstein et al., "the predominant pattern among drug users who are also delinquent was for initial drug use to follow delinquency or to occur simultaneously, rather than for drug use to precede delinquency" (1986: 51).

Taken at face value, prior longitudinal research leads to the conclusion that crimes cause drug use (robbery causes addiction?). It also leads to the more reasonable conclusion that crime and drug use have common causes, and eventually it leads to our conclusion that crime and drug use are the same thing—that is, manifestations of low self-control. If we are correct, longitudinal research designed to determine the causal relationship between crime and drug use is a waste of time and money.

Peer group influences. In Chapter 7, we considered the connection between self-control and involvement in delinquent gangs. Our theory is consistent with the Gluecks' hypothesis (1950) that delinquency causes association with other delinquents (i.e., "birds of a feather flock together"). This hypothesis reverses the causal order from that asserted by differential association theory, according to which association with delinquents is a major or, in some versions, the sole cause of delinquency. Clearly, this would seem to be a case made for longitudinal research, with its ability to solve questions of causal order: Which comes first, delinquency or association with delinquents?

Current longitudinal research replicates the standard cross-sectional finding of a correlation between the respondent's delinquency and the respondent's report of the delinquency of his friends (Elliott, Huizinga, and Ageton 1985). Blumstein et al. seem to take the causal-order issue as resolved, stating that "several longitudinal studies report that association with delinquent friends is clearly related to participation in serious criminal behavior at later ages" (1986: 53).

This statement illustrates the difficulties encountered in using longitudinal designs in the absence of clear research questions that pay proper attention to alternative hypotheses. Quantitative research presupposes ideas that direct the collection, analysis, and interpretation of data. Absent such ideas, neither causal-order nor spuriousness issues are likely to be resolved, whether the study is cross-sectional or longitudinal. For example, the "finding" that delinquent friends are present before "participation in serious criminal behavior" is hardly evidence contrary to the birds-of-a-feather hypothesis, since it would also be predicted by that hypothesis—which, after all, asserts that people first become delinquents, then find delinquent friends and commit delinquent acts, including "serious criminal" acts. Unless this alternative hypothesis is acknowledged in the collection, analysis, and interpretation of data, the fact that a study is longitudinal will mean nothing in terms of the likelihood that it will add to existing knowledge.

One longitudinal study purports to have considered these issues and to have collected evidence bearing on the temporal-order issue. Elliott, Huizinga, and Ageton (1985) present a test of an "integrated theory," the major feature of which is the idea that the sole cause of persistent delinquency is the delinquency of one's friends. The study uses a longitudinal design in a national probabiiity self-report survey, with six waves of data already collected through 1983. Does this study shed new light on the delinquency/delinquency-of-friends question?

Which comes first, according to the National Youth Survey, delinquency of friends or delinquency? Interestingly, Elliott, Huizinga, and Ageton (1985: 99) argue that their longitudinal design inhibits rather than facilitates an unambiguous test of the causal-order question, noting that their theory presupposes more rapid changes than their longitudinal design will accommodate. The actual test of the theory, then, as mentioned (see also Chapter 7), is a composite cross-sectional/longitudinal design, where involvement with delinquent peers and self-reported delinquency are measured at the same time. It is not surprising that Elliott et al. find a strong correlation between self-reported delinquency and involvement with delinquent friends. This strong correlation has been reported in similar cross-sectional research for at least 35 years. The Elliott et al. interpretation of the relation, with lags and cross lags, is more complex than those produced by earlier research. Its causal status is not, however, more definitive.

This summary of some of the social and demographic correlates of crime leads us to conclude that the causal-order problem is an illusion that largely disappears when it is addressed one variable at a time. We find no evidence that existing longitudinal research has resolved any issue of causal order more adequately than has cross-sectional research. On the contrary: the complexities of analysis introduced by longitudinal data have tended to interfere with the straightforward resolution of what turn out to be largely conceptual issues.

Treatment and Criminal Justice Interventions

According to Farrington, "longitudinal studies are useful in investigating the effects of particular events or life experiences on the course of development. A central question in criminology concerns the effects of different penal treatments on criminal careers" (1979: 310–11). Farrington then goes on to describe a research design that blends features of a true experiment (random assignment to treatment and control groups) with the pre- and post-treatment measures provided by the longitudinal design.

We do not wish to quarrel with the ideal design for evaluating the effects of treatment in the criminal justice system. We note only that evaluation-design issues have been carefully and fully explicated (e.g., Logan 1972; Cook and Campbell 1979) and that the admitted strength of these designs says nothing about the value of longitudinal designs that share none of their features beyond repeated measurement.

Longitudinal research in crime and delinquency is by definition nonexperimental. Active intervention by the investigator and random assignment of subjects to treatment and control groups are not part of these designs and should not be used to justify them. More important, features of longitudinal research should not be presented as though they were part and parcel of powerful experimental or quasi-experimental designs.

Longitudinal research frequently reports finding treatment and justice-system intervention effects on behavior. For example, several studies report that intervention (arrest, conviction, fines, institutionalization) is followed by greater delinquency among those dealt with by the system (Williams and Gold 1972; Wolfgang, Figlio, and Sellin 1972; Farrington 1979). There are, however, good reasons to be suspicious of these alleged effects (see Gottfredson and Hirschi 1987b: 598–602). The best reason is that they are typically not found when more powerful experimental designs are employed.

The Effects of Ordinary Life Events

A considerable source of the attraction of the longitudinal design is its ability to track individuals through ordinary institutional experiences, such as entering and leaving school, entering and leaving marriage, finding and losing a job, and becoming a parent. The design assumes that these events may have a causal impact on criminal behavior and that the task is to study the interplay between subject characteristics (e.g., social class) and characteristics of the institutional experience (e.g., marriage to a delinquent as opposed to a nondelinquent spouse [Farrington 1986a]) as they jointly influence the probability of delinquency.

It seems to us that concern with the *conditions* under which life events affect criminal behavior should follow evidence that such events do in fact affect criminal behavior. The evidence that such events are important is, in our view, not nearly as strong as advocates of developmental studies of crime and delinquency would have us believe (see Chapters 6 and 7). In logic, the problem of determining the effect of these ordinary life experiences is identical to that encountered in determining the effects of delinquent peers on delinquent behavior. Associations with delinquents are not "accidental" or, in research terminology, random. Also not random, it may be argued, is marriage to a nondelinquent spouse, persistence in a good job, or an educational or vocational program. Nor is the age at which these events take place accidental or random. In fact, many theories would argue that the characteristics of people associated with these events are also associated with crime and delinquency. Indeed, we would go so far as to argue that crime-relevant characteristics of people cause all of these events.

If our theory is true, then reports from longitudinal research of a causal impact of ordinary life events on crime are wrong. Neither perspective is unambiguously supported or refuted by a correlation between ordinary events and delinquency. What is required is either random assignment to such events (or complete assignment to them, as in the World War II "assignment" of almost all young men to a "job"; see Chapter 7) or careful control of relevant personal characteristics (coupled with adequate variation in assignment; i.e., there must be enough "good workers" out of work and enough "bad workers" continuously employed to allow the relevant comparisons). The obvious difficulty in finding the requisite natural variation seems to us evidence for the view that the longitudinal/developmental assumption that such events are important neglects its own evidence on the stability of personal characteristics (West and Farrington 1977; Farrington 1979, 1986a; Loeber 1982). In the latter case, the "cross-sectional" survey (which can, it might be recalled, ask people "when" and "how long" questions) is more likely to be adequate than the longitudinal study with an equivalent budget. The funds used to follow the same people over an extended period of time can be used to collect more information on more people at one point in time, thus facilitating the application of modern, sophisticated multivariate statistics to such problems. Advocates of longitudinal research acknowledge the utility of such techniques (Farrington 1979), but the design of existing longitudinal studies unfortunately inhibits their application, in part by creating the illusion that the longitudinal design somehow makes them unnecessary. Given the centrality of the dispute between the personality and the institutional views of crime causation, unqualified recommendations for more longitudinal studies (Farrington, 1979, 1986a, 1986b; Tracy, Wolfgang, and Figlio 1985; Blumstein et al. 1986; Farrington, Ohlin, and Wilson 1986) are once more hard to justify.

The problems facing the researcher can be illustrated by consideration of the effects of marriage on crime. As is extensively documented, crime rates tend to rise until late adolescence and then to decline. The general decline in crime is coincident with a variety of life events that seem inconsistent with criminal behavior, such as a job, marriage, and the accumulation of material goods. This coincidence has suggested to many criminologists that these events are responsible for the decline in crime (e.g., Greenberg 1979, 1985; Baldwin 1985; Farrington 1986a). Existing research, however, contradicts the hypothesis that the decline in crime with age is due to such events, since the decline occurs whether or not these events occur (Hirschi and Gottfredson 1983). The inability of life events to explain the age distribution of crime suggests that these events are not themselves causes of crime. This conclusion is contrary to the basic substantive justification for the longitudinal design.

Longitudinal researchers counter with the following argument:

Some factors only apply at certain ages. For example, the relation between marriage and crime cannot be studied among 10-year-olds, who cannot get married, any more than the relation between truancy and crime can be studied among 60-year-olds. Other factors may have different meanings at different ages. . . . It seems implausible to argue that all variables are related to crime in the same way at all ages. [Farrington 1986a: 229]

Similarly, it is argued that:

there are different relationships with offending at different ages. For example, . . . Farrington (1986[b]) reported that if a child, up to age 10, had parents who had been convicted, this was one of the best predictors of that child offending at ages 14 through 16 and 17 through 20, but did not predict offending at ages 10 to 13. West (1982) reported that if a delinquent married between ages 18 and 21, marriage had no effect on offending between these ages, while marriage between 21 and 24 (to a noncriminal woman) led to a decrease in offending between these ages. It is implausible to propose that a variable such as marriage should have the same effect on offending at all ages. [Farrington, Ohlin, and Wilson 1986: 27]

This combination of logical and data-based argument is, at first glance, persuasive. Marriage and truancy would not be expected to have the same effect or the same meaning for children as for old people. The issue, however, is their empirical relation to crime, a relation that needs to be established before it can be used as part of a *logical* refutation of the age-invariance thesis. If truancy, marriage, and stable employment are causes of crime at an early age, and *if there are no equivalents of these variables at later ages*, then the causes of crime indeed vary from one age to another. What needs to be established in the first instance, therefore, is the causal influence of these variables at any age. This has not been done, and arguments that assume it has been or could be done remain speculative rather than logical.

For that matter, establishing the causal influence of a variable that is apparently meaningful only at one time in the life course would not clinch the case that the causes of crime are age-specific. The variable in question may have other forms or analogs. For example, school truancy is not the only form of truancy. Indeed, runaways were once called "home truants," and joblessness may in some cases be a radical form of truancy. Clearly, being "absent without leave" (AWOL) from military service is the logical equivalent of school truancy, although it takes place when school truancy is no longer possible. If our argument is correct, the idea that certain factors operate only at certain ages merely reflects inadequate conceptualization of the causes of crime. (In response to this argument, Blumstein, Cohen, and Farrington "wonder . . . what the functional equivalent of marriage might be at age 8" [1988b: 65]. The answer to this question of course depends on the function of marriage at any age. Since we do not ascribe a crime-prevention function to marriage, we are in no position to guess what its age-8 equivalents might be. However, we suspect that the question properly specified would not be nearly as difficult as Blumstein et al. take it to be. All studies of enduring phenomena encounter similar difficulties. They solve them by merely conceptualizing the underlying causes.)

Such conceptual equivalents, however, need not be adduced in the present case, since the empirical evidence for the argument that the causes of crime vary by age is not persuasive. The principal findings of differential causation by age come from the West and Farrington longitudinal study (1977). The argument for a differential effect of parental criminality depending on the age of the child is not convincing. All differences are in the same direction, and the differences among the differences are insignificant. (No test of the statistical significance of the difference is reported.) The correct conclusion from the data presented is that the effect of parental criminality is the *same* at all ages. If it were not the same, we would have to explain why one of the major causes of crime is not correlated with "early onset" but appears to produce its effects from four to ten years after exposure to it.

The marriage finding is even less persuasive. The subjects in the London study were not randomly assigned to marital statuses, let alone to delinquent and nondelinquent wives, and we therefore have no reason to believe that a meaningful "age by marriage by type of marriage" interaction has been discovered in the London longitudinal study. When such an interaction is discovered, in our view the burden is on the researcher to show that it is replicable and theoretically nontrivial.

Prevalence and Incidence; Participation and Lambda

A major attraction in the contemporary call for longitudinal research is that it offers the opportunity to distinguish clearly between ordinary offenders and career criminals—in other words, the opportunity to study "the dimensions of active criminal careers" (Blumstein et al. 1986: 55). Advocates of the longitudinal design stress the fact that the "crime rate" can be "decomposed" into several components. The crime rate is a function of both the number of persons in the population committing crimes (the prevalence of crime) and the number of crimes they commit. When the denominator of the rate consists of the total number of people in the population, the first rate is traditionally called the prevalence rate and the second the incidence rate of crime. Modern criminal-career researchers alter the traditional incidence measure by using "the number of active criminals" as the denominator to produce individual frequency rates, or what they call *lambda*.

All of these statistics can be computed from cross-sectional and longitudinal designs. For example, the annual crime rates reported by the *Uniform Crime Reports* (e.g., U.S. Department of Justice 1985) and the National Crime Survey are cross-sectional estimates of the incidence of crime. When researchers divide subjects into delinquents and nondelinquents (however delinquency is measured), a prevalence statistic may be calculated. When the number of persons committing at least one criminal act and the number of acts they have committed are known, one can calculate lambda, whatever the research design. The traditional tendency among researchers has been to treat prevalence and incidence as interchangeable and lambda as derivative (Gottfredson and Hirschi 1986). The current preference among longitudinal researchers is for prevalence and lambda, with the traditional incidence measure being seen as derivative (Farrington 1979; Wilson and Herrnstein 1985; Blumstein et al. 1986).

The interest of the longitudinal community in prevalence and lambda stems not from the idea of interchangeability but from the idea that these measures may have distinct causes. "The factors that distinguish participants from nonparticipants could well be different from the factors that distinguish among participants, in terms of their offending frequency" (Blumstein et al. 1986: 54). Put in other terms, the criminal-career researcher assumes that the causes of the second crime *may* differ from the causes of the first and third crimes, that offenders who commit five crimes may differ from those who commit two or twelve, and that differences among offenders are as significant for the causation of crime as differences between offenders and nonoffenders. Nor does this exhaust the complexities introduced by interest in differences among offenders over time. The offender who moves from petty theft to rape to vandalism may differ in causal terms from the offender who starts with aggravated assault and moves to bicycle theft and shoplifting. Since such sequences are significant to criminal-career research and by definition take place over time, they help justify longitudinal research. Lambda is also attractive to those interested in crime-control policies that focus on the individual offender.

The career-criminal perspective introduces a distinction not unlike that found routinely in medical research. For example, medical researchers studying the causes of heart disease can focus on people who have suffered heart attacks and attempt to find factors indicative of multiple attacks, or they can focus on the general population and attempt to find factors distinguishing people who suffer from those who do not suffer heart attacks. In the first case they deal with a population whose behavior and treatment has been much affected by the initial heart attack. In the second case they deal with a population whose "causal history" has not been contaminated by efforts to correct the medical problem of interest. Researchers concentrating on the first group will likely formulate policies for the individualized treatment of heart attack patients and will explore all sorts of operative techniques, drugs, and mechanical devices (thereby attracting great attention and resources to their efforts). To the extent that such policies are successful, the lives of some heart attack victims will be prolonged. Researchers studying the prevalence of heart attacks, in contrast, will attempt to identify manipulable causes of heart attacks, such as smoking, lack of exercise, and excessive cholesterol. To the extent that such research is successful, it will prolong the lives of a great many people, including, in all likelihood, heart attack victims. The statistics of human longevity are driven much more by prevalence than by lambda factors.

There is no reason to believe that the same logic does not apply to crime. Our theory would predict that the correlates of the prevalence of crime are also correlates of crime incidence. That is, our theory assumes that the causes of criminal acts are the same regardless of the number of such acts. It also assumes that the stable characteristics of individuals that "cause" crime do not thereby produce "stable" or "consistent" criminal behavior.

We have previously investigated the data bearing on this question (Gottfredson and Hirschi 1988a). Here we briefly summarize the results of that investigation and describe its implications for the crime-criminality perspective.

Standard research determines the criminality of people by counting the number of criminal acts they have committed in a specified period. The aim is to account for variation in the measure of criminality. Ordinarily, researchers assume as we do that the causes of one offense are the same as the causes of others—that is, "crime" or "criminality" is a continuous variable. (They need not assume, of course, that the difference been twenty and thirty acts is ten times greater than the difference between two and three acts.) They also typically assume that the causal system producing criminality is likely to remain stable over time unless acted on by an outside force. Such assumptions have well-known statistical and theoretical advantages and are capable of direct, meaningful testing. Researchers vary in where they draw the line between offenders and nonoffenders and in how many levels of offenders they wish to acknowledge. The actual decisions on these issues are typically guided by inspection of the data and by previous research. Because measurement decisions depend on the research question, the method of measurement, and the frequency of the offense in the population at issue, they are made prior to examination of the data only with great risk.

As noted, the opposite point of view is advocated by the career perspective. In that perspective, the fundamental cutting point is between people who have committed at least one offense and those who have committed none. Beyond this cutting point (i.e., among offenders), counting procedures are much like those followed by researchers outside the career perspective.

To examine the significance of these many distinctions, we use data from the Richmond Youth Project (Hirschi 1969), which collected police records and self-report data on 2,587 males and self-report data on 1,488 females. The official data are counts of offenses recorded in police files, whatever the subsequent disposition of the case. The large sample and the large number of serious offenses recorded and reported are sufficient to allow examination of the prevalence-incidence distinction.

In Table 7, Column 1 represents the number of offenses committed by males in the sample. This column, commonly called a frequency distribution, is, in ordinary terminology, the "incidence" of crime (I). Career researchers decompose this distribution on the grounds that it *may* be misleading. Following their logic, Column 2 divides the sample into two groups, those who have and those who do not have a recorded offense. In career terms, this distribution is called "partici-

TABLE 7

Measures of Incidence (I), Participation (P), and Frequency (λ) by Type of Offense and Source of Data, Males Aged 13–18

Number of offenses	Official records, all offenses			Official records, serious offenses[a]		
	I	P	λ	I	P	λ
	(1)	(2)	(3)	(4)	(5)	(6)
0	1,630	1,630	—	2,280	2,280	—
1	396	957	396	214	307	214
2	211	—	211	41	—	41
3	111	—	111	33	—	33
4	66	—	66	5	—	5
5	49	—	49	6	—	6
6+	124	—	124	8	—	8
Total sample	2,587	2,587	957	2,587	2,587	307
Total offenses/ offenders	3,067	957	3,067	509	307	509
Mean	1.19	.37	3.20	.20	.12	1.66

Number of offenses	Official records, theft			Self reports[b]		
	I	P	λ	I	P	λ
	(7)	(8)	(9)	(10)	(11)	(12)
0	2,220	2,220	—	724	724	—
1	232	367	232	643	1,757	643
2	73	—	73	482	—	482
3	23	—	23	343	—	343
4	18	—	18	171	—	171
5	6	—	6	79	—	79
6+	15	—	15	39	—	39
Total sample	2,587	2,587	367	2,481	2,481	1,757
Total offenses/ offenders	660	367	660	3,949	1,757	3,949
Mean	.26	.14	1.80	1.59	.71	2.25

SOURCE: Richmond Youth Survey data (Hirschi 1969: 54–62, 298–99).
[a]Robbery, burglary, and assault.
[b]Six item scale, with reference period "ever." Responses coded "yes" or "no."

pation" (P). (Recall that participation is said to be of interest in prevention or in theories of deviance or trivial offending but to have little value in research focused on the effects of criminal justice policy.)

Column 3 shows the distribution of offenses among those who have committed offenses, referred to in career terms as "frequency" or lambda (λ). The central distinction of the career model can thus be represented by the formula:

$\lambda = I,$

where $I \geq 1$, or $P = 0$.

The difference between the two measures is that one includes the value 0, nonoffenders, while the other does not. Where interest focuses on the causes of the difference between 0's (nonoffenders) and any other number (offenders, however defined), lambda does not apply.[1]

Another measurement issue addressed by the data in Table 7 is the treatment of serious as opposed to trivial offenses or to all offenses without regard to seriousness. Because robbery, burglary, and assault are universally considered to be serious offenses, Column 4 lists the count of these offenses for the sample as a whole. Serious counts too can be transformed without difficulty into participation and lambda equivalents (Columns 5 and 6).

The most common subdivision of crimes is of course that between person and theft offenses. Column 7 thus lists the distribution of theft offenses, with Columns 8 and 9 showing the participation and lambda measures of the theft count.

Finally, Table 7 shows the same three distributions for a standard six-item self-report measure based on the same sample (Columns 10–12). The participation measure is particularly problematic for self-report data because the bulk of the sample will report at least some offenses and thus fall within the offender category.

We are now in position to examine the consequences of these distinctions for the correlates of "crime." Researchers familiar with

---

[1] Blumstein, Cohen, and Farrington (1988b: 58) complain that we misunderstand what they call "individual crime rate," "frequency," or "lambda." They go on to define frequency or lambda as: "the number of crimes an active offender commits in a unit of time"—which does not appear to be all that difficult to understand or all that different from the definition we use. Apparently, however, it is crucial that lambda be measured precisely as it exists in the minds of those inventing it. Otherwise, the observed results cannot be used to say anything about the behavior of the true lambda (see Blumstein, Cohen, and Farrington 1988b: 58–64). Why little modifications of a measure should make such a difference here when large modifications of measures typically make little difference elsewhere in social science, Blumstein et al. do not say. And of course they cannot show that these little modifications do make a difference because they, like the rest of us, are only guessing about what we will find when we at last measure lambda correctly.

the statistical implications of restricting the range of the dependent variable for correlation coefficients can predict the results of this exercise. They will be impressed if these distinctions are sufficiently strong to shine through statistical tendencies to the contrary. They will also be impressed if *for no theoretical reason* the prevalence-incidence distinction produces results contrary to established statistical tendencies.

Table 8 depicts seven common correlates and their relation to the twelve measures of crime. Crime is measured first with official records (Columns 1–9) and then with self-reports (Columns 10–12). The number of cases on which the correlations are based vary from measure to measure, with the range of sample sizes shown at the bottom of each column. (Sex is shown only for self-report data.) Two standard measures of statistical association, Pearson's r and gamma, are reported for each comparison. (Unless otherwise noted, Pearson's correlations in the table are significant at the .05 level. The sample is described in Table 7.)

Inspection of the correlations in Table 8 yields two conclusions. First, they are substantively the same from one career measure to another. Contrary to career-model predictions, the researcher could here focus on incidence, on participation, or even on lambda in its various definitions without concern. There is some variation in the correlation coefficients in Table 8, but the direction, pattern, and relative magnitude of the correlations is much the same for all measures. In general, then, and consistent with the crime and criminality perspective, substantive conclusions about the causes and correlates of crime in Table 8 do not depend on career distinctions. Second, there is one important, easily predictable limitation to this conclusion: Generally, as one moves from participation to lambda to lambda for serious offenses, the correlations become smaller, eventually approaching insignificance as sample sizes also decline. The career paradigm thus pursues ever smaller correlations based on ever smaller sample sizes, with nothing but a statistical test to tell us whether the results are meaningful.

If we ask, "Would researchers studying *participation* measures be misled about the correlates of lambda?," the answer would be "no." In other words, to the extent this research is generalizable (and the findings of Table 8 are among the most heavily replicated in the field), findings based on standard measures are fully applicable to "active offenders," "serious offenders," "career criminals," and indeed to all of the categories and types of offenders said to be worthy of special study by advocates of the career model. Advocates of this model thus

TABLE 8

Correlations (Pearson's r and gamma) Between Outside Variables and Incidence (I), Participation (P), and Frequency (λ) Measures of Crime

		Official records, all offenses[a]			Official records, serious offenses[a]		
Outside variable		I	P	λ	I	P	λ
		(1)	(2)	(3)	(4)	(5)	(6)
Race	r	.21	.25	.16	.17	.20	.10
	gamma	.46	.51	.24	.57	.58	.16
Smoke	r	.21	.25	.15	.14	.16	.06*
	gamma	.47	.52	.28	.47	.48	.21
Drink	r	.20	.23	.16	.14	.16	.09*
	gamma	.44	.48	.16	.46	.47	.26
Date	r	.14	.21	.07	.10	.11	.10*
	gamma	.38	.42	.10	.34	.34	.32
GPA	r	-.21	-.28	-.13	-.15	-.18	-.07*
	gamma	-.35	-.38	-.17	-.36	-.37	-.10
Friends picked up	r	.21	.26	.14	.15	.16	.15
	gamma	.37	.41	.21	.37	.38	.30
Number of cases		1,858–2,587	1,858–2,587	699–957	1,858–2,587	1,858–2,587	206–307

		Official records, theft[a]			Self reports[a]		
Outside variable		I	P	λ	I	P	λ
		(7)	(8)	(9)	(10)	(11)	(12)
Race	r	.24	.27	.19	.04	.02*	.04
	gamma	.67	.67	.42	.06	.03	.08
Smoke	r	.16	.15	.17	.35	.23	.30
	gamma	.42	.42	.27	.51	.58	.44
Drink	r	.16	.15	.15	.41	.26	.36
	gamma	.42	.43	.15	.60	.69	.51
Date	r	.11	.11	.12	.29	.22	.22
	gamma	.31	.31	.22	.40	.46	.34
GPA	r	-.13	-.14	-.11	-.15	-.10	-.13
	gamma	-.27	-.28	-.18	-.14	-.15	-.12
Friends picked up	r	.16	.18	.10	.43	.29	.36
	gamma	.38	.39	.13	.46	.53	.39
Number of cases		1,858–2,587	1,858–2,587	250–367	1,784–2,481	1,784–2,481	1,274–1,757
Sex	r				.28	.25	.21
	gamma				.48	.51	.43
Number of cases					2,201	2,201	1,370

SOURCE: Richmond Youth Project data (Hirschi 1969).
[a]The three variables are defined and their distributions shown in Table 7.
*Correlation not significant at .05 level.

have no reason to question the relevance of prior research to questions of the utility and validity of their own "paradigm."

Interestingly, Blumstein, Cohen, and Farrington (1988a) summarize our point of view as a testable hypothesis that turns out to be consistent with Table 8: "If they [Gottfredson and Hirschi] are right, all criminal career features will be interrelated, and the correlates and predictors of participation, for example, will have to be the same as the correlates and predictors of frequency and career length" (p. 5). At the same time, they summarize their own point of view as a testable hypothesis that turns out to be inconsistent with the data in Table 8: "In the criminal career approach, by contrast, the different criminal career features can each have different correlates and predictors and they are not necessarily interrelated" (ibid.).

Prior research agrees with the results of Table 8 that the correlates of crime are robust over method of measurement, crime types, crime seriousness, and even limitations of range. In fact, substantial consensus on the basic correlates of crime has developed in the face of considerable dispute about their theoretical meaning.

Criminal Events as Measures of Criminality

We do not mean, however, that some measures of crime and criminality are not better than others. On the contrary, our position suggests that criminal acts or events may not be the best measures of criminality, especially by themselves.

First of all, such events are insufficiently numerous at all stages of the life course to allow comparable measures from one age to another. For example, very young children are incapable of criminal acts, as are in many cases the elderly. To study the propensity to crime among such groups, it would therefore be necessary to adopt alternative measures. Second, such events are insufficiently numerous among some groups to allow study of criminality among them, even during high-rate periods. Women and some ethnic groups pose particular problems in this regard (for example, the Richmond Youth Project did not collect police data on females because too few of them had criminal records). Third, such events are often insufficiently numerous (when measured by official or process data) even among high-rate groups to allow treatment of criminality as a continuous variable. Finally and most seriously, such events often depend on opportunity factors that are, to some extent, independent of the criminality of the actor. When they involve the action of officials as well as of the offender, such events may be even further removed from the criminality of the actor.

Self-Reported Criminal Acts as Measures of Criminality

If we ask, "Would researchers who prefer self-report measures be misled by the comparisons in Table 8?," the answer would be "no." The results do not depend on the method of measurement. Once again, however, this does not require the conclusion that all methods of measurement are equally appropriate from the crime and self-control perspective.

If officially recorded events are factorially complex in that they reflect environmental opportunities and the behavior of officials as well as the propensities of the actor, self-reported events are also factorially complex in different ways. Self reports reflect factorially complex events as well as criminality. They also reflect the influence of criminality on the task of conceptualizing and disclosing one's behavior. (Questionnaires and interviews appear to have differential validity depending on the criminality of the respondent. Thus, the higher the level of criminality, the lower the validity of crime measures [Hindelang, Hirschi, and Weis 1981], as our perspective would predict.) Taken together, the limitations of official and self-report counts of criminal acts as measures of criminality are sufficient to suggest that a new or alternative method be developed.

Research Design and the Theory of Crime

The longitudinal study is a consequence of particular theories or orientations toward the causes of crime. Theories that see crime as a consequence of developmental processes or stages, as an occupation or state one moves into and out of, or as the consequence of positive learning by malleable individuals all suggest the desirability or necessity of following individuals over time.

Our theory sees crime as a consequence of relatively stable characteristics of people and the predictable situations and opportunities they experience. It does not presume that major changes in criminal activity are associated with entry into or exit from roles, institutions, or organizations. It may therefore be adequately tested at any point in the life course. The preferred age of subjects will depend on expected distributions of the important variables.

What is clear, therefore, is that the theoretical point being tested to a large extent determines the appropriateness of a research design. The reverse is true as well: advocacy of a particular research design almost by definition entails acceptance of a theory of crime. Thus researchers favoring longitudinal research designs must assume that transitions from one state to another (e.g., from being single to being married) produce changes in crime. They must assume that the specific character of institutional arrangements or social relations will have an impact on crime (e.g., that being married to a nondelinquent wife will have good consequences whereas being married to a delinquent wife will have bad consequences independent of the initial propensities of the husband). Such theories may of course be correct or incorrect. But their truth is problematic, and what needs to be understood is that these theories and not methodological virtue may be behind the preference for the longitudinal design.

Although theoretical notions are implicit in the decision to advocate longitudinal designs, explicit theories of crime are extremely rare among longitudinal researchers. One finds them proposing to examine the effects of becoming unemployed, dropping out of school, or getting married, but the theoretical justification for these interests appears typically to be nothing more than the commonsense notion that these factors "should make a difference." When pressed, longitudinal researchers tend to be eclectic and to fall back on theories traditionally used to explain cross-sectional results. Thus, for example, in his attempt to explain changes in crime over the life course, David Greenberg (1979) proposes a model combining traditional strain/social-control ideas. Elliott, Huizinga, and Ageton (1985) combine three standard sociological theories (strain, control, and differential association) to provide structure to the National Youth Survey. And Farrington (1986b) combines subcultural, opportunity, social-learning, social-control, and differential association theories to produce a four-stage processual model of delinquency.

The "theoretical" appeal of longitudinal research apparently lies in its implicit promise to take us to the scene of the crime, to allow study of the person before, during, and after the event. Frequent measurement is interpreted as measurement directly relevant to the causal chain involving crime and as measurement sufficiently detailed to allow us to understand the meaning of events to those participating in them.

In practice, "frequent" measurement becomes once-a-year or once-every-six-months measurement. More frequent measurement would be prohibitively expensive, even if the size of the study sample were not increased to provide the cases necessary to study the rare combinations of life events produced by such frequent measurement. For example, in any given *week*, only a very small portion of an adolescent sample would be expected to drop out of school, to use marijuana for the first time, or to acquire new delinquent friends. Even assuming perfect correlations between such activities and subsequent crime, the sample sizes would in all likelihood be too small to allow rejection of the null hypothesis. Thus, even if the theory guiding such frequent-measurement research were true, the data collected to test it could not falsify or verify the theory.

However, frequent measurement remains a seductive justification for longitudinal research. Because we tend to equate behavioral and causal sequences, we imagine that observation of the former will automatically reveal the latter. Put another way, we assume that "complete" observation is all that is necessary to understand causal processes. Unfortunately, nothing could be further from the truth. We can observe offenders every hour of every day and still not know the causes of their behavior. Facts require a context for their interpretation. Even longitudinal facts do not speak for themselves. Observation, as Charles Darwin reminded us, must be for or against some view if it is to be useful. As of now, it seems to us, the longitudinal research tradition has no unique findings or compelling theory about the causes of crime that it could use to justify more detailed or more frequent observation.

In the cross-sectional view of crime, differences across people and their life circumstances are sufficiently stable over time that day-to-day variability is uninteresting or likely to be nothing more than measurement error. In this view, apparently large changes in circumstance are themselves perfectly predictable from the explanation of crime itself. Lack of perseverance in school, in a job, or in an interpersonal relationship are simply different manifestations of the personal factors assumed to cause crime in the first place. Taking up with delinquent friends is another example of an event without causal significance. Since such "events" are predictable consequences of the causes of crime, there is little or no point in monitoring them.

Differences in propensity to crime are also sufficiently stable over time that they need not be continually reassessed. Given basic stability in the causal system, the particular slice of it that one examines is determined by considerations of (1) sampling efficiency: it makes sense to concentrate research at the point in life where the crime rate is maximally variable; (2) measurement adequacy: some subjects are more suitable than others for questionnaire surveys, record searches, or experimental interventions; (3) policy relevance: for example, understanding crime among the elderly is of limited practical significance; and (4) sampling costs: for example, young people are preferred because they are easier to find and to induce to cooperate.

In one version of the cross-sectional view, differences in crime rates by age are due to age itself (see Chapter 6). This view leads to an interest in the causes of crime that do not operate on the propensity to crime previously mentioned but on the differences in the likelihood of criminal acts among persons equal in criminal propensities. For example, holding propensity constant, areas with a curfew for teenagers would be expected to have lower crime rates than areas without such a curfew. Holding propensity constant, communities in which schools enforce attendance rules would be expected to have lower crime rates than communities in which such rules were ignored. Interest in questions of such obvious policy relevance can only be satisfied by research based on samples sufficiently large and variable to allow control for differences in propensity to crime, samples far beyond the reach of feasible longitudinal designs. (Moreover, since such findings can be produced without delay, they are likely to be of greater policy relevance than those produced by standard longitudinal research.)

At first glance, it seems reasonable to argue in favor of both approaches to research and policy. If time and money were unlimited, and if there were no opportunity costs from a policy focusing on lambda, we would agree with this position. Since this is not the case, we believe the present emphasis of longitudinal research leads us to overlook more promising avenues for criminal justice policy. Criminal-career researchers argue that criminal justice policy is restricted to criminal offenders and cannot attend to the general population. According to this line of reasoning, policies directed at family, school, and environmental design are not "criminal justice" policies and are therefore irrelevant topics of research for federal agencies charged with crime control. Obviously, we do not agree.

Conclusions

The thesis of this chapter has been that there must be an intimate connection between the conceptualization of a problem and the design of research focused on that problem. Fads and fashions of research design in criminology come and go, and the current emphasis on the prospective longitudinal design may therefore be expected to do the same. This state of affairs is a consequence of the devotion to a form of positivism that relentlessly pursues "facts" for their own sake. We believe there is a higher form of positivism that explicitly recognizes the need to frame its research agenda in terms of existing knowledge rather than in terms of the assumption that nothing has been hitherto discovered.

The crime and self-control perspective is in fact based on three general facts that any research design would have to take into account. For purposes of discussion, we can express these facts in abstract methodological terms:

1. Indicators of crime and deviance are consistently positively correlated among themselves. It is therefore possible to construct highly reliable general measures of crime (*versatility* or *reliability*).

2. These composite measures of crime are highly stable over time. People having a high degree of criminality at one time will tend to have a high degree of criminality later in life (*stability*).

3. Composite measures of crime follow a predictable path over the life course, rising to a peak in late adolescence and declining sharply thereafter throughout life (*age effect*).

Put briefly, criminology possesses a dependent variable that is broad or general, stable from the early years of life, and predictably variable over time. From these facts, much about research design and measurement follows. For example, to be useful, longitudinal studies must be underway before the age at which crime can be reliably measured. Otherwise, such studies cannot measure their independent variables prior to manifestation of their dependent variable, nor can they examine an environment that has not been itself influenced by individual differences in criminality. For example, during the period of life addressed by most longitudinal studies, the school experiences and friendship patterns are inextricably linked to individual differences in delinquency. Given this state of affairs, it is obvious that longitudinal designs are not *a priori* superior to (or even different from) cheaper and more efficient cross-sectional designs.

If the interesting variability in crime (i.e., variability that cannot be explained by nonmanipulable variables such as age, sex, and ethnicity) appears at relatively young ages, it is going to be difficult to ascribe such variation to institutional experiences occurring later in life. Furthermore, if the phenomenon of "criminality" is present at the time that longitudinal research gets under way, no correlational study of the manifestations of this phenomenon can shed light on its causal priority vis-à-vis other phenomena.

The versatility or measurement-reliability finding may be expressed as empirical evidence of the existence of an underlying construct, a construct we refer to as self-control. If we are correct, or if any general underlying construct is consistent with the data, all efforts to categorize or typologize crime and related behaviors cannot survive standard tests of convergent and discriminant validity. Put in terms of current discussions of incidence and prevalence, the assertion by some criminologists that the concept of crime can itself be divided into two concepts, each of which possesses the quality of discriminant validity, is strictly contrary to the facts. Similarly, such longitudinal ideas as offense escalation, crime switching, and career specialization are all negated by the fact of versatility (as are designs meant to facilitate study of these "phenomena").

As discussed throughout this book (especially Chapter 6), the age effect has similarly important consequences for the design and interpretation of research. Since the causes of crime do not vary by age, the causes of crime may be studied at any age. The age selected should therefore depend on questions of research quality and efficiency as well as on questions of public policy.

The research and proposals for research discussed in this chapter illustrate the dangers of a science unguided by substantive concepts. They also illustrate the costs of ignoring the substantive knowledge of criminology. The theory we have described is, to our minds, compatible with the major substantive contributions of prior research—contributions that have themselves survived the most rigorous scientific tests of replication, reliability, validity, and generalizability.

12

Implications for Public Policy

We have taken the view throughout this book that conceptions of crime and criminality are critical for evaluations of crime-control policy. In Chapter 2 we described the elements of typical crimes and showed how remote they are from the operations of the criminal justice system. In Chapter 5 we spelled out the implications of our concepts of crime and criminality for the structure of the family and the school. In Chapter 10 we described the general irrelevance of policing and enforcement operations for organized crime. Clearly, the general thrust of the public policy implications of our theory is counter to the prevailing view that modifications of the criminal justice system hold promise for major reductions in criminal activity. In this chapter, we focus specifically on major contemporary criminal justice policies and evaluate their likely effect according to the crime and self-control perspective.

Several features of the crime and self-control perspective are relevant to the evaluation of current or proposed criminal justice policies because they diverge sharply from the views informing these policies. First, our perspective emphasizes the stability of differences in self-control across the lifespan, differences that are established very early in life. Because low self-control arises in the absence of the powerful inhibiting forces of early childhood, it is highly resistant to the less powerful inhibiting forces of later life, especially the relatively weak forces of the criminal justice system. The common expectation that short-term changes in the probabilities of punishment (such as arrest) or in the severity of punishment (such as length of sentence) will have a significant effect on the likelihood of criminal behavior misconstrues the nature of self-control.

Second, our perspective emphasizes the considerable diversity of acts and behaviors that flow from low self-control and the extent to which such acts therefore have a common etiology. Because the within-person causes of truancy are the same as the within-person causes of drug use, aggravated assault, and auto accidents, it follows that the criminal justice system is at best a weak cause of any one of them. It follows further that efforts to target one of these acts as an important determinant of other acts (e.g., drug use as a cause of crime; truancy as a cause of delinquency) are unlikely to be successful.

Third, our theory suggests that the motive to crime is inherent in or limited to immediate gains provided by the act itself. There is no larger purpose behind rape, or robbery, or murder, or theft, or embezzlement, or insider trading. Therefore policies that seek to reduce crime by the satisfaction of theoretically derived wants (e.g., equality, adequate housing, good jobs, self-esteem) are likely to be unsuccessful. (The evidence on rehabilitation discussed below is overwhelmingly consistent with our point of view.) Because offenders do not have overwhelming impulses to commit crime, our theory suggests that some limited benefit can accrue to programs that focus on variables necessary to the commission of particular criminal or deviant acts. That is, a reduction in burglary, computer theft, or car theft will not be followed by compensatory increases in other crimes. Our theory does not predict displacement from crime type to crime type, from simple to sophisticated crime, or from one geographical area to another.

Finally, our theory recognizes the large changes that naturally occur over the life span in the likelihood of committing criminal acts. Policies that do not attend to this highly predictable circumstance are likely to mistake natural change for program effectiveness or to waste considerable resources treating or incapacitating people without benefit to them or to society.

Most criminal justice policies lack rigorous theoretical justification. How do they fare when evaluated on the basis of expectations derived from a theory of crime and self-control?

American criminal justice policy has passed through several phases in recent decades (von Hirsch 1985). Throughout most of the twentieth century, positivistic assumptions prevailed and the criminal justice system pursued rehabilitation as its major goal. It was assumed that offenders could be changed into law-abiding citizens by a variety of therapeutic techniques. It also assumed that, unless they were treated, they would continue in their criminal activities. These assumptions gave considerable discretion to those imposing sentences on offenders, allowing judges to base the length of the sentence on the amount of treatment thought to be required for the offender as well as on the seriousness of the offense and the danger posed by the offender to the community. The positivistic assumptions provided part of the justification for probation and parole, for the creation of a separate justice system for juveniles, and for an expanded role for experts (psychologists, psychiatrists, and social workers) in the criminal justice system.

In the mid-1970's, however, research was progressively interpreted as showing that treatment had little or no effect and that the presumed diagnostic power of the experts could not be documented. On inspection, it turned out that the juvenile and adult justice systems were more similar than different (and that the offenders in them were difficult to distinguish, apart from age). As a result, at least within the academic community, the rehabilitation model fell into disfavor. The positivism that justified rehabilitation could have been used to justify "restraining" offenders whether or not they could be treated (since it suggests that it is possible to predict future misbehavior), but the link between positivism and rehabilitation was so strong that the "failure" of rehabilitation led to a search for a new justification for sentencing decisions.

In the late 1970's, therefore, the deterrence school rose to prominence. Although positivism finds the deterrence perspective contrary to its assumptions about human nature (and contrary to its interpretation of research on the effectiveness of punishment), the leaders of the U.S. policy establishment were no longer traditional criminological positivists. Some were economists, who brought with them the classical assumption that "crime could effectively be reduced . . . [only] through sentencing policies aimed at intimidating potential offenders more efficiently" (von Hirsch 1985: 7). Others were operations researchers or lawyers, people who do not share the positivistic assumptions about the causes of human behavior. Their influence was sufficiently strong that the National Academy of Sciences sponsored a panel to investigate the factual basis for a deterrence policy. The conclusions of the panel were cautiously optimistic, reporting that in general the evidence supported the idea of deterrence over the idea that deterrence has no effect (Blumstein, Cohen, and Nagin 1978). Perhaps because the panel studied only work on the effects of criminal justice system sanctions and ignored a considerable body of research within the larger deterrence tradition, its report did not lead to increased interest in deterrence as a viable public policy. Instead, the panel's work on incapacitation captured the interest of policymakers.

Since the early 1980's, incapacitation has been a major focus of attention. Incapacitation policy is based on the obvious conclusion that an offender in prison is not committing crimes in the community. Incapacitation does not seek to change the offender or the likelihood that he will commit crimes. Rather, it simply seeks to limit his opportunities to commit crimes. Incapacitation therefore assumes continuity in offending, at least among those most responsible for the crime problem. Because our theory explicitly accepts the idea of long-term continuity in the behavior of people, it may appear to be consistent with the idea of incapacitation. Because our theory also explicitly accepts the idea that crime can be predicted from behavior in adolescence or earlier, it may in fact appear to be grounds for considerable optimism about the effectiveness of such incapacitation. For that matter, since rehabilitation and treatment share with incapacitation the idea of focusing intervention on individuals with a high propensity to crime (incapacitation denies the opportunity to offend, treatment reduces the proclivity to offend), our theory could be construed as supportive of the prospects for treatment as well. In fact, however, our theory predicts the failure of both of these crime-control policies. We begin by considering selective incapacitation.

Modern Interest in Incapacitation

Contemporary interest in the idea of incapacitation can be traced to the rediscovery of an old positivistic idea applied to criminology (recall Lombroso): the idea that offenders can be usefully divided into types according to the frequency with which they commit criminal acts. This idea leads to attempts to identify chronic, habitual, or career criminals. If the crime problem is largely the work of a few highly active criminals, then the problem can be controlled by identification and incapacitation of them. Thus the question to be answered by research is, how general or widespread is involvement in criminal acts?

In 1972, Wolfgang, Figlio, and Sellin published a study of the criminal records of about 10,000 boys in Philadelphia. This study traced the boys from birth to age 18 and counted the number of times they had been arrested and convicted. The 10,000 boys had committed 10,214 offenses by age 18, an average of slightly more than one offense per boy. But these offenses were not evenly distributed among the boys in the sample. Indeed, only one-third of the boys had committed any offenses at all, suggesting that the average delinquent was responsible for about three offenses. But these offenses were not evenly distributed among the delinquents in the sample. Indeed, one-sixth of the delinquents were responsible for more than half of the offenses committed by all delinquents. Wolfgang refers to these boys, 6 percent of the entire sample, as "chronic offenders."

Such a concentration of offending among a small segment of the population suggested to many policymakers that the crime rate could be cut in half by isolating these chronic offenders and preventing them from engaging in criminal acts. In other words, the rediscovery of the chronic offender directed attention away from crime prevention aimed at the population as a whole and toward a small group thought to be responsible for a disproportionate share of crime.

This new direction in crime-control policy appears to have a number of attractive features. It suggests that, with minimal money and effort, sizable reductions in the crime rate can be achieved. Since the focus is on chronic, habitual, or career criminals, there would be few legal or ethical problems with a policy that isolates them from society. Since the number of career criminals is small, it may be possible to reduce the scope of the criminal justice system at all levels, from police to prisons. Instead of a large and unwieldy system passively accepting a mixture of occasional, petty, and serious offenders, this new policy would create an efficient system where resources could be focused on the dangerous few. Finally, this new system would take the criminal justice system out of the business of dealing with social problems and put it to work doing what it alone can do: identifying and removing from circulation people whose continued freedom would jeopardize the safety of the community.

Evaluating Selective Incapacitation Policy

Implementation of a selective incapacitation policy requires identification of chronic offenders before they have committed the crimes that define them as chronic offenders. It would be of little value to incapacitate such offenders after they have committed their crimes. Thus a threshold requirement for implementation of selective incapacitation policy is a scheme or mechanism whereby we can predict with sufficient accuracy a habitual or sustained pattern of offending.

What would such a scheme look like? First, it would have to meet fairly high standards of accuracy. After all, people with scores indicating that they are a threat to society are going to be deprived of liberty. Second, it would have to use evidence of dangerousness that is public, easily or consistently measurable, and socially and legally acceptable. Third, it would have to use evidence available prior to commission of the acts that identification is designed to prevent. Finally, the measuring device could not be subject to manipulation by potentially dangerous subjects.

What are the prospects of developing predictive procedures that satisfy these requirements? Interestingly enough, researchers had explored the prospects for predicting delinquency long before the idea of selective incapacitation came on the scene. These efforts demonstrate that delinquency can be predicted with sufficient accuracy to justify benign or minimal intervention. For example, in the Cambridge-Somerville Youth Study (McCord and McCord 1959) it was shown that boys predicted to be delinquent at age eleven were considerably more likely actually to become delinquent than boys predicted at the same age to be nondelinquent. By scientific standards, these predictions are a remarkable achievement. However, a majority of those predicted to be delinquent turned out not to be seriously delinquent after ten years, and harsh or restrictive treatment of the entire group predicted to be delinquent could by no means be justified. These predicted delinquents who turn out to be nondelinquents are known as "false positives." In the absence of perfect prediction, there will always be such false positives, a fact that has led some scholars to argue that predictive punishments are necessarily unjust (von Hirsch 1985). In any event, the existence of false positives in the Cambridge-Somerville Youth Study is good evidence that the best available prediction strategies do not satisfy the "accuracy" standard when they are applied before criminal acts take place.

An examination of the factors used to predict delinquency from an early age quickly reveals that these predictive schemes fail to satisfy the social-legal acceptability criterion as well. Thus, although social scientists have been able to establish reliable and valid predictors of crime and delinquency, these predictors typically do not themselves justify harsh intervention. For example, a major predictor of subsequent criminality is a tendency to push and shove other kids. Other predictors are unsatisfactory relations with one's parents or other authorities, the use of alcohol and tobacco, and even the age of the individual (since young people are more likely than old people to commit criminal acts). Clearly none of these traits or behavior tendencies would in and of themselves justify incarceration. It is not surprising, therefore, that the incapacitation tradition has focused attention on behavior that lends itself more readily to intervention by the criminal justice system.

Behavior that is consistent with incapacitation by the criminal justice system is, by definition, illegal behavior. Thus the search for predictors acceptable on one criterion tends to lead to predictors unacceptable by another criterion. The effort to prevent illegal behavior by incapacitation must await the commission of illegal acts before it can get under way. How much and what kinds of illegal behavior are required for effective prediction of subsequent illegal behavior?

As we have seen, it is easily established that the greater the frequency of criminal activity in the past, the greater the frequency of criminal activity in the future. For example, Shannon (1981) shows that there is a strong correlation between past and future delinquent behavior, a correlation that has been reported many times in the literature (see Chapter 6). To illustrate the strength of this correlation, Shannon notes that almost two-thirds of those who have as many as five criminal offenses before age eighteen will have five or more criminal offenses in the dozen or so years thereafter. Clearly, the policy of selective incapacitation would take advantage of this relation. The problem arises, however, that the criminal justice system has always reserved its harshest sanctions for offenders with a prior record. In fact, apart from the seriousness of the instant offense, prior record is the best predictor of the actions of the criminal justice system. That is, all things being equal, offenders with prior records are more likely to be arrested, prosecuted, and sentenced to harsh treatment than those without such records.

Although such an outcome is consistent with all penal philosophies and certainly comes as no surprise, it presents the idea of selective incapacitation with a special problem: how to improve on a system that is already highly selective and that uses the very criteria of selection recommended by the goal of incapacitation.

Given this problem, advocates of selective incapacitation can focus on two groups of offenders: those unnecessarily incapacitated (on purely predictive grounds) by the current system, and those whose behavior justifies greater incapacitation than that provided by the current system. Focus on the first of these groups reveals an obvious problem. As mentioned, the best predictor of sentence severity or probability of incarceration is the gravity of the current offense. Thus, under the current system, those guilty of murder or forcible rape have the highest probability of incarceration, regardless of prior record. Although most such offenders do have prior records, some do not. A strict incapacitation policy would suggest that these first-time murderers and rapists not be incarcerated, a policy obviously at odds with other goals of the criminal sanction, such as retribution.

As a consequence of this problem, selective incapacitation in practice focuses on the second group and attempts to identify high-rate or chronic offenders who now escape the notice of the criminal justice system. On its face, such an undertaking seems doomed to failure. It is instructive, therefore, to examine studies devoted to the discovery of *secret* career criminals.

The most famous example of such research is that by Peter Greenwood (1983). Greenwood identifies seven variables in the construction of a scale for the identification of high-rate offenders:

1. Incarceration for more than half of the two-year period preceding the most recent arrest.
2. Prior conviction for the crime type that is being predicted.
3. Juvenile conviction prior to age 16.
4. Commitment to a state or federal juvenile facility.
5. Heroin or barbiturate use in the two-year period preceding the current arrest.
6. Heroin or barbiturate use as a juvenile.
7. Employment for less than half of the two-year period preceding the current arrest. [1983: 260]

This scale, intended for the prediction of high-rate offenders qualified for selective incapacitation, was constructed on the basis of interviews with a sample of imprisoned offenders. It has been the object of considerable criticism (see von Hirsch 1985 for a full discussion). For example, there was no validation of the predictive ability of the scale, which was, the reader will note, constructed by interviews with people already incapacitated. It cannot then provide information on those people of most interest—that is, people who currently avoid incarceration. As developed, the scale also violates our rule that the prediction device not be manipulable by those whose behavior is being predicted. (Interviewees might be inclined to deny behavior that would add to the length of their sentence.)

Nonetheless, it is interesting to learn what factors appear to discriminate between high- and low-rate offenders, according to the Greenwood scale. It cannot escape notice that these factors tend to overlap to the point that they may be considered measures of the same thing—that is, of prior record of illegal conduct. As indicated above, decisionmakers in the criminal justice system now pay considerable attention to prior record in making their incarceration decisions. Explicit, mandatory attention to prior record would systematize decisionmaking and would therefore increase its visibility and equity (Gottfredson and Gottfredson 1988), but it would not be ex-

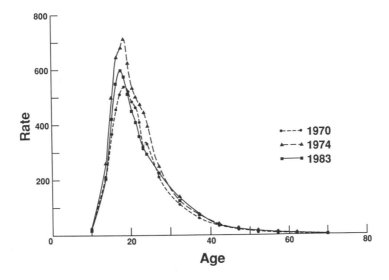

Fig. 14. Arrest Rates by Age of Males for Robbery (per 100,000), United States, 1970, 1974, and 1983. From Gottfredson and Hirschi 1986: 223.

pected greatly to increase the system's ability to isolate the so-called career criminal.

There are, however, even more fundamental difficulties in this method of identifying targets for selective incapacitation that have heretofore escaped the notice of the criminal justice system. By the time such "targets" have been identified by Greenwood's procedures, they will have been incarcerated as adults; in other words, they will have moved well beyond the age of maximum offending. It is therefore doubtful that large reductions in the crime rate (the goal of selective incapacitation) could be achieved by marginal increases in the incarceration of offenders. Thus Greenwood's scale fails also to satisfy the requirement that the prediction instrument allow *prediction* of high-rate criminality.

The decline in crime with age in fact suggests that, for maximum effectiveness, incapacitation should be focused on the age period just prior to the rapid onset and peaking of crime. Figure 14 shows the age distribution of robbery offenders as indicated by FBI arrest statistics for 1970, 1974, and 1983. Clearly, these statistics suggest that, were intervention to be made on the basis of potential incapacitation effects, such intervention would take place at an early age, probably around thirteen or fourteen. The ethical issues raised by the apparent advantage of incapacitating young people usually preclude further investigation of the actual mechanics of such a policy. This creates the impression that selective incapacitation has an ace in the hole, a card that it could play were it not prevented from doing so on ethical grounds.

Does selective incapacitation have such a card? One way to find out is to ask researchers favoring this policy to devise a maximally efficient system free of ethical concerns. Incapacitate as you will, they may be told. Would they lock up youths of thirteen and fourteen? If so, which ones?

Obviously, such predictive devices as Greenwood's would be in-applicable. What might be used instead? The Cambridge-Somerville type of scale, we have previously shown, would also not achieve the required efficiency, since it would entail locking up too many non-delinquents. Apparently, the only choice left is to base the decision on prior criminal acts. So, putting these facts together, the "ace in the hole" becomes the policy of incarcerating thirteen and fourteen year olds on their first offense. Yet as Wolfgang, Figlio, and Sellin (1972) have shown, almost half of all offenders are one-time-only offenders, and it would again seem inefficient to incapacitate people who will, if left alone, commit no more offenses. Given the large number of one-time offenders (a third of the Wolfgang et al. sample by age eighteen), such a strategy would be inconceivable in any event. We are therefore forced to move the selection point to *two* offenses, not just one, and to consider the consequences of this selection policy.

Recall that a maximally efficient incapacitation policy does not in-carcerate those who pose too little risk. This suggests that no one-time offender be incarcerated and that all two-time offenders be incarcer-ated. Again, however, the policy suggested is inconceivable. No mat-ter how little risk is posed by them, some first-time offenders must on grounds of justice or deterrence be punished by imprisonment. And, since more than a third of two-time offenders do not commit a third offense by the time they are eighteen years old (Wolfgang, Figlio, and Sellin 1972), we are again treating many low-rate offenders as though they were high-rate offenders. And so on as the number of offenses increases.

At some point, of course, almost any policy will suggest that mul-tiple recidivists merit incarceration. Also note that the accumulation of a record sufficient to justify imprisonment will typically take time, that offenders with such records will not be thirteen or fourteen years old but will have passed beyond the peak age of crime. Therefore, the logic of selective incapacitation falls of its own weight. We cannot predict relative criminal activity until the absolute likelihood of such activity has declined to the point that our prediction is of little practical value.

The Career Criminal

We find the conclusion about selective incapacitation to be inescapable, and therefore neither to be celebrated nor to be mourned. Others find it unacceptable, however, and they seek strategies for identifying career criminals: offenders whose patterns of criminal activity deviate from those for the general population of offenders, criminals active in crime long after their colleagues have retired (Blumstein et al. 1986). Although considerable research effort has concentrated on the search for such offenders, we believe this effort has yielded little in the way of positive results (Gottfredson and Hirschi 1986, 1988a). Public policies, of course, do not necessarily turn on research results, and the many special career-criminal units in prosecutors' offices and police departments were firmly established before the academic search for the career criminal got under way. Such units seek to assign special priority to the arrest and prosecution of those with lengthy prior records. This activity has considerable appeal to the media, to politicians, and to the general public. It suggests that some segment of the offender population is worthy of concentrated, sophisticated effort. Although there is reason to doubt that such units have any effect on the crime problem, influential policymakers do not share our view. For example, the director of the National Institute of Justice, James Stewart, favors attack on the career criminal as a key to crime reduction:

Research in the 1970's confirmed, for example, the existence of the career criminal. Following up on this important insight the Institute supported surveys to gauge the impact of the high-rate offender on crime and criminal justice operations. From this basic knowledge came the idea of focusing criminal justice resources selectively on the career criminals. Today, the concept of the career criminal is entrenched in criminal justice—a dramatic rethinking of policy and practice. Now research is examining ways to identify these offenders more accurately, moving toward the recommendation of one recent study that concluded that public safety would clearly benefit from incarcerating a larger proportion of high-risk probations and prisoners, and for longer periods of time. [1987: iii]

Given its alleged centrality to crime control, the idea of the career criminal would appear to merit careful scrutiny. Those who favor concentration on career criminals do not have anything to say about the nature of crime. They must therefore find something of special value in the idea of a career (recall the discussion of economic positivism in Chapter 4). What is the meaning of the idea of a career? Whether applied to dentistry, college teaching, or crime, the concept of a career implies several things. It suggests a beginning, as in "When did you become a teacher?," and an end, as in "When did you quit teaching?" Given a beginning and an end, the career concept also implies variable duration or length, as in "How long did you (or how much longer do you plan to) teach?" Once given, careers may be characterized along many dimensions, such as area of specialization (e.g., logic and the scientific method), amount of time and effort devoted to them (half time), level of accomplishment (professor), productivity (.19 articles a year), current direction (down), overall shape (peaked early), and time out for other activities (sabbatical, administration). Once the decision to apply career terminology has been made, it is relatively straightforward to construct a career model and to outline the research necessary to estimate its parameters (Blumstein et al. 1986: fig. 1-1).

Indeed, it turns out that the career idea was applied to crime almost from the beginning of positivism. The biological positivists had their "habitual" offenders; the psychological positivists had their psychopaths; and sociological positivists had the professional criminal. Glueck and Glueck focused on the criminal career through a lengthy series of research projects. And, in perhaps the major piece of positivistic research in modern criminology, Wolfgang, Figlio, and Sellin (1972) devote considerable attention to such career questions as onset, escalation, and termination.

When the Gluecks introduced explicit career terminology, the idea appeared to have potential merit. Fifty years ago it was reasonable to guess that individual offenders might engage in more serious crimes or at least in more specialized crimes as they grew older. Fifty years ago it was reasonable to assume that concepts of onset, duration, and desistance might lead to a better understanding of the crime problem. Today, however, it is not reasonable to wonder whether individual offenders engage in progressively more serious offenses as they grow older; research on the topic shows that they do not (e.g., Glueck and Glueck 1940, 1968). Today, it is not reasonable to assume that offenders tend to specialize in particular types of crime; research shows that they do not (e.g., Wolfgang, Figlio, and Sellin 1972: 163; Blumstein and Cohen 1979: 585; Hindelang, Hirschi, and Weis 1981).

If offenders do not specialize in particular types of crime, if they do not become progressively more criminal or more skilled in crime as the years pass, and if they do not make enough money from crime to live, then how do we account for the continued interest in career criminals or for the crime-control programs based on the presumption that they exist? Research devoted to criminal careers now centers on discovering a subgroup of offenders whose rate of criminal activity remains constant at a high level for an unusually long period of time—that is, well into adulthood.

As a result, the relation between age and crime (see Chapter 6) is fundamental to an assessment of the career paradigm and its implications for crime-control policy. In fact, the strong decline in crime with age directly challenges the validity of the career paradigm. The serious, predatory offenses said to be of interest to the career paradigm are in fact typically committed by young people, some of whom go on committing them for awhile, but most of whom spend their declining years (late twenties) running afoul of the authorities over alcohol, drugs, and family squabbles. In perhaps their last word on the subject, after a lifetime of research on it, the Gluecks reported among *delinquents* a "substantial reduction in criminalism, especially of the more serious kind" during the 25–31 age range, and they noted that those offenders who do not during this period "achieve . . . maturity . . . tend to commit petty misdemeanors often associated with *disintegration* of organism and morale" (1968: 151–52, emphasis in original).

Offenders in prison (presumably people of special interest to the criminal justice system) commit fewer infractions of the rules as they grow older (see Chapter 6; see also Glueck and Glueck 1940: 319). Research on offenders in the community repeatedly shows that they reduce the level of their criminal activity as they age. The parole follow-up literature, easily construed as research on serious offenders, has always found steep declines in offending as parolees age (see, e.g., Glaser 1964: 474), so much so that age is typically included as a major predictor of success on parole. When a large sample of California parolees was followed for eight years after release, and when only those still free in the community were considered, the violation rate for "major new offenses" declined precipitously with number of years since release (Gottfredson and Gottfredson 1980: 265).

Perhaps the most thorough study specifically addressing the question of the stability of offending over age is reported by Rudy Haapanen (1987). Haapanen collected fifteen- to twenty-year follow-up data on a large sample of serious offenders in California. His conclusions are to the point and contrary to the notion of a career criminal:

Our longitudinal data allowed us to look not only at simple indices of involvement in crime but also at 'career' characteristics, such as breadth of involvement and the extent of repetition for particular crime types. These analyses showed that for this large sample of serious offenders, both the kinds of crimes for which they were arrested and the rate of arrest clearly differed by race and clearly declined with age. [1987: iii]

The career-criminal idea—the idea that crime does not decline with age among active offenders or that crime *may* not decline with age among active offenders (as advanced by Blumstein, Cohen, and Farrington 1988a, 1988b)—flies in the face of much evidence to the contrary.

Rehabilitation

If there is current enthusiasm for incapacitation as a crime-control policy, the same cannot be said for rehabilitation. Among academicians, the conclusion that rehabilitation programs have been extensively tried and have been found wanting is generally accepted. Although claims for the success of particular programs continue to be reported (e.g., Murray and Cox 1979) and the quality of the research on program effectiveness leaves much to be desired (see Gottfredson 1979; Sechrest, White, and Brown 1979), the enthusiasm for treatment that accompanied the development of positivism has been replaced by profound pessimism in most quarters of the academic community.

The assumptions necessary for successful treatment are in many respects identical to those necessary for successful incapacitation. To avoid having to "treat" the entire population, it is necessary to identify in advance of their highest levels of criminality those persons most likely to engage in crime. To avoid having serious conflict with justice concerns, it is necessary to wait until clearly illegal acts have been committed before commencing treatment. To avoid doing it all for nothing, it is necessary to institute and complete treatment well before the offender stops committing crimes of his own accord. Thus the "window of opportunity" for successful treatment programs is very narrow, whatever the potential effectiveness of the treatment program. This window is so narrow that most treatment programs in fact appear to work: offenders normally change their behavior in the late teens, regardless of what has happened to them.

In our view, treatment need not be derived from or consistent with a theory of crime causation. Most positivistic theories are silent with respect to treatment. On inspection, however, most imply that standard treatment programs will be ineffective. It is, therefore, an illegitimate criticism of positivistic theories and the crime-causal research they generate to say that they have spawned or somehow supported ineffective treatment efforts. Even so, because positivism itself claims to seek factors conducive to crime that are beyond the offender's control, factors that may therefore be changed with or without the consent of the offender, it brings much of this criticism down on itself. Our theory would be consistent with efforts to teach the offender self-control, but all indications are that such teaching is highly unlikely to be effective unless it comes very early in development (see Chapter 5). Given the ineffectiveness of natural learning environments in teaching self-control, we would not expect the artificial environments available to the criminal justice system to have much impact.

The interventions we have in mind would normally be regarded as prevention rather than treatment. They assume that trouble is likely unless something is done to train the child to forego immediate gratification in the interest of long-term benefits. Such training must come from adults, but these adults need not be trained in one or another of the various academic treatment disciplines. Instead, they need only learn the requirements of early childhood socialization, namely, to watch for and recognize signs of low self-control and to punish them. Effective and efficient crime prevention that produces enduring consequences would thus focus on parents or adults with responsibilities for child-rearing. Such intervention does not suffer from coming too soon or too late in relation to when crime is committed; it does not suffer from potential illegality; and few serious objections can be raised to it on justice grounds.

Note that our theory does not call for specific interventions for specific kinds of offenders. So far as we can see, there is no evidence that ordinary child-rearing practices (see Chapter 5) are inappropriate or inapplicable to any segment of the population.

Other treatments may occupy the time and energy of an incarcerated population, provide living-condition benefits to inmates, and even facilitate recruitment of staff to the correctional system, but it is unlikely that criminal justice system rehabilitation programs will themselves reduce criminal behavior sufficiently to justify their cost.

The Police

We have stressed throughout this book the ordinary character of ordinary crime: no planning, no skill, no organization, no resources, no success. An obvious opportunity coupled with a lack of self-control is all that is required. The offender sees a momentary opportunity to get something for nothing and he siezes it. These facts delineate the natural limits of law enforcement.

The idea that investigative talent or expenditure is worthwhile is contrary to our expectations and is, for that matter, contrary to empirical research (Sherman 1983). The idea that a substantial effect on the crime rate can be achieved simply by increasing the numbers of police—and thereby restricting opportunities—is also contrary to our theory and to empirical research. The police are not a factor in the overwhelming number of robberies, burglaries, assaults, homicides, thefts, or drug deals (see the literature summarized in Sherman 1983). In the bulk of these offenses, the offender does not know or care about the probability of being observed by the police.

An adequate police force is necessary to *respond* to criminal activity; it is necessary to control traffic and crowds; and it is necessary to respond to medical emergencies, lost children, loud noise, and unruly neighbors. These are all important functions in their own right, and we would not argue for doing away with them. However, such functions are not the primary focus of police ideology or of its demands for support. On the contrary, when the issue is the division of the public purse, the police focus on their crime-control function.

As our view suggests, no evidence exists that augmentation of police forces or equipment, differential patrol strategies, or differential intensities of surveillance have an effect on crime rates. Also consistent with our view is the lack of evidence supporting the effectiveness of police undercover activities aimed at identification of professional thieves and fences (the so-called "sting" operations). As pointed out in Chapter 10, such programs make assumptions about offenders (level of skill, organization, and commitment to criminal means of livelihood) that are untrue. The common result of such expensive and time-consuming operations is the capture of a number of ordinary "losers," many of whom may have very low self-control but few of whom, if accurately described by the police in media representations, would engender public support for such programs.

Our view emphasizes the youthfulness of offenders. The police view, in contrast, emphasizes the hardened (and therefore mature adult) criminal. Our view emphasizes the versatility of offenders. The police view leads to the creation of burglary units, robbery squads, vice patrols, and arson investigators. Such specialization within police forces can have adverse consequences. For example, when the police focus their attention on a "rapist," they tend to forget that the offender in question is also likely to be a burglar, a drug user, a petty thief, a drunk driver, and a school dropout. Whenever the commission of a particular offense leads to the conclusion that the search is for that type of offender, mistakes are likely to be made.[1]

Gun Control

To own a gun costs money. To own a good gun costs a lot of money. The purchase of guns on the legitimate market requires effort, paper work, and sometimes a short delay. Guns are inconvenient to carry and require awkward permanent storage. Further, guns are useless without ammunition, which also costs money and requires storage. At the same time, guns are relatively lightweight, easily portable over short distances, and likely to be one of the most valuable unprotected small objects in a dwelling or household, along with stereos and VCRs. (Also like stereos and VCRs, one gun is enough for most purposes.)

In light of these facts, and in light of our theory of crime, it is not surprising that interviews with convicts who reported committing crimes with a gun reveal that the majority obtain their weapons from people like themselves (rather than through legitimate channels), that they tend to possess expensive, well-made guns (as opposed to "Saturday Night Specials") originally stolen from dwellings, that the purpose of the weapon was to make victim resistance less likely, and that fear of other people was a principal justification for carrying a weapon (Wright 1986).

In combination, these facts suggest the limits of gun-control policies that would focus on the regulation of legitimate gun sales or ownership. Offenders do not use these mechanisms for obtaining or transferring ownership of guns. To the extent they would be inclined to do so, it seems likely that current natural controls on the legitimate market (such as price and inconvenience) are sufficient to deter the vast majority of ordinary offenders from using this market to obtain

---

[1] An example of this sort of mistake occurred in Tucson, Arizona, in the summer of 1986, when the police sought the "prime-time rapist," an individual thought to be responsible for a series of break-in rapes during the early evening hours. These break-ins involved burglary, robbery, drug use, kidnaping, assault, and auto theft, as well as rape. But the police investigation focused on finding a clever "rapist." In the end, the person responsible for these rapes turned out to be a long-term offender with a substantial juvenile record, including a period of incarceration for theft from automobile dealerships, who lived a short distance from most of his victims. A tip to the police from one of his drug connections led eventually to his identification. When surrounded, he reportedly said "I never hurt anybody" and committed suicide. Prior to the incidents in question, he had no record for sex offenses.

a gun for the purpose of committing a crime. (The rewards of most ordinary crimes would not cover the down payment on a good-quality handgun.) Part of the reason for the ineffectiveness of legitimate-market controls is the easy availability of guns on the underground market, with offenders willing to part with surplus (stolen) guns quite inexpensively.

Recall that our picture of "ordinary" homicide suggested that in one common case the offender uses a handy gun to rid himself of an irritating companion. In the other case, the gun is actually used when its threat value fails to intimidate the victim sufficiently. In both cases, in our view, the homicide would be less likely to occur were no gun available. As mentioned, however, this does not mean that ordinary gun-control legislation would be expected to have an impact on the rate of either type of homicide. In neither case was the gun originally purchased for the purpose of committing the crime. In the former case, the gun was probably purchased for self-defense (and perhaps on the underground market), or it may even have been purchased for sporting purposes. In the latter case, the gun was almost certainly acquired through the underground economy, and the range of weapons suitable for this purpose is so large that effective regulation of retail sales is difficult to imagine. (Given our thesis, a total ban on guns or ammunition would have an important effect on the number of crimes involving intimidation and personal injury.)

The Reduction of Crime in a Free Society

Both the classical and the positivistic theories gave the burden of crime control to the state. Whereas the classicists would accomplish such control through the operation of the criminal justice system, the positivists would accomplish it through programs designed to eliminate the personal and social motives for crime. In both cases, the state remains central to the crime-control enterprise. (In both cases, the state is the substantive as well as the formal cause of crime.)

We offer an alternative view, a view in which the state is neither the cause of nor the solution to crime. In our view, the origins of criminality of low self-control are to be found in the first six or eight years of life, during which time the child remains under the control and supervision of the family or a familial institution. Apart from the limited benefits that can be achieved by making specific criminal acts more difficult, policies directed toward enhancement of the ability of familial institutions to socialize children are the only realistic long-term state policies with potential for substantial crime reduction.[2]

Conclusions

When we began this book, we hoped to resolve the historical division between the classical school, on the one hand, and the scientific or positive school, on the other. Initially we thought we could accomplish our purpose simply by noting that the classical theory was as "scientific" as the theories advanced by positivism and that the ideas of criminality implicit in positive theories could be applied to the classical image of crime. With little effort, therefore, we hoped to combine one tradition's image of crime with the other tradition's image of the criminal and produce thereby a truly general theory. This turned out to be not so simple.

From classical thought, we derived a theoretical image of crime that turned out to be remarkably consistent with data on actual criminal acts. This image stressed simplicity and the immediate gratification of universal desires, with little concern for long-term consequences. It had the added advantage that it accurately described many acts that we have long known go together with crime, such as accidents and the legal use of drugs. Even though the classical image of the criminal event was consistent with such observations, it had problems of its own and seemed impossible to reconcile with positivistic images of the criminal. We therefore could not simply adopt without modification the classical image as presented by current champions of it; in describing criminal choice, they give too much power to political sanctions and too much credence to the similarity between crime and labor-force participation. Research on crime has for some time shown that family sanctions govern criminal activity and that the phrase "careers in crime" is oxymoronic.

When we turned to the positivistic disciplines for an image of criminality, we discovered that they had constructed a criminal inconsistent with the research literature they had themselves produced. For example, we know that criminal tendencies arise early in life, that they are reasonably stable over the life course, and that the diversity of deviant acts is the only "pattern" that can be identified. Yet the

[2]We do not restrict the meaning of "familial institution" to the traditional family unit composed of a natural father and mother. The socialization function does not, in our view, require such an institution. It does, however, require responsible adults committed to the training and welfare of the child.

disciplines, we discovered, are far better at promoting their own interests than at identifying a defensible image of the offender. Thus
they describe criminal choice as resulting from the pursuit of such
long-term problems as employment, social status, group solidarity,
and mental conflict. As a result, much of the research generated by
these disciplines is beyond the reach of their own explanations of
crime.

In the end, we adopted a theory of self-control. This theory traces
the important restraints on criminal conduct to child-rearing practices, allows the diversity of criminal activity, predicts its stability over
long periods of time, and is comfortable with the simplicity and immediacy of the benefits associated with it. The self-control theory
seems to us to organize the facts about crime, whether demographic,
social, or institutional, in a coherent manner, telling us which are
important and which are not worthy of further attention. It also tells
us about the design and conduct of research, suggesting areas of
exploration that may yield important results and those that in all
likelihood will not. Our theory also resolves for criminology the persistent problem of typologies, of special types of crime and criminals,
of special criminologies for every time and place. Finally, our theory
provides a coherent base from which to judge and design public
policy on crime. Contemporary crime policies, from criminal-career
programs to modifications in policing, from selective incapacitation to
the drug-crime connection, all have their roots in positivistic conceptions of the offender. According to the theory of self-control, none of
these programs is likely to have much of an impact on the crime
problem. Effective policy must deal with the attractiveness of criminal
events to potential offenders and with child-rearing practices that
produce self-control.

Every book must end somewhere. Had we unlimited time, space,
and imagination, we believe we could go much further tracing the
implications of our general theory of crime. For example, left unex-
plored here are its implications for the nature and origins of values,
for the distinction between criminal and civil law, for intergroup conflict, and for the structure and functioning of complex organizations,
be they educational, legal, or economic. After all, a general theory of
crime must be a general theory of the social order.

Although from time to time throughout the book we have raised
competing theories of crime, systematic treatment of the differences
between our view and these alternatives must also be deferred. We
do not believe that our theory is "just another rehash of rational-
choice theory," that it is inconsistent with the reasonable assump-

tions of any discipline, or that it can be easily falsified by facts that we have not discussed here, but we admit that we have been more concerned about presenting a point of view than about defending it from critical attack. The study of crime is too important to be diverted by arguments about theory ownership or disciplinary boundaries. In the end, we will be happy if our theory helps renew some intellectual interest in criminology, a field that once engaged the finest minds in the community.

References Cited

Adler, Freda. 1981. *The Incidence of Female Criminality in the Contemporary World*. New York: New York University Press.

Akers, Ronald L. 1973. *Deviant Behavior: A Social Learning Approach*. Belmont, Calif.: Wadsworth. 2d ed., 1977.

———. 1984. "Delinquent Behavior, Drugs, and Alcohol: What Is the Relationship?" *Today's Delinquent*, 3: 19–47.

———. 1987. "A Social Behaviorist's Perspective on Integration of Theories of Crime and Deviance." Paper presented at the Albany Conference on Theoretical Integration in the Study of Deviance and Crime. State University of New York at Albany, Department of Sociology.

Archer, Dane, and Rosemary Gartner. 1984. *Violence and Crime in Cross-National Perspective*. New Haven: Yale University Press.

Aschaffenburg, Gustav. 1913. *Crime and Its Repression*. Boston: Little, Brown.

Bachman, Jerald G., Robert L. Kahn, Martha T. Mednick, Terrence N. Davidson, and Lloyd D. Johnston. 1967. *Youth in Transition*. Vol. 1. Ann Arbor: University of Michigan, Institute for Social Research.

Baldwin, John. 1985. "Thrill and Adventure Seeking and the Age Distribution of Crime: Comment on Hirschi and Gottfredson." *American Journal of Sociology*, 90: 1326–30.

Bandura, Albert. 1973. *Aggression: A Social Learning Analysis*. Englewood Cliffs, N.J.: Prentice Hall.

———. 1986. *Social Foundations of Thought and Action*. New York: Prentice Hall.

Beccaria, Cesare. 1963 [1764]. *On Crimes and Punishments*. Indianapolis: Bobbs-Merrill.

Becker, Gary. 1974. "Crime and Punishment: An Economic Approach." In *Essays in the Economics of Crime and Punishment*, edited by G. Becker and W. Landes (pp. 1–54). New York: Columbia University Press.

Becker, Howard S. 1963. *Outsiders*. New York: Macmillan.

Beeley, Arthur L. 1954. "A Social-Psychological Theory of Crime and Delinquency: A Contribution to Etiology." *Journal of Criminal Law, Criminology, and Police Science*, 45: 391–99.

Beirne, Piers. 1983. "Generalization and Its Discontents." In *Comparative Criminology*, edited by I. Barak-Glantz and E. Johnson (pp. 19–38). Beverly Hills, Calif.: Sage.

Bentham, Jeremy. 1970 [1789]. *An Introduction to the Principles of Morals and Legislation*. London: The Athlone Press.

Bequai, August, 1987. "Justice Department Sends Warning to White-Collar Criminals." *Arizona Daily Star*, March 15, p. F3.

Berk, Richard A., Kenneth J. Lenihan, and Peter H. Rossi. 1980. "Crime and Poverty: Some Experimental Evidence from Ex-Offenders." *American Sociological Review*, 45: 766–86.

Blau, Judith R., and Peter M. Blau. 1982. "The Cost of Inequality: Metropolitan Structure and Violent Crime." *American Sociological Review*, 47: 114–29.

Bloch, Herbert, and Gilbert Geis. 1970. *Man, Crime, and Society*. New York: Random House.

Block, Richard. 1984. *Victimization and Fear of Crime: World Perspectives*. Washington, D.C.: USGPO.

Blumstein, Alfred, and Jacqueline Cohen. 1979. "Estimation of Individual Crime Rates from Arrest Records." *Journal of Criminal Law and Criminology*, 70: 561–85.

———. 1987. "Characterizing Criminal Careers." *Science*, 237: 985–91.

Blumstein, Alfred, Jacqueline Cohen, and David P. Farrington. 1988a. "Criminal Career Research: Its Value for Criminology." *Criminology*, 26: 1–36.

———. 1988b. "Longitudinal and Criminal Career Research: Further Clarifications." *Criminology*, 26: 57–74.

Blumstein, Alfred, Jacqueline Cohen, and Daniel Nagin. 1978. *Deterrence and Incapacitation: Estimating the Effects of Sanctions on the Crime Rate*. Washington, D.C.: National Academy Press.

Blumstein, Alfred, Jacqueline Cohen, Jeffery Roth, and Christy Visher. 1986. *Criminal Careers and "Career Criminals."* Washington, D.C.: National Academy Press.

Bohman, M. 1972. "A Study of Adopted Children, Their Background, Environment, and Adjustment." *Acta Pediatrica Scandinavia*, 61: 90–97.

Braithwaite, John. 1981. "The Myth of Social Class and Criminality Reconsidered." *American Sociological Review*, 46: 36–57.

———. 1985. "White Collar Crime." *Annual Review of Sociology*, 11: 1–25.

Brantingham, Paul, and Patricia Brantingham. 1984. *Patterns in Crime*. New York: Macmillan.

Bureau of Justice Statistics. 1986. *Tracking Offenders: White Collar Crime*. Washington, D.C.: U.S. Department of Justice.

Burgess, Robert L. 1980. "Family Violence: Implications from Evolutionary Biology." In *Understanding Crime*, edited by T. Hirschi and M. Gottfredson (pp. 91–101). Beverly Hills, Calif.: Sage.

Burgess, Robert L., and Ronald K. Akers. 1966. "A Differential Association—Reinforcement Theory of Criminal Behavior." *Social Problems*, 14: 128–47.

Campbell, Donald, and Julian Stanley. 1963. *Experimental and Quasi-Experimental Designs for Research*. Chicago: Rand-McNally.

Chambliss, William. 1969. *Crime and Legal Process*. New York: McGraw-Hill.

Christiansen, Karl O., and S. G. Jensen. 1972. "Crime in Denmark—A

Statistical History." *Journal of Criminal Law, Criminology, and Police Science*, 63: 82–92.

Clark, John P., and Richard C. Hollinger. 1983. *Theft by Employees in Work Organizations*. Washington, D.C.: U.S. Department of Justice.

Clarke, Ronald V. 1983. "Situational Crime Prevention: Its Theoretical Basis and Practical Scope." In *Crime and Justice: An Annual Review of Research*, vol. 4, edited by M. Tonry and N. Morris (pp. 225–56). Chicago: University of Chicago Press.

Clarke, Ronald V., and Derek B. Cornish. 1983. *Crime Control in Britain: A Review of Policy Research*. Albany: State University of New York Press.

Clinard, Marshall, and Richard Quinney. 1973. *Criminal Behavior Systems: A Typology*. New York: Holt, Rinehart and Winston.

Cline, Hugh. 1980. "Criminal Behavior over the Life Span." In *Constancy and Change in Human Development*, edited by O. G. Brim and J. Kagan (pp. 641–74). Cambridge, Mass.: Harvard University Press.

Cloninger, Robert, and Irving Gottesman. 1987. "Genetic and Environmental Factors in Antisocial Behavior Disorders." In *The Causes of Crime: New Biological Approaches*, edited by S. Mednick, T. Moffitt, and S. Stack (pp. 92–109). Cambridge, Engl.: Cambridge University Press.

Clotfelter, Charles T. 1983. "Tax Evasion and Tax Rates: An Analysis of Individual Returns." *The Review of Economics and Statistics*, 65: 363–73.

Cloward, Richard, and Lloyd Ohlin. 1960. *Delinquency and Opportunity*. New York: The Free Press.

Cohen, Albert K. 1955. *Delinquent Boys: The Culture of the Gang*. New York: The Free Press.

Cohen, Albert K., Alfred Lindesmith, and Karl Schuessler. 1956. *The Sutherland Papers*. Bloomington: Indiana University Press.

Cohen, Lawrence E., and David Cantor. 1981. "Residential Burglary in the United States: Lifestyle and Demographic Factors Associated with the Probability of Victimization." *Journal of Research in Crime and Delinquency*, 18: 113–27.

Cohen, Lawrence E., and Marcus Felson. 1979. "Social Change and Crime Rate Trends: A Routine Activity Approach." *American Sociological Review*, 44: 588–608.

Cohen, Lawrence E., and Kenneth Land. 1987. "Age and Crime: Symmetry vs. Asymmetry, and the Projection of Crime Rates Through the 1990's." *American Sociological Review*, 52: 170–83.

Colvin, Mark, and John Pauly. 1983. "A Critique of Criminology: Toward an Integrated Structural-Marxist Theory of Delinquency Production." *American Journal of Sociology*, 89: 513–51.

Conklin, John E. 1972. *Robbery and the Criminal Justice System*. Philadelphia: Lippincott.

———. 1986. *Criminology*. 2d ed. New York: Macmillan.

Cook, Philip J. 1986. "The Demand and Supply of Criminal Opportunities." In *Crime and Justice: An Annual Review of Research*, edited by M. Tonry and N. Morris (pp. 1–27). Chicago: University of Chicago Press.

Cook, Thomas, and Donald Campbell. 1979. *Quasi-Experimentation*. Boston: Houghton Mifflin.

Cornish, Derek B., and Ronald V. Clarke. 1986. *The Reasoning Criminal*. New York: Springer-Verlag.

Cressey, Donald R. 1953. *Other People's Money*. New York: The Free Press.
———. 1969. *Theft of the Nation*. New York: Harper and Row.
———. 1986. "Why Managers Commit Fraud." *Australian and New Zealand Journal of Criminology*, 19: 195–209.
Crowe, Raymond. 1975. "An Adoptive Study of Psychopathy: Preliminary Results from Arrest Records and Psychiatric Hospital Records." In *Genetic Research in Psychiatry*, edited by R. Fieve, D. Rosenthal, and H. Brill (pp. 95–105). Baltimore: Johns Hopkins University Press.
Currie, Elliott. 1985. *Confronting Crime: An American Challenge*. New York: Pantheon Books.
Curtis, Lynn A. 1974. *Criminal Violence: National Patterns and Behavior*. Lexington, Mass.: D. C. Heath.
Darwin, Charles. 1859. *The Origins of Species*. New York: D. Appleton and Company.
———. 1874 [1871]. *The Descent of Man*. New York: Merrill and Baker.
DeFleur, Lois B. 1970. *Delinquency in Argentina*. Pullman: Washington University Press.
Douglas, J. W. B., J. M. Ross, W. A. Hammond, and D. G. Mulligan. 1966. *British Journal of Criminology*, 6: 294–302.
Edelhertz, Herbert. 1970. *The Nature, Impact and Prosecution of White Collar Crime*. Washington, D.C.: National Institute of Law Enforcement and Criminal Justice.
Ehrlich, Isaac. 1974. "Participation in Illegitimate Activities: An Economic Analysis." In *Essays in the Economics of Crime and Punishment*, edited by G. Becker and W. Landes (pp. 68–134). New York: Columbia University Press.
Elliott, Delbert, Suzanne S. Ageton, and David Huizinga. 1978. "1977 Self-Reported Delinquency Estimates by Sex, Race, Class, and Age." Mimeographed. Boulder, Colo.: Behavioral Research Institute.
Elliott, Delbert, and David Huizinga. 1983. "Social Class and Delinquent Behavior in a National Youth Panel." *Criminology*, 21: 149–77.
Elliott, Delbert, David Huizinga, and Suzanne Ageton. 1985. *Explaining Delinquency and Drug Use*. Beverly Hills, Calif.: Sage.
Elliott, Delbert, and Harwin Voss. 1974. *Delinquency and Dropout*. Lexington, Mass.: D. C. Heath.
Ellis, Desmond, Harold G. Grasmick, and Bernard Gilman. 1974. "Violence in Prisons: A Sociological Analysis." *American Journal of Sociology*, 80: 16–43.
Ellis, Lee. 1982. "Genetics and Criminal Behavior." *Criminology*, 20: 43–66.
Empey, LaMar T. 1982. *American Delinquency*. Homewood, Ill.: Dorsey.
Erickson, Maynard, and Gary F. Jensen. 1977. "'Delinquency Is Still Group Behavior!': Toward Revitalizing the Group Premise in the Sociology of Deviance." *Journal of Criminal Law and Criminology*, 68: 262–73.
Ermann, M. David, and Richard Lundman. 1982. *Corporate and Governmental Deviance: Problems of Organizational Behavior in Contemporary Society*. 2d ed. New York: Oxford University Press.
Eron, Leonard. 1987. "The Development of Aggressive Behavior from the Perspective of a Developing Behaviorism." *American Psychologist*, 42: 135–42.

Eysenck, Hans. 1964. *Crime and Personality*. London: Routledge and Kegan Paul.

———. 1977. *Crime and Personality*. Rev. ed. London: Paladin.

———. 1989. "Personality and Criminality: A Dispositional Analysis." In *Advances in Criminological Theory*, edited by W. S. Laufer and F. Adler (pp. 89–110). New Brunswick, N.J.: Transaction.

Farrington, David. 1973. "Self Reports of Deviant Behavior: Predictive and Stable?" *Journal of Criminal Law and Criminology*, 64: 99–110.

———. 1978. "The Family Backgrounds of Aggressive Youths." As cited in D. Olweus, "Stability of Aggressive Reaction Patterns in Males: A Review." *Psychological Bulletin*, 86 (1979): 852–75.

———. 1979. "Longitudinal Research on Crime and Delinquency." In *Crime and Justice: An Annual Review of Research*, vol. 1, edited by N. Morris and M. Tonry (pp. 289–348). Chicago: University of Chicago Press.

———. 1986a. "Age and Crime." In *Crime and Justice: An Annual Review of Research*, vol. 7, edited by M. Tonry and N. Morris (pp. 189–250). Chicago: University of Chicago Press.

———. 1986b. "Stepping Stones to Adult Criminal Careers." In *Development of Antisocial and Prosocial Behavior*, edited by D. Olweus, J. Block, and M. Radke-Yarrow (pp. 359–84). New York: Academic Press.

Farrington, David, Lloyd Ohlin, and James Q. Wilson. 1986. *Understanding and Controlling Crime*. New York: Springer-Verlag.

Feeney, Floyd. 1986. "Robbers as Decision-Makers." In *The Reasoning Criminal*, edited by D. B. Cornish and R. V. Clarke (pp. 53–71). New York: Springer-Verlag.

Felson, Marcus. 1987. "Routine Activities and Crime Prevention in the Developing Metropolis." *Criminology*, 25: 911–31.

Felson, Marcus, and Michael Gottfredson. 1984. "Social Indicators of Adolescent Activities Near Peers and Parents." *Journal of Marriage and the Family*, 46: 709–14.

Ferraro, Gina Lombroso. 1972 [1911]. *Criminal Man*. Montclair, N.J.: Patterson Smith.

Ferri, Enrico. 1897. *Criminal Sociology*. New York: D. Appleton and Company.

Flanagan, Timothy. 1979. "Long-Term Prisoners." Ph.D. diss., State University of New York at Albany.

———. 1981. "Correlates of Institutional Misconduct Among State Prisoners." Mimeographed. Albany, N.Y.: Criminal Justice Research Center.

Freeman, Richard B. 1983. "Crime and Unemployment." In *Crime and Public Policy*, edited by J. Q. Wilson (pp. 89–106). San Francisco: Institute for Contemporary Studies.

Friday, Paul. 1973. "Problems in Comparative Criminology." *International Journal of Criminology and Penology*, 1: 151–60.

Geis, Gilbert, and Colin Goff. 1983. "Introduction." In *White Collar Crime: The Uncut Version*, by E. H. Sutherland (pp. ix–xxxiii). New Haven: Yale University Press.

Geis, Gilbert, and Robert Meier, eds. 1977. *White Collar Crime*. New York: The Free Press.

Geis, Gilbert, Henry Pontell, and Paul Jesilow. 1987. "Medicaid Fraud." In *Controversial Issues in Crime and Justice*, edited by J. E. Scott and T. Hirschi (pp. 17–39). Newbury Park, Calif.: Sage.

Gibbons, Donald. 1973. *Society, Crime and Criminal Careers*. Englewood Cliffs, N.J.: Prentice Hall.

Glaser, Daniel. 1964. *The Effectiveness of a Prison and Parole System*. New York: Bobbs-Merrill.

———. 1978. *Crime in Our Changing Society*. New York: Holt, Rinehart and Winston.

Glenn, Norval. 1981. "Age, Birth Cohorts, and Drinking: An Illustration of the Hazards of Inferring Effects from Cohort Data." *Journal of Gerontology*, 36: 362–69.

Glueck, Sheldon, and Eleanor Glueck. 1930. *500 Criminal Careers*. New York: Knopf.

———. 1934. *500 Delinquent Women*. New York: Knopf.

———. 1940. *Juvenile Delinquents Grown Up*. New York: Commonwealth Fund.

———. 1950. *Unraveling Juvenile Delinquency*. Cambridge, Mass.: Harvard University Press.

———. 1968. *Delinquents and Nondelinquents in Perspective*. Cambridge, Mass.: Harvard University Press.

Goddard, Henry H. 1914. *Feeble-Mindedness: Its Causes and Consequences*. New York: Macmillan.

Gold, Martin. 1970. *Delinquent Behavior in an American City*. Belmont, Calif.: Brooks/Cole.

Golden, Reid M., and Steven F. Messner. 1987. "Dimensions of Racial Inequality and Rates of Violent Crime." *Criminology*, 25: 525–41.

Goring, Charles. 1913. *The English Convict*. Montclair, N.J.: Patterson Smith.

———. 1919. *The English Convict*. Rev. ed. London: His Majesty's Stationery Office.

Gottfredson, Michael. 1979. "Treatment Destruction Techniques." *Journal of Research in Crime and Delinquency*, 16: 39–54.

———. 1984. *Victims of Crime: The Dimensions of Risk*. London: HMSO.

———. 1986. "Substantive Contributions of Victimization Surveys." In *Crime and Justice: An Annual Review of Research*, edited by M. Tonry and N. Morris (pp. 251–87). Chicago: University of Chicago Press.

Gottfredson, Michael, and Don Gottfredson. 1980. *Decisionmaking in Criminal Justice*. Cambridge, Mass.: Ballinger.

———. 1988. *Decisionmaking in Criminal Justice*. 2d ed. New York: Plenum.

Gottfredson, Michael, and Travis Hirschi. 1986. "The True Value of Lambda Would Appear to Be Zero." *Criminology*, 24: 213–34.

———. 1987a. *Positive Criminology*. Newbury Park, Calif.: Sage.

———. 1987b. "The Methodological Adequacy of Longitudinal Research on Crime." *Criminology*, 25: 581–614.

———. 1988a. "Science, Public Policy, and the Career Paradigm." *Criminology*, 26: 37–55.

———. 1988b. "Career Criminals and Selective Incapacitation." In *Controversial Issues in Crime and Justice*, edited by J. E. Scott and T. Hirschi (pp. 199–209). Newbury Park, Calif.: Sage.

———. 1988c. "A Propensity-Event Theory of Crime." In *Advances in Criminological Theory*, vol. 1, edited by F. Adler and W. Laufer (pp. 57–67). New Brunswick, N.J.: Transaction.

Gough, Harrison G. 1948. "A Sociological Theory of Psychopathy." *American Journal of Sociology*, 53: 359–66.

Gove, Walter R. 1980. *The Labelling of Deviance: Evaluation of a Perspective.* 2d ed. Beverly Hills, Calif.: Sage.

Greenberg, David F. 1979. "Delinquency and the Age Structure of Society." In *Criminology Review Yearbook*, edited by S. L. Messinger and E. Bittner (pp. 586–620). Beverly Hills, Calif.: Sage.

———. 1981. *Crime and Capitalism: Readings in Marxist Criminology.* Palo Alto, Calif.: Mayfield.

———. 1985. "Age, Crime, and Social Explanation." *American Journal of Sociology*, 91: 1–21.

Greenwood, Peter. 1983. "Controlling the Crime Rate Through Imprisonment." In *Crime and Public Policy*, edited by J. Q. Wilson (pp. 251–69). San Francisco: Institute for Contemporary Studies.

Guttman, Louis. 1977. "What Is Not What in Statistics." *The Statistician*, 26: 81–107.

Haapanen, Rudy A. 1987. *Selective Incapacitation and the Serious Offender: A Longitudinal Study of Criminal Career Patterns.* Sacramento: California Department of the Youth Authority.

Harris, Anthony. 1977. "Sex and Theories of Deviance: Toward a Functional Theory of Deviant Type-Scripts." *American Sociological Review*, 42: 3–16.

Hartshorne, Hugh, and Mark May. 1928. *Studies in the Nature of Character.* New York: Macmillan.

Herrnstein, Richard. 1983. "Some Criminogenic Traits of Offenders." In *Crime and Public Policy*, edited by J. Q. Wilson (pp. 31–52). San Francisco: Institute for Contemporary Studies.

Hindelang, Michael J. 1971. "Age, Sex, and the Versatility of Delinquent Involvements." *Social Problems*, 18: 522–35.

———. 1973. "Causes of Delinquency: A Partial Replication and Extension." *Social Problems*, 20: 471–87.

———. 1976. *Criminal Victimization in Eight American Cities.* Cambridge, Mass.: Ballinger.

———. 1978. "Race and Involvement in Common Law Personal Crimes." *American Sociological Review*, 43: 93–109.

———. 1981. "Variations in Sex-Race-Age Specific Incidence Rates of Offending." *American Sociological Review*, 46: 461–74.

Hindelang, Michael, Michael R. Gottfredson, and James Garofalo. 1978. *Victims of Personal Crime.* Cambridge, Mass.: Ballinger.

Hindelang, Michael, Travis Hirschi, and Joseph Weis. 1981. *Measuring Delinquency.* Beverly Hills, Calif.: Sage.

Hirschi, Travis. 1969. *Causes of Delinquency.* Berkeley: University of California Press.

———. 1979. "Separate and Unequal Is Better." *Journal of Research in Crime and Delinquency*, 16: 34–38.

———. 1983. "Crime and the Family." In *Crime and Public Policy*, edited by J. Q. Wilson (pp. 53–68). San Francisco: Institute for Contemporary Studies.

Hirschi, Travis, and Michael Gottfredson. 1983. "Age and the Explanation of Crime." *American Journal of Sociology*, 89: 552–84.

———. 1986. "The Distinction Between Crime and Criminality." In *Critique and Explanation: Essays in Honor of Gwynne Nettler*, edited by T. F. Hartnagel and R. Silverman (pp. 55–69). New Brunswick, N.J.: Transaction.

———. 1987. "Causes of White Collar Crime." *Criminology*, 25: 949–74.

———. 1988a. "Toward a General Theory of Crime." In *Explaining Criminal Behaviour*, edited by W. Buikhuisen and S. A. Mednick (pp. 8–26). Leiden: E. J. Brill.

———. 1988b. "A General Theory of Crime for Cross-National Criminology." In *Proceedings of the Fifth Asian-Pacific Conference on Juvenile Delinquency* (pp. 44–53). Taipei, Taiwan.

Hirschi, Travis, and Hanan Selvin. 1967. *Delinquency Research*. New York: The Free Press.

Hirschi, Travis, and Rodney Stark. 1969. "Hellfire and Delinquency." *Social Problems*, 17: 202–13.

Hobbes, Thomas. 1957 [1651]. *Leviathan*. Oxford: Basil Blackwell.

Hope, Timothy. 1985. *Implementing Crime Prevention Measures*. Home Office Research Study no. 86. London: HMSO.

Hough, Michael. 1987. "Offenders' Choice of Target: Findings from Victim Surveys." *Journal of Quantitative Criminology*, 3: 355–69.

Hough, Michael, and Pat Mayhew. 1985. *Taking Account of Crime: Key Findings from the 1984 British Crime Survey*. Home Office Research Study no. 85. London: HMSO.

Huesmann, L. Rowell, Leonard Eron, Monroe Lefkowitz, and Leopold Walder. 1984. "Stability of Aggression over Time and Generations." *Developmental Psychology*, 20: 1120–34.

Hutchings, Barry, and Sarnoff Mednick. 1977. "Criminality in Adoptees and Their Adoptive and Biological Parents: A Pilot Study." In *Biosocial Bases of Criminal Behavior*, edited by S. Mednick and K. O. Christiansen (pp. 127–43). New York: Gardner.

Jensen, Gary F., and Raymond Eve. 1976. "Sex Differences in Delinquency: An Examination of Popular Sociological Explanations." *Criminology*, 13: 427–48.

Johnson, Elmer, and Israel Barak-Glantz. 1983. *Comparative Criminology*. Beverly Hills, Calif.: Sage.

Johnson, Richard E. 1979. *Juvenile Delinquency and Its Origins*. Cambridge, Engl.: Cambridge University Press.

Johnston, Lloyd D., Jerald Bachman, and Patrick M. O'Malley. 1978. *Monitoring the Future*. Ann Arbor: Institute for Social Research, University of Michigan.

Johnston, Lloyd D., Patrick M. O'Malley, and Jerald Bachman. 1984. *Highlights from Drugs and American High School Students 1975–1983*. Washington, D.C.: U.S. Department of Health and Human Services.

Jonsson, G. 1967. *Delinquent Boys, Their Parents and Grandparents*. Copenhagen: Munksgaard.

Kandel, Denise B. 1978. *Longitudinal Research on Drug Use*. Washington, D.C.: Hemisphere.

Kelly, DeLos. 1982. *Creating School Failure, Youth Crime, and Deviance*. Los Angeles: Trident Shop.

Klein, Malcolm. 1971. *Street Gangs and Street Workers*. Englewood Cliffs, N.J.: Prentice Hall.

———. 1984. "Offense Specialization and Versatility Among Juveniles." *British Journal of Criminology*, 24: 185–94.

Klockars, Carl B. 1974. *The Professional Fence*. New York: The Free Press.

———. 1988. "Police and the Modern Sting Operation." In *Controversial Issues in Crime and Justice*, edited by J. E. Scott and T. Hirschi (pp. 95–112). Newbury Park, Calif.: Sage.

Kornhauser, Ruth. 1978. *Social Sources of Delinquency*. Chicago: University of Chicago Press.

Lasley, James R. 1987. "Toward a Control Theory of White Collar Offending." Unpublished manuscript. Claremont, Calif.: Department of Criminal Justice, Claremont Graduate School.

Laub, John H. 1983. "Urbanism, Race, and Crime." *Journal of Research in Crime and Delinquency*, 20: 183–98.

Lemert, Edwin. 1951. *Social Pathology*. New York: McGraw-Hill.

Loeber, Rolf. 1982. "The Stability of Antisocial and Delinquent Child Behavior: A Review." *Child Development*, 53: 1431–46.

Loeber, Rolf, and Thomas Dishion. 1983. "Early Predictors of Male Delinquency: A Review." *Psychological Bulletin*, 94: 68–99.

Loeber, Rolf, and Magda Stouthamer-Loeber. 1986. "Family Factors as Correlates and Predictors of Juvenile Conduct Problems and Delinquency." In *Crime and Justice: An Annual Review of Research*, vol. 7, edited by M. Tonry and N. Morris (pp. 29–149). Chicago: University of Chicago Press.

Logan, Charles. 1972. "Evaluation Research in Crime and Delinquency: A Reappraisal." *Journal of Criminal Law, Criminology, and Police Science*, 63: 378–98.

Lombroso, Cesare. 1918 [1899]. *Crime: Its Causes and Remedies*. Rev. ed. Boston: Little, Brown.

Mabli, Jerome, Charles Holley, Judy Patrick, and Justina Walls. 1979. "Age and Prison Violence." *Criminal Justice and Behavior*, 6: 175–86.

Mason, Robert, and Lyle D. Calvin. 1978. "A Study of Admitted Income Tax Evasion." *Law and Society Review*, 13 (Fall): 73–89.

Matsueda, Ross. 1986. "The Dynamics of Belief and Delinquency." Paper presented at the annual meetings of the American Sociological Association.

Matza, David. 1964. *Delinquency and Drift*. New York: Wiley.

Mayhew, Pat. 1984. "Target-Hardening: How Much of an Answer?" In *Coping with Burglary*, edited by R. V. G. Clarke and T. Hope (pp. 29–44). Boston: Kluwer-Nijhoff.

Mayhew, Pat. 1987. *Residential Burglary: A Comparison of the United States, Canada, and England and Wales*. Washington, D.C.: National Institute of Justice.

Mayhew, Pat M., Ronald V. Clarke, A. Sturman, and J. M. Hough. 1976. *Crime as Opportunity*. Home Office Research Study no. 34. London: HMSO.

McClintock, Frederick H., and H. Howard Avison. 1968. *Crime in England and Wales*. London: Heinemann.

McCord, Joan. 1979. "Some Child-Rearing Antecedents of Criminal Behavior in Adult Men." *Journal of Personality and Social Psychology*, 37: 1477–86.

McCord, William, and Joan McCord. 1959. *Origins of Crime: A New Evaluation of the Cambridge-Somerville Study*. New York: Columbia University Press.

McGarrell, Edmund F., and Timothy J. Flanagan, eds. 1985. *Sourcebook of Criminal Justice Statistics—1984*. Washington, D.C.: USGPO.

Mednick, Sarnoff. 1977. "A Bio-social Theory of the Learning of Law-Abiding

Behavior." In *Biosocial Bases of Criminal Behavior*, edited by S. Mednick and K. O. Christiansen (pp. 1–8). New York: Gardner.

———. 1987. "Introduction." In *The Causes of Crime: New Biological Approaches*, edited by S. A. Mednick, T. E. Moffitt, and S. A. Stack (pp. 1–6). Cambridge, Engl.: Cambridge University Press.

Mednick, Sarnoff, and Karl O. Christiansen, eds. 1977. *Biosocial Bases of Criminal Behavior*. New York: Gardner.

Mednick, Sarnoff, William Gabrielli, and Barry Hutchings. 1983. "Genetic Influences in Criminal Behavior: Some Evidence from an Adoption Cohort." Paper presented at the annual meetings of the American Society of Criminology, Denver, Colorado.

———. 1984. "Genetic Influences in Criminal Convictions: Evidence from an Adoption Cohort." *Science*, 224: 891–94.

———. 1987. "Genetic Factors in the Etiology of Criminal Behavior." In *The Causes of Crime: New Biological Approaches*, edited by S. A. Mednick, T. E. Moffitt, and S. A. Stack (pp. 74–91). Cambridge, Engl.: Cambridge University Press.

Megargee, Edwin, and M. Bohn. 1979. *Classifying Criminals*. Beverly Hills, Calif.: Sage.

Merton, Robert. 1938. "Social Structure and 'Anomie.'" *American Sociological Review*, 3: 672–82.

Miller, Judith. 1982. *National Survey on Drug Abuse: Main Findings 1982*. Washington, D.C.: U.S. Department of Health and Human Services, National Institute of Drug Abuse.

Morris, Norval, and Gordon Hawkins. 1970. *The Honest Politician's Guide to Crime Control*. Chicago: University of Chicago Press.

Murray, Charles A., and Louis A. Cox, Jr. 1979. *Beyond Probation: Juvenile Corrections and the Chronic Delinquent*. Beverly Hills, Calif.: Sage.

Nagel, Ilene H., and John Hagan. 1983. "Gender and Crime: Offense Patterns and Criminal Court Sanctions." In *Crime and Justice: An Annual Review of Research*, vol. 4, edited by M. Tonry and N. Morris (pp. 91–144). Chicago: University of Chicago Press.

National Institute of Mental Health. 1982. *Research Highlights 1982*. Vol. 1. Washington, D.C.: U.S. Department of Health and Human Services.

Neison, Francis G. P. 1857. *Contributions to Vital Statistics*. London: Simpkin, Marshall.

Nettler, Gwynne. 1984. *Explaining Crime*. 3d ed. New York: McGraw-Hill.

———. 1982. *Killing One Another*. Cincinnati, Ohio: Anderson.

Newman, Graeme. 1976. *Comparative Deviance: Perception of Law in Six Cultures*. New York: Elsevier.

Newman, Oscar. 1972. *Defensible Space: Crime Prevention Through Urban Design*. New York: Macmillan.

New York State. 1976. *Characteristics of Inmates Under Custody*. Albany, N.Y.: Department of Correctional Services, Division of Programming Planning, Evaluation, and Research.

———. *New York State Statistical Yearbook*. 1979–80 edition. Albany, N.Y.: Division of the Budget.

Normandeau, Andre. 1968. *Trends and Patterns in Crimes of Robbery*. Ph.D. diss., University of Pennsylvania.

Olweus, Dan. 1979. "Stability of Aggressive Reaction Patterns in Males: A Review." *Psychological Bulletin*, 86: 852–75.

Ong, Jin Hui. 1986. "Drug Abuse Among Juveniles." In *Proceedings of the Fourth Asian-Pacific Conference on Juvenile Delinquency* (pp. 122–36). Seoul, Korea.

Orsagh, Thomas, and Ann D. Witte. 1981. "Economic Status and Crime: Implications for Offender Rehabilitation." *Journal of Criminal Law and Criminology*, 72: 1055–71.

Parmelee, Maurice. 1918. *Criminology*. New York: Macmillan.

Parsons, Talcott. 1957. *The Social System*. New York: Macmillan.

Patterson, Gerald R. 1980. "Children Who Steal." In *Understanding Crime*, edited by T. Hirschi and M. Gottfredson (pp. 73–90). Beverly Hills, Calif.: Sage.

Petersilia, Joan. 1980. "Criminal Career Research: A Review of Recent Evidence." In *Crime and Justice: An Annual Review of Research*, vol. 2, edited by M. Tonry and N. Morris (pp. 321–79). Chicago: University of Chicago Press.

Posner, Richard. 1977. *Economic Analysis of Law*. 2d ed. Boston: Little, Brown.

President's Commission on Law Enforcement and Administration of Justice. 1967. *The Challenge of Crime in a Free Society*. Washington, D.C.: USGPO.

Rand, Michael, Patsy Klaus, and Bruce Taylor. 1983. "The Criminal Event." In *Report to the Nation on Crime and Justice* (pp. 1–16). Washington, D.C.: U.S. Department of Justice.

Reiman, Jeffrey. 1979. *The Rich Get Richer and the Poor Get Prison*. New York: Wiley.

Reiss, Albert J., Jr. 1967. *Studies in Crime and Law Enforcement in Major Metropolitan Areas*. Vol. 1. Field Surveys III. Washington, D.C.: President's Commission on Law Enforcement and Administration of Justice.

———. 1976. "Settling the Frontiers of a Pioneer in American Criminology: Henry McKay." In *Delinquency, Crime, and Society*, edited by J. F. Short (pp. 64–88). Chicago: University of Chicago Press.

———. 1988. "Co-offending and Criminal Careers." In *Crime and Justice: An Annual Review of Research*, vol. 10, edited by M. Tonry and N. Morris (pp. 117–70). Chicago: University of Chicago Press.

Reiss, Albert J., Jr., and Albert Biderman. 1980. *Data Sources on White-Collar Law-Breaking*. Washington, D.C.: U.S. Department of Justice.

Reppetto, Thomas A. 1974. *Residential Crime*. Cambridge, Mass.: Ballinger.

Reuter, Peter. 1983. *Disorganized Crime: The Economics of the Visible Hand*. Cambridge, Mass.: MIT Press.

Riley, David, and Margaret Shaw. 1985. *Parental Supervision and Juvenile Delinquency*. Home Office Research Study no. 83. London: HMSO.

Robins, Lee. 1966. *Deviant Children Grown Up*. Baltimore: Williams and Wilkins.

Robins, Lee. 1978. "Aetiological Implications in Studies of Childhood Histories Relating to Antisocial Personality." In *Psychopathic Behavior*, edited by R. Hare and D. Schalling (pp. 255–71). New York: Wiley.

Rojek, Dean, and Maynard Erickson. 1982. "Delinquent Careers." *Criminology*, 20: 5–28.

Rosenquist, Carl, and Edwin Megargee. 1969. *Delinquency in Three Cultures*. Austin: University of Texas Press.

Rosenthal, Robert, and L. Jacobson. 1968. *Pygmalion in the Classroom*. New York: Holt, Rinehart and Winston.

Rossi, Peter, E. Waite, C. Bose, and Richard Berk. 1974. "The Seriousness of Crimes, Normative Structure and Individual Differences." *American Sociological Review*, 39: 224–37.

Rowe, Alan R., and Charles R. Tittle. 1977. "Life-Cycle Changes and Criminal Propensity." *Sociological Quarterly*, 18: 223–36.

Rowe, David, and D. Wayne Osgood. 1984. "Heredity and Sociological Theories of Delinquency: A Reconsideration." *American Sociological Review*, 49: 526–40.

Rutter, Michael, and Henri Giller. 1984. *Juvenile Delinquency: Trends and Perspectives*. New York: Guilford.

Sampson, Robert J. 1985. "Race and Criminal Violence: A Demographically Disaggregated Analysis of Urban Homicide." *Crime and Delinquency*, 31: 47–82.

———. 1987. "Urban Black Violence: The Effect of Male Joblessness and Family Disruption." *American Journal of Sociology*, 93: 348–82.

Schoff, Hannah Kent. 1915. *The Wayward Child*. Indianapolis: Bobbs-Merrill.

Sechrest, Lee, Susan O. White, and Elizabeth D. Brown, eds. 1979. *The Rehabilitation of Criminal Offenders: Problems and Prospects*. Washington, D.C.: National Academy of Sciences.

Sellin, Thorsten. 1938. *Culture Conflict and Crime*. New York: Social Science Research Council.

Shannon, Lyle. 1978. "Predicting Adult Criminal Careers from Juvenile Careers." Paper presented at the 30th meeting of the American Society of Criminology, Dallas.

———. 1981. *Assessing the Relationship of Adult Criminal Careers to Juvenile Careers. Final Report*. Washington, D.C.: National Institute of Juvenile Justice and Delinquency Prevention.

Shavit, Yossi, and Ayre Rattner. 1988. "Age, Crime, and the Early Life Course." *American Journal of Sociology*, 93: 1457–70.

Shaw, Clifford, and Henry McKay. 1931. *Social Factors in Juvenile Delinquency*. Washington, D.C.: USGPO.

———. 1942. *Juvenile Delinquency and Urban Areas*. Chicago: University of Chicago Press.

Sherman, Lawrence W. 1983. "Patrol Strategies for Police." In *Crime and Public Policy*, edited by J. Q. Wilson (pp. 145–63). San Francisco: Institute for Contemporary Studies.

Sherman, Lawrence W., and Richard A. Berk. 1984. "The Specific Deterrent Effects of Arrest for Domestic Assault." *American Sociological Review*, 49: 261–72.

Short, James F. 1987. "Exploring Integration of the Theoretical Levels of Explanation: Notes on Juvenile Delinquency." Paper presented at the Albany Conference on Theoretical Integration in the Study of Deviance and Crime, State University of New York at Albany, Department of Sociology.

Short, James F., and Fred L. Strodtbeck. 1965. *Group Process and Gang Delinquency*. Chicago: University of Chicago Press.

Siegel, Larry J., and Joseph J. Senna. 1981. *Juvenile Delinquency*. St. Paul, Minn.: West.

Silberman, Charles E. 1978. *Criminal Violence, Criminal Justice.* New York: Random House.

Simon, Rita J. 1975. *Women and Crime.* Lexington, Mass.: Lexington Books.

Skinner, Burrhus F. 1953. *Science and Human Behavior.* New York: Macmillan.

Skogan, Wesley. 1979. "Crime in Contemporary America." In *Violence in America,* edited by H. Graham and T. Gurr (pp. 375–91). Beverly Hills, Calif.: Sage.

Social Science Citation Index, 1966–1984 editions. Philadelphia, Pa.: Institute for Scientific Information.

Sparks, Richard F., Hazel G. Genn, and David J. Dodd. 1977. *Surveying Victims: A Study of the Measurement of Criminal Victimization.* New York: Wiley.

Steffensmeier, Darrell, Emilie Allan, Miles Harer, and Cathy Streifel. 1989. "Age and the Distribution of Crime." *American Journal of Sociology,* 94: 803–31.

Stewart, James K. 1987. "Foreword." In *Research Program Fiscal Year 1988.* Washington, D.C.: National Institute of Justice.

Stinchcombe, Arthur. 1964. *Rebellion in a High School.* Chicago: Quadrangle.

Sutherland, Edwin. 1924. *Criminology.* Philadelphia: Lippincott.

––––––. 1937. *The Professional Thief.* Chicago: University of Chicago Press.

––––––. 1939. *Principles of Criminology.* Philadelphia: Lippincott.

––––––. 1940. *White Collar Crime.* New Haven: Yale University Press.

––––––. 1983. *White Collar Crime: The Uncut Version.* New Haven: Yale University Press.

Sutherland, Edwin, and Donald Cressey. 1978. *Principles of Criminology.* 10th ed. Philadelphia: Lippincott.

Suttles, Gerald D. 1968. *The Social Order of the Slum.* Chicago: University of Chicago Press.

Tannenbaum, Frank. 1938. *Crime and the Community.* Boston: Ginn.

Teresa, Vincent. 1973. *My Life in the Mafia.* New York: Doubleday.

Thomas, William I. 1923. *The Unadjusted Girl.* New York: Harper.

Thrasher, Frederic. 1927. *The Gang: A Study of 1313 Gangs.* Chicago: University of Chicago Press.

Tittle, Charles R. 1980. *Sanctions and Social Deviance.* New York: Praeger.

––––––. 1988. "Two Empirical Regularities (Maybe) in Search of an Explanation: Commentary on the Age/Crime Debate." *Criminology,* 26: 75–85.

Tittle, Charles, Wayne Villemez, and Douglas Smith. 1978. "The Myth of Social Class and Criminality." *American Sociological Review,* 43: 643–56.

Toby, Jackson. 1979a. "Delinquency in Cross-Cultural Perspective." In *Juvenile Justice: The Progressive Legacy and Current Reforms,* edited by L. T. Empey (pp. 105–49). Charlottesville: University Press of Virginia.

––––––. 1979b. "The New Criminology Is the Old Sentimentality." *Criminology,* 16: 516–26.

Tracy, Paul, Marvin Wolfgang, and Robert Figlio. 1985. *Delinquency in Two Birth Cohorts.* Washington, D.C.: U.S. Department of Justice.

Trasler, Gordon. 1980. "Aspects of Causality, Culture and Crime." Paper presented at the Fourth International Seminar at the International Center of Sociological, Penal and Penitentiary Research and Studies, Messina, Italy.

––––––. 1987. "Some Cautions for the Biological Approach to Crime Causation." In *The Causes of Crime: New Biological Approaches*, edited by S. A. Mednick, T. E. Moffitt, and S. A. Stack (pp. 7–24). Cambridge, Engl.: Cambridge University Press.

Turk, Austin T. 1969. *Criminality and the Legal Order*. Chicago: Rand-McNally.

Turner, Stanley. 1969. "Delinquency and Distance." In *Delinquency: Selected Studies*, edited by T. Selling and M. Wolfgang (pp. 11–27). New York: Wiley.

U.S. Department of Justice. 1979. *Uniform Crime Reports for the United States*. Washington, D.C.: USGPO.

———. 1981. *Uniform Crime Reports for the United States*. Washington, D.C.: USGPO.

———. 1985. *Uniform Crime Reports for the United States*. Washington, D.C.: USGPO.

Vaughan, Diane. 1983. *Controlling Unlawful Organizational Behavior*. Chicago: University of Chicago Press.

Vold, George. 1979. *Theoretical Criminology*. 2d ed., prepared by Thomas Bernard. New York: Oxford University Press.

von Hirsch, Andrew. 1985. *Past or Future Crimes*. New Brunswick, N.J.: Rutgers University Press.

Wadsworth, Michael F. J. 1979. *Roots of Delinquency: Infancy, Adolescence and Crime*. Oxford: Martin Robertson.

Waller, Irvin, and Norman Okihiro. 1978. *Burglary: The Victim and the Public*. Toronto: University of Toronto Press.

Warren, Marguerite. 1981. *Comparing Male and Female Offenders*. Beverly Hills, Calif.: Sage.

West, Donald. 1982. *Delinquency: Its Roots, Careers, and Prospects*. London: Heinemann.

West, Donald, and David Farrington. 1973. *Who Becomes Delinquent?* London: Heinemann.

———. 1977. *The Delinquent Way of Life*. London: Heinemann.

Wheeler, Stanton, David Weisburd, and Nancy Bode. 1982. "Sentencing the White Collar Offender." *American Sociological Review*, 47: 641–59.

Wheeler, Stanton, David Weisburd, Elin Waring, and Nancy Bode. 1988. "White Collar Crime and Criminals." *American Criminal Law Review*, 25: 331–56.

Wiatrowski, Michael D., David B. Griswold, and Mary K. Roberts. 1981. "Social Control Theory and Delinquency." *American Sociological Review*, 46: 525–41.

Wilbanks, William. 1986. *The Myth of a Racist Criminal Justice System*. Belmont, Calif.: Brooks/Cole.

Will, George. 1987. "Keep Your Eye on Giuliani." *Newsweek*, March 2, p. 84.

Williams, Jay, and Martin Gold. 1972. "From Delinquent Behavior to Official Delinquency." *Social Problems*, 20: 209–29.

Wilson, James Q. 1975. *Thinking About Crime*. New York: Basic Books.

Wilson, James Q., and Richard Herrnstein. 1985. *Crime and Human Nature*. New York: Simon and Schuster.

Winchester, Stuart, and Hilary Jackson. 1982. *Residential Burglary: The Limits of Prevention*. London: HMSO.

Witkin, Herman, Sarnoff Mednick, Fini Schulsinger, Eskild Bakkestrom, Karl Christiansen, Donald Goodenough, Kurt Hirschhorn, Claes Lundsteen,

David Owen, John Philip, Donald Rubin, and Martha Stocking. 1977. "Criminality, Aggression, and Intelligence among XYY and XXY Men." In *Biosocial Bases of Criminal Behavior*, edited by S. Mednick and K. O. Christiansen (pp. 165–87). New York: Gardner.

Witte, Ann D., and Diane F. Woodbury. 1985. "The Effect of Tax Laws and Tax Administration on Tax Compliance: The Case of the U.S. Invidividual Income Tax." *National Tax Journal*, 38: 1–13.

Wolfgang, Marvin. 1961. "Quantitative Analysis of Adjustment to the Prison Community." *Journal of Criminal Law, Criminology, and Police Science*, 51: 608–18.

Wolfgang, Marvin, and Franco Ferracuti. 1967. *The Subculture of Violence: Towards an Integrated Theory in Criminology*. Beverly Hills, Calif.: Sage.

Wolfgang, Marvin, Robert Figlio, and Thorsten Sellin. 1972. *Delinquency in a Birth Cohort*. Chicago: University of Chicago Press.

Wolfgang, Marvin, Robert Figlio, and Terence Thornberry. 1978. *Evaluating Criminology*. New York: Elsevier.

Wright, James D. 1986. "The Armed Criminal in America." Research in Brief. U.S. Department of Justice, National Institute of Justice. November.

Yablonsky, Lewis. 1962. *The Violent Gang*. New York: Macmillan.

Zeisel, Hans. 1982. "Disagreement over the Evaluation of a Controlled Experiment." *American Journal of Sociology*, 88: 378–96.

Zimring, Franklin. 1981. "Kids, Groups and Crime: Some Implications of a Well-Known Secret." *Journal of Criminal Law and Criminology*, 72: 867–85.

Zink, Theodore. 1958. "Are Prison Troublemakers Different?" *Journal of Criminal Law, Criminology, and Police Science*, 48: 433–34.

Index

von Hirsch, A., 256, 262
Voss, H., 223

Wadsworth, M., 145
Waller, I., 219
Warren, M., 144, 147–48
Weis, J., 29, 40, 74, 91, 146, 150, 154, 249
West, D., 96, 98–101, 138, 164, 167, 172, 222, 230, 237
Wheeler, S., 196
White-collar crime, 38–40, 146, 180–201
Wilbanks, W., 150
Wilson, J.: (1975) 7; (with Farrington and Ohlin, 1986) 50, 165–66, 222, 237–38; (with Herrnstein, 1985) 16, 43, 58, 60, 65, 70, 87–88, 108–17

passim, 124, 133, 139, 150, 173, 240
Winchester, S., 25
Witkin, H., 62
Witte, A., 163, 195
Wolfgang, M., 74, 76, 91, 123–29 *passim*, 151, 170, 173, 215, 226–27, 236–37, 258, 264
Working mothers, 104
Wright, J., 271

XYY chromosome, 62

Yablonsky, L., 151, 159, 207

Zeisel, H., 163
Zimring, F., 139, 158, 205

Library of Congress Cataloging-in-Publication Data

Gottfredson, Michael R.
   A general theory of crime.

   Includes bibliographical references.
   1. Criminology—Methodology.   I. Hirschi, Travis.
II. Title.
HV6018.G68 1990   364   89-22027
ISBN 0-8047-1773-7
ISBN 0-8047-1774-5 (pbk.)   L7422

∞   This book is printed on acid-free paper